Growing *Luca*
ORCHIDS

Vandas, dendrobiums and ┘

Growing ORCHIDS

Book Three
Vandas, Dendrobiums and others

J. N. Rentoul

Lothian Publishing Company Pty Ltd
Melbourne Sydney Auckland

First published 1982
by Lothian Publishing Company Pty. Ltd.,
4 Tattersalls Lane, Melbourne 3000.

© J. N. Rentoul 1982
Reprinted 1984

National Library of Australia
Cataloguing-in-Publication Data:

Rentoul, J. N. (James Noel), 1909-
Growing orchids-vandas, dendrobiums and others

Bibliography.
Includes index.
ISBN 0 85091 156 7
ISBN 0 85091 155 9 (pbk)

1. Orchid culture. I. Title.
635.9'3415

Typeset and printed in Hong Kong
through Bookbuilders Ltd

Contents

The three volumes of *Growing Orchids* are dedicated to Madge Rentoul, whose inspiration and help made them possible.

Introduction — Orchids and Names

'We now proceed to give an account of the species of another of that large genera of orchids which fill our collections with their species and whose names are to be found scattered through so many books that even the most skilful botanist can scarcely know where to search for them or when his inquiry is exhausted.'

Those were the words of John Lindley in contemplating another stage in his working life. In his span of sixty-six years he was considered by contemporaries the outstanding figure in the orchid world. In the late twentieth century this reputation is enhanced when the size of his contribution is reviewed. The son of a nurseryman, John Lindley worked for more than forty years in a voluntary capacity in the intensely competitive field of orchid culture, taxonomy and its revision — a part-time occupation in a life spent with plants.

John Lindley — tranquility with age.

The truth of the words of the opening paragraph has also been brought home in the writing of the three books *Growing Orchids*; with the search through literature and by correspondence bringing to light all the inconsistencies, the confusion and the sometimes egocentric edicts of some taxonomists and their imitators, whose idea seems to be to confuse even further the endless list of names that pour out each year. It would be a mistake, however, to think that orchids are alone in this madness.

When Lindley was asked to review several genera with a view to amending their names because of obvious linkage he sought to avoid the task, saying: 'I should have all the amateurs up in arms against me. They have had bother enough to get the existing names into their heads'. There is little doubt that the greater part of the orchid-growing world will echo those thoughts. Perhaps some of the crusaders for reclassification and renaming in the twentieth century might have been more understanding and forbearing had they known of Lindley's analysis. It is scarcely an admirable or clever thing to insist on total or even partial eclipse of a name which has been adequate for generations of growers. Too often the cause is perhaps personal gratification or the ambition to reach immortality through taxonomy.

The correction of Latin grammar by purists is perhaps a little more understandable, particularly when it means only the elimination of a consonant or dropping of a vowel. A notable instance is *Cattleya trianae*. Rolfe, another of the outstanding British botanists closely associated with orchids and Editor of *The Orchid Review*, may be quoted:

'A discussion has recently taken place as to whether *Cattleya trianae* or *trianaei* is the correct spelling, both methods finding advocates. The question seems to me an exceedingly simple one, as the word Triana requires no change of termination in Latinising. The nominative singular is Triana and the "a" must be changed into "ae" in the genitive — thus Triana's cattleya becomes *Cattleya trianae*. Strangely enough, one writer on the question says: "Not all the customs of the English can make *trianaei* correct". But why saddle the English with the error? It was Reichenbach who originated it, though there are still some who follow the error. By the way, *The Orchid Review* has never adopted the erroneous method.' Rolfe's edict has not lasted, although *The Orchid Review* followed it through until 1982. It will be noted that Rolfe's spelling has been followed through this book and judged on past performance it is not unlikely that it will return once again into general use, because the horticultural world is full of enthusiasts who are continually bringing changes in nomenclature and spelling before conferences which determine these things. The reinstatement of the letter 'i' into such names as *Phalaenopsis schilleriana* is typical.

Names may be utterly confusing to non-orchid growers and growers alike when they fail to understand why so many different cymbidiums, for example, bear the same name. The grex *Cymbidium* Anita is an example. It usually becomes clear on explaining all the changes which cross-pollination of some five species could have on further cross-pollinations. *Cymbidium* Anita comprises many fine clones, some of which are distinguished by varietal names. This point is frequently perverted by the use of these varietal names instead of the grex name and it is common to find plants labelled with the varietal name instead of the registered title.

The importance of names could have been more thoroughly appreciated from the time all species were cross-pollinated, regardless of the genus. But, regrettably, this point was frequently missed. To understand how this came about one must go back to *The Orchid Stud Book,* by Rolfe and Hurst, few copies of which would now be available anywhere in the world. In this book many misconceptions and incorrect entries of parentage were corrected, principally because Robert Allen Rolfe, like Dr John Lindley, was intensely interested in species orchids and knew them well. Both Rolfe and Lindley were intuitive and analytical and accepted nothing which they did not implicitly believe. They were frequently correct in assessments of uncertain and disputed parentage and corrected the entries wherever possible. If it were not for their enthusiasm and attention the hybridising fields of the late twentieth century would be far more impregnated with errors than they are and little reliance could be placed on the names from which so many cross-pollinations emerge.

This comes down to a personal level for all orchid growers with the small pieces of plastic or other material which are stuck into the potting mix at the edge of each pot. The names which occasionally appear on some of these labels are humorous, ridiculous and frequently illegible. One of the first things to remember when plants are bought, propagated, catalogued and even tortured by some of the methods we use is that the label is more important than the plant — without it the plant is nothing.

In writing these books there is no doubt at all in my mind that some of the names used will not meet with approval by some people, both orchid growers and taxonomists. Hundreds of books and papers were consulted, read through, accepted or rejected to maintain as correct a result as possible. In the course of the research many strange things were encountered, some contentious, some long solved and others debatable still. One fact which emerged is that it is impossible to keep up with the changes the would-be successors to Lindley and Reichenbach seek to impose on the orchid-growing community. These correctors should have some regard for the words of Lindley which were quoted in the fourth paragraph of the introduction.

John Lindley is mentioned frequently in the three books and unfortunately, like other noteworthy contemporaries, left no biography of consequence. He was born in 1799 and died in 1865, when Reichenbach succeeded to the kingdom. However, he was to prove a frustrating successor, with the extraordinary last act of locking away his papers and specimens to decay for twenty-five years. It would be wrong to imagine that these two men contributed everything, as they were assisted by hundreds of individuals to reach their conclusions and name their names.

In orchids, as with all other plants, pronunciation is always good for a verbal battle. With some people it is the result of carelessness and the 'can't be bothered' attitude which is at the root of their difficulties, but at the same time the taxonomists of the past three hundred years have not helped to achieve a better understanding of names, with the orchidophiles not least to blame.

Pronunciation brings understanding, but I am always reminded of a short poem printed many, many years ago in reference to cyclamen:

How shall we sound its mystic name
Of Greek descent and Persian fame?
Shall "y" be long and "a" be short,
Or will the "y" and "a" retort?
Shall "y" be lightly rippled o'er
Or should we emphasise it more?
Alas! The doctors disagree,
For "y" is a doubtful quantity.
Some people use it now and then
As if 'twere written "sickly-men";
But as it comes from kuklos, Greek,
Why not "kick-laymen", so to speak?
The gardener, with his ready wit,
Upon another mode has hit,
He's terse and brief, long names dislikes,
And so he renders it as "sykes".

It is little wonder that we have Slippers and Odontos and Dens and Cats — at least they take the sting out of the scorpion of orchid names. In these books some attempt has been made to give the derivation of many names and if the interest of readers extends beyond these books they should buy the book by Schultes and Pease which is listed in the bibliography. It is well worth the effort of hunting it down.

3

Calanthe

The genus was named by Robert Brown in 1821 when investigating the flora of Australia, according to Veitch. The name is derived from the two Greek words *kalos* and *anthe* which signify a beautiful flower.

Although *Calanthe triplicata* (syn. *Calanthe veratrifolia*) was the species on which the genus was founded, *Calanthe brevicornu* was among the early discoveries when Dr Nathaniel Wallich found it in Nepal about 1820. This orchid, however, was not flowered in collections until Sir Joseph Hooker sent plants to the Kew Gardens in England about 1838-40. *Calanthe triplicata* was flowered in Colville's Chelsea nursery somewhere about 1822 or 1823 following receipt of a batch of plants from Alan Cunningham in Australia which also contained some dendrobiums, including *Dendrobium speciosum*.

Calanthes are close relatives of phaius and are common to many countries, with the principal concentration of the genus in the Indo-Asian region. They comprise two distinct groups, one which retains its leaves while the other commonly discards all or most of its foliage as the flower spikes develop. There is little relationship between habitat conditions and those under which the plants grow and flower in cultivation, but the two may be comparative if good conditions are provided.

Calanthes were the first recorded hand-pollinated hybrid orchids to be flowered. Dominy, one of the gardeners in the Veitch establishment, impregnated the green-leafed species *Calanthe masuca* with the pollen of *Calanthe furcata,* another green-leafed species. *Calanthe furcata* is similar in most respects to *Calanthe veratrifolia*. *The Gardeners' Chronicle* of 1858 recorded the event and Rolfe and Hurst, in *The Orchid Stud Book,* published in 1909, recognised it as the first man-made orchid hybrid to flower.

This was a momentous incident, although little importance is given to it in this century. *The Gardeners' Chronicle* describes it:

Dr Lindley writes: "On the 28th October Mr James Veitch, jun., of the Exotic Nursery, Chelsea, brought to the writer of this memorandum a flower of a Calanthe which combined the peculiar hairy forked spur and deeply lobed lip of the white *Calanthe furcata*, with the violet colour and broad middle lobe of the lip of *C. masuca*. One might have said that the flowers were just intermediate between the two... It appears to have been raised in the Exeter Nursery by Mr Dominy, Messrs Veitchs' indefatigable and very intelligent foreman, between *C. masuca* and *C. furcata*. The seed was obtained in 1854 by crossing these two species, was immediately sown, and in two years the seedlings were in flower. Nor is it the least remarkable circumstance connected with this production that it grows and flowers freely, while *C. masuca* is a 'shy' plant. We therefore propose with much pleasure that the name of the hybrid be *Calanthe* Dominyi, in order to put upon record the name of the first man who succeeded in this operation."

Dominy was inspired by Dr John Harris, a surgeon who practised near the Veitch nursery in Exeter and who was probably a constant visitor to the nursery, where no doubt he was amazed by the various plants which came to

Veitch's glass-houses from all over the world. Dominy had by this time hand-pollinated all sorts of orchids, but the calanthe happened to flower first.

Botanists of the period, including perhaps John Lindley, were at first unimpressed by the hybrids as they imagined them to be mules or sterile. Some of the fraternity were openly hostile and condemnatory. However, the swelling tide soon engulfed them and even such purists as James Bateman had in the end to concede their importance.

Bateman, one of the outstanding men of the nineteenth century, in proposing a vote of thanks to Mr Veitch for a paper delivered at an orchid conference at South Kensington in 1885, said:

'I am sure that he, and Mr Dominy also, will know and appreciate the effort it costs me to make this proposal, for I have been brought up with the strongest abhorrence of hybridisers. (Laughter.) I fell into evil hands early in life. My first orchid-growing friend was Mr Huntley. When I paid Mr Huntley a visit at his snug rectory in Huntingdonshire he pointed out to me his cacti and his orchids and said: "I like those plants; in fact, they are the only plants I grow, because those fiends (meaning the hybridisers) cannot touch them." (Laughter.) You must make a little allowance for a botanist, for hybridisers do give botanists a lot of trouble. (Laughter.) But however strong my prejudices were, I must confess that when I saw such plants as the cattleyas downstairs, if I was not convinced I was at all events shut up. (Laughter.) I have the greatest pleasure in moving the vote of thanks to Mr Veitch. (Applause.)'

John Dominy
(Photo courtesy *The Orchid Review*)

Bateman echoed the surprise and impression which the hybrids of the period created among botanists and growers alike. However, throughout his lifetime he never really became reconciled to the work of men like Dominy and in his own collections rigorously barred hybrids and concentrated solely on species orchids.

Other hybrid calanthes quickly appeared, with *Calanthe* Veitchii (*C. rosea* x *C. vestita*) in 1859, and still cultivated in the 1980-90 decade. This, unlike the first hybrid, was bred from the deciduous calanthes. The natural growing counterpart of this cross-pollination was later found by Boxall, who sent it from Indo-Asia to Hugh Low & Co. in 1893.

Hybrids were even generated between the two types, green-leafed and deciduous, with *Calanthe* Elwesii (*C. regnieri* x *C. veratrifolia*), which was flowered and named in 1903, one of the well-known examples.

By the time Rolfe and Hurst had published their *Orchid Stud Book* in 1909 twenty-one hybrids had been named and in the usual confusion of those years, over thirty other names were known for the same orchids. In *Sander's Orchid Hybrid List* in 1945 the confusion still had not been eliminated and more than ninety distinct cross-pollinations had been named, the worst example of which was *Calanthe* Sedenii.

Many of the hybrids raised in the period of their popularity, from discovery until the 1900 era, are still cultivated for their graceful, beautiful spikes of flower which often grow up to a metre tall, the flowers at the apex of the spike opening consecutively as it elongates. Inbreeding was a feature of their development, with examples such as *Calanthe* ruby (*C.* Sedenii x *C. vestita*) showing wide divergence of color from deep ruby red to pure white.

The habit of these orchids in casting their leaves may alarm some growers as they yellow off, but it has nothing to do with culture or overwatering. Almost total root loss accompanies this phase of their cycle and there is little use applying water or nutrients in order to boost the flower size or number. The spikes have been made or marred by the culture applied over their growth stages from shoot to flower opening.

While the deciduous types grow more easily in semi-tropical to sub-tropical climates, they will grow and flower quite well in cattleya conditions in cooler climates. More attention to the preliminary and closing phases of their growth, however, may have to be paid to them in such climates, with no great fluctuations in temperature in the later stage of their growing cycle. In their dormant period the pseudo-bulbs will stand quite cold conditions with no harm as they have neither leaves nor roots in this stage, but a lift out of dormancy, once started, must be continuous and not subject to a stop-and-go type of cultivation. An early lift out of dormancy may be induced by standing the pseudo-bulbs in a small pot into which a loose pad of sphagnum moss has been placed. The pot may then be stood in the warmest part of the glass-house or in a hot-box until roots are visible on the new growths, when they should be potted into a growing mix.

The deciduous calanthes, unlike most orchids, do not mind being divided into single or double pseudo-bulbs. They have a peculiar bottle shape in many of the species and hybrids, with a marked neck near the apex of the bulb. This is convenient for attaching them to a small stake with a 'twisty' to secure them in primary growing stages.

Potting mix for these pseudo-bulbs should be similar to that for cymbidiums but would be improved by adding a few small knobs of very old, hard cow or sheep manure. As the new growths show roots they should be potted into such a mix. If too much manure is added it may burn the roots in their tender shoot stage. The pot should not be too large, although by the later stages of growth in good conditions it may be nearly filled by the root system. About 10 or 12 centimetre diameter pots for normal pseudo-bulbs should be adequate. The pseudo-bulbs are usually greyish green colored and about 10 to 12 centimetres high. Good drainage is essential and a preference could be expressed for clay pots crocked to some 2 to 3 centimetres of their depth.

Once in full growth the plants should be grown quickly in good light conditions, sparingly watered until the root system is developing rapidly, then in the warmer months of their growth period the plants may be freely watered, preferably in the evening, and grown in a fresh but humid atmosphere.

With animal manure included there is no necessity to use liquid nutrients until the new growths are about half-way to maturity, and in this stage very weak applications of liquid nutrients such as Aquasol with fish emulsion or Maxicrop added will boost plant strength and flower size and numbers.

The green-leafed, non-deciduous calanthes mostly originate in cooler climates and *Calanthe triplicata*, despite its widespread habitat, which runs through temperate to sub-tropical countries including Australia, is most adaptable provided it is not grown too cold. Frequently because orchids grow in what look like uncongenial conditions the same type of treatment is meted out in cultivation. A more thorough analysis of the environment would soon show that it was rather special. Natural growing plants would mostly be found in beds of detritus and rotting vegetation and some of this type of material should be included in potting mixes. Cymbidium mixes are a good basic, but should have more added breakdown material such as oak leaf included for calanthes. Good drainage is essential, although the plants do not mind 'wet feet' in their stronger growing stages.

The root systems of the green-leafed calanthes are completely unlike the almost annual type found on the deciduous calanthes. They are somewhat like cymbidium roots and the leafed pseudo-bulbs will remain vigorous only as long as the root systems last. The foliage reflects the type of cultivation to which they are subjected, with blackened areas or minor spotting indicating that conditions are too cold or too wet, the humidity too high and air circulation inadequate. Even *Calanthe triplicata*, which flowers about Christmas time in

Australia, will not withstand poor cultivation methods such as wet and dry, hot and cold in too great a degree or poor light, although it is an inhabitant of the denser lower floor forest. Like phaius, they are almost swamp plants, but even swamps dry up at certain times of the year. Some difference between pot conditions and swamp conditions, however, should be appreciated.

Generally plants like phaius and calanthes are taken on as second-grade subjects in collections which are too big or poorly planned. They suffer second-rate treatment and are first to be neglected. While they may not have the image of cattleyas, they are still orchids and entitled to treatment as such.

Vanda

This genus was named by Jones in 1795 and, unlike many of the genera with Greek or Latin derived names, has reference to the species itself. It is derived from a Sanskrit word attached to *Vanda roxburghii* or to morphologically similar orchids. Sanskrit is the ancient language of India and bears a relationship to their modern languages similar to that of Latin to modern English.

Euanthe

This genus of apparently only one member was named by Schlechter in 1914. The derivation is a Greek word meaning blooming, given for the showy flowers. In the opinion of many orchid growers and even some botanists the name is superfluous and *Euanthe sanderana* could well have been left in its previous generic category of vanda.

The vanda family is large, complex and diverse and includes all the associated members listed in the hybridising section. They all belong to the monopodials, with continuously lengthening main stems from which side-shoots may emerge to elaborate the plant into multiple growths, an attribute more common in species than in most hybrids. The foliage is varied from the broader channelled leaves of phalaenopsis and similar genera to narrow, deeply grooved and almost cylindrical foliage of the so-called terete-stemmed vandas and aerides. In general these terete-foliaged plants will grow in much brighter light than those with broad, flat foliage. Each type is a basic or fundamental development from the environment in which it has been growing for so many untold periods of time.

The area covered by this group of plants is widespread, extending from northern India right through Asia in an arc ending in southern Australia and some islands to the east of that continent. In that sweep they grow in climates as disparate as it would be possible to imagine, from the fierce heat of the tropics almost to snow conditions in the Burma-India sector. Morphologically they vary from the small plants of *Sarcochilus ceciliae* to occasional members with long foliage and massive proportions.

The flowers of the family vary in size from minute saccolabiums and such to what could be regarded as normal vanda size of some 6 to 8 centimetres (about 2½ to 3½ inches) in species and very much larger in some of the hybrid vandas. Most of the flowers are long lasting if grown and maintained in the correct environments; some are scented, others most disappointing in this attribute. The flowers are produced on racemes or spikes which originate from the main stems in similar fashion to the roots, the buds in tight little knots on the ends of the stems as they grow, with the labellum and chin or spur tucked in toward the stems on the inside of the clusters. As the spikes develop the buds spread out, turn through arcs of about 180 degrees like most of the resupinate species and open with the labellum as the lowest part of the flowers. The labellums of some are attractive, on others mere decadent segments with none of the attraction of cattleya and other labellums.

There is a distinct difference between flowers from terete-foliage vandas and those of the broad-leafed species and it is an advantage when buying plants, seedlings or hybrid propagations or offshoots to know something about the background and breeding of such orchids. Flowers of both types are included in the illustrations. While the two types have been frequently hybridised and cross-pollinated, vandas which carry the broad-leaf characteristics in general have the better shaped flowers. For instance, *Vanda* Katsura came from the two hybrids *Vanda* Beebe Sumner and *Vanda* Rothschildiana. Both these vandas go back through their breeding lines to the species vandas *tricolor* and *coerulea* and *Euanthe sanderana,* so one could expect pink to buff flowers or even lilac and blue tints. All of these species have broad leaves. The flowers of *Vanda tricolor* are white with pink to red-purple or red-brown spotting; *Vanda coerulea* is blue with deeper blue reticulations and *Euanthe sanderana* buff to pink and brown-red with darker reticulations. With that combination many things are possible, but the flowers should be of fair to good shape, as outlined in the illustrations.

The introduction of terete-foliage vandas to such a combination would probably result in terete or semi-terete foliage and a rather open flower as the main chance, with gaps between the segments where no gaps are desired. Even *Euanthe sanderana*, dominant as it is, has little effect on terete-foliage tendencies.

Another example of background study, introducing another genus, is *Aeridovanda* Kalya, which used *Aerides odorata* with two infusions of *Vanda sanderana* or *Euanthe sanderana* and one each of *Vanda luzonica* and *Vanda manila*. It is what is known as an inter-generic cross-pollination and was aimed at producing a miniature vanda-type flower with a possible red intensification from *Aerides odorata*. It should be selected for color and miniaturisation, which is a dreadful but expressive word.

A further example is *Ascocenda* Medasand, which also uses two infusions of *Euanthe sanderana*, one of *Vanda coerulea* and one of *Ascocentrum curvifolium*, which is illustrated. It was aimed at producing miniature hybrids with possibilities for coppery or orange-red flowers with the added beauty and half-size of the vandas, which it did to perfection.

The hybridists use *Vanda coerulea* or *Euanthe sanderana* when they seek size, and the way in which the resultant progeny have been reselected and further cross-pollinated is obvious on looking at the flowers produced in the 1970-80 period. Color is difficult to predict but as it follows two principal lines, which are the blue of *Vanda coerulea* and the color range of *Euanthe sanderana*, singly or in combination, it is almost certain that the reticulations present in these two species flowers will always be apparent.

Knowledge of vandas by European races is of the order of only some 200 years, while the native races in the countries where they were natural have known and used them for countless years. *Vanda roxburghii* (R. Brown), syn. *Vanda tessellata* (Roxburgh) was the founding species of the genus and it is featured in the literature of India, Ceylon and Burma from antiquity. It is variable and illustrated in the photographs both as a pastel of the type form and as an intensely colored form. *Vanda tessellata* was grown and flowered by Sir Joseph Banks about 1819, a year or a little more before he died. He should need no introduction to Australians as he was one of the outstanding botanists who surveyed the flora of Australia in its formative years from 1780 to 1820. In India this vanda grew mostly on mango or ficus trees, but is widespread over the Indo-Asian area and grows on other host trees and occasionally rock surfaces. A tropical lowland orchid, it was named by Dr Roxburgh, director of Calcutta Botanic Gardens from about 1797 to 1814. He introduced many orchids to cultivation in India, England and Europe. *Vanda tessellata* grows and flowers almost continuously in its habitats, where it has among other colloquial names the title 'Rasna Nai' and is used medicinally in various ways by the native population.

Unlike *Vanda tessellata*, which for some growers of the early nineteenth century posed no cultural hazards, *Vanda coerulea,* one of the most beautiful of the genus, has always bothered people who try to cultivate it. In order that its habitat peculiarities may be made plain, some space is devoted to it. *Vanda coerulea* was discovered by the botanist-explorer W. Griffith in the Khasia Hills, Assam, north-eastern India, an area known for species orchids of all types.

Sir Joseph Hooker, writing in 1850, makes it all sound too easy:

'We left Nurtiung on the 4th October, 1850, and walked to Pomrang. Near the village of Lernai oak woods are passed in which *Vanda coerulea* grows in profusion, waving its panicles of azure flowers in the wind... The dry grassy hills which it inhabits are elevated 3000 to 4000 feet, the trees are small and very sparingly leafed, so that the vanda which grows on their dry limbs is fully exposed to the sun, rain and wind. There is no moss or lichen on the branches with the vanda, whose roots sprawl over the rough bark. The atmosphere is on the whole humid and extremely so during the rains, but there is no damp heat or stagnation in the air and at flowering season the temperature ranges between 60 and 80 degrees, there is much sunshine and both air and bark are dry during the days. In July and August during the rains the temperature is a little higher than above, but in the winter it falls much lower and hoar-frost forms on the ground.'

It all reads so simply, yet how can a plant which endures all those extremes be so hard to cultivate? Part of the answer lies in the fact that the conditions created in most glass-houses are too protective and do not offer these extremes in the right sequence. The fact, also, that most glass-houses do not have sufficient air flow about the plants could be a contributing factor.

The last part of Sir Joseph Hooker's report has an all too familiar ring: 'We collected seven men's loads of this superb plant for the Royal Gardens at Kew, but owing to unavoidable accidents and difficulties few specimens reached England alive.'

Sander's collector Micholitz worked in the area and sent several very large consignments back to his employers, but most of these also were soon to perish.

Vanda coerulea is common to several areas of India and Burma and generally it is found in localities which align with the description of Sir Joseph Hooker. Micholitz worked right through the Shan States in Burma, which embraced at that time several areas now known under other names. He said that the best plants came from these regions.

Vanda coerulea is an orchid which must be grown individually and while it is impossible to model its culture entirely on descriptions of its habitats, some features should be copied. For example, a good air flow should be given throughout the year and a reasonable temperature supplied. The hoar-frost part is beyond the control of most growers, but accompanying this stage there were most certainly either breezes or wind. Most growers are plagued by short, knotty root systems, black patches on the leaves occasioned by stagnant conditions, apparent cold intolerance and gradual shortening of the leaf structure never normally as long as the usual run of broad-leaf vandas. The type of conditions seems such that few other orchids could survive in them and unless the plants offer such a challenge that it cannot be denied, *Vanda coerulea* is best left out of the general collection with time given to hybrids instead. In early years of *Vanda coerulea* cultivation entire glass-houses were frequently given over to this species. One of the illustrations indicates how easily this vanda fits into a habitat by sheer chance. (See page 57.)

In order to break the apparent intractability of *Vanda coerulea* many sibling pollinations have been made and raised — that is, seedlings from two or more parents, usually clones selected because they appeared more amenable to artificial culture. While it is an "A" line procedure along the lines of the graph in *Growing Orchids — Book Two*, very fine flowers resulted and a number of tractable clones were produced. One cannot help subscribing to the common view that such sibling techniques allied to glass-house culture does indeed produce plants quite unlike those from habitats. While it cannot be proved or disproved easily, this is a comforting thought to have in mind when buying *Vanda coerulea*.

For those who would like to try this difficult orchid, here is something on which to model a cultural procedure. Writing first-hand from residence in *Vanda coerulea* territory, a student has this to say: '*Vanda coerulea* grows here on several species of trees from 10 to 40 feet above the ground. As a general rule the rainfall averages about 45 inches and falls from the middle of April to the end of September fairly regularly. Some heavy showers come in October and generally a wet spell of a few days in either November or December. It flowers from the end of July to late in September... The roots grow to 2 feet or more in length and adhere closely to the bark of the tree. It does not appear to mind whether the wood is dead or not.' That, of course, is a northern hemisphere program. Transpose the months by half a year for its southern equivalent.

The foregoing seems to indicate that the plants should succeed better on sections of branches of rough, permanent barked trees like oaks or casuarinas rather than to attempt to grow them in loose conglomerates of bark and charcoal and similar materials in pots or slat baskets.

Leaving *Vanda coerulea* for easier prospects, and showing that conservation is not a new idea, Charles Power, writing about the orchid from India in 1921, had this to say: 'It was only the timely action of the Shillong government that really saved the species from extinction... It is satisfactory to note that no collector may now take away more than a dozen plants and these only by special permission and on payment of a royalty of 1 rupee per plant.'

William Griffith found this beautiful orchid growing on gordonia trees in the Khasia Hills in 1837 and his choice in naming it *coerulea* would be hard to improve on.

Although the genus contains many broad-leaf vandas, few of them are of consequence so far as the average grower is concerned. *Vanda tricolor* is, however, important as a component of many of the hybrids produced over a long period. It was discovered in Java by the Veitch collector Thomas Lobb in 1846 and named by Lindley in his usual simplistic style, denoting the number of colors in combination. It is basically off-white to a yellowish tint in the petals and sepals, red-brown markings covering these segments, and with a purple labellum. The separate variety *Vanda tricolor* var. *suavis* has red-purple spotting instead of brownish to yellowish red and the labellum usually is not as pronounced in color.

The original discoverer of the vanda was Blume, who found it growing on palm trees in Java. His discovery was not noted at any of the herbariums or registries so his name of *Vanda suaveolens* was rejected. *Vanda tricolor* grows at about 500 to 1500 metres elevation (about 1500 to 5000 feet) on teak as well as other trees and is fairly hardy but not frost-resistant. The two varieties were common to the same areas of the island and, according to Sir Joseph Hooker, the only difference was in color of the flowers. Yet for a considerable time they were considered and listed as separate species and their conjunction was only for a matter of some years in the 1970 period. Both have a delightful perfume and lasting qualities as cut flowers beyond that of most of the species and the hybrids.

Vanda tricolor has also been noted as growing in northern Australia but no real confirmation of this had been arrived at when this book was put together. The brief report and description indicates that it may be a retrograde form which, if found, could be given a separate species name in the same way as *Vanda whitei* which grows in the Cape York area.

The Philippines' *Vanda luzonica* is morphologically similar to *Vanda tricolor*. It was discovered and named by the collector Loher about 1905, but remained something of a mystery species until it was described and catalogued by R.A. Rolfe about ten years later. His material and description came from an Australian grower named Hugh Dixon, of 'Sidney' (as it appears in the literature of the time). Writing of his plants in 1914, Dixon had this to say: 'The plant in habit is very much like the vandas of this section. The mauve markings on the segments of the flower in the photo are not nearly so pronounced as on the flower itself, although the plate was panchromatic. The markings are violet, though on account of the tinge of yellow on the white ground it looks a darker mauve. The plants do well in the warm end of the intermediate house.' What would Hugh Dixon have given for some Agfacolor!

Several American growers, among them Albert Burrage, had this vanda brought to their attention in a magnificent display of Philippine orchids at an exhibition at Panama about the same period. They obtained plants and had marked success in cultivating what at that time was a 'new orchid'.

Albert Burrage was one of the leading American growers in the early years of the twentieth century. He had a magnificent collection, including a large number of odontoglossums. He was president of the Massachusetts Horticultural Society and in 1925 arranged one of the most outstanding displays ever seen in America. He was a strong advocate of simple cultivation principles and had a penchant for cymbidiums. He was also noted for his wonderful collection of literature, pictures and lithographs of orchids, possibly the greatest ever assembled by an orchid grower.

Since the discovery of so many natural hybrids among the plants imported from Central and South America, most observant people interested in orchids were always on the lookout for similar occurrences in plants imported from the Asian and Indian habitats. In vandas they were not disappointed for long, because in 1894 a stranger turned up in a parcel of *Vanda coerulea* and *Vanda bensoni* consigned to Charlesworth, Shuttleworth & Co. in England. Rolfe suggested that it was a natural hybrid of the two. Another plant came to light in a consignment which arrived at Hugh Low's nursery about the same time. Both plants bore flowers which were reticulated like those of *Vanda coerulea*, but the overall color was pale with rose-purple color intrusions about the tips and edges of the petals and sepals, the overall size being about 6 to 7 centimetres (about 2½ inches).

Vanda bensoni (Bateman) was discovered by a British army general after whom it was named. He found it in light but deciduous jungle in the Burmese lowlands, where it was associated with *Saccolabium gigantea* and *Rhyncostylis retusa*, in a climate where the temperature frequently reached some 45 degrees Celsius (about 112 degrees Fahrenheit). Its flowers are smaller than those of *Vanda coerulea,* pale yellow-green spotted with red-brown and with a bluish labellum.

Several other similar plants were found in consignments sent to European nurseries, one of which originated in Linden's nursery in Brussels and was named *Vanda amoena*. It was subsequently identified as another plant of the natural hybrid *Vanda charlesworthii*.

Vanda coerulea is a dominant species which leaves its 'fingerprints' on subsequent generations to an astonishing degree. In *Vanda amoena,* as in *Vanda charlesworthii*, there was little doubt as to its parentage, although the other side was uncertain for a little while. The close association of the species in habitats led to a fairly certain guess as to the other parent. The hybrids in general bear witness to the dominance of *Euanthe sanderana* in equal proportions, neither it nor *Vanda coerulea* surrendering its identity.

Vanda denisoniana was discovered by the same man who found *Vanda bensoni*, but at a considerably higher altitude of 700 to 1000 metres (about 2250 to 3500 feet) in the Arracan Mountains of Burma. It grew in an average temperature of some 20 to 25 degrees Celsius (about 70 to 80 degrees Fahrenheit) and with an annual rainfall of about 2.5 metres (100 inches). This climate, although seasonal to a degree, was never dry. Never a popularly grown vanda like some of the others, in its early history considerable numbers of plants were collected and sent to England and Europe, where they joined the other contemporary species vandas in special glass-houses devoted entirely to the genus. It was noted early that these plants were greedy for room and their wandering root systems made them unsuitable to share space with other than their own kind. *Vanda denisoniana* is color variable from off-white to the red-brown of the illustrated plant. As a species for a collection of that type of orchid, which is a thing fancied by a lot of growers of the 1970-80 decade, this vanda is a beautiful addition, but unfortunately the plants obtainable are much smaller than the specimens originally collected, some of which were magnificent, with up to ten or twelve 'leads' carrying 100 or more flowers. Such plants would take many years to cultivate and possibly the ambition is seldom achieved.

General Benson also found *Vanda coerulescens* in the same area but at a lower elevation, growing on deciduous trees. This vanda has always been considered the poor relative of *Vanda coerulea*, with its petals and sepals lightly tesselated, the color rather washy but the labellum a very deep blue. It was first found by the collector Griffith but lost again for many years. It is usually a summer flowering species, rarely appearing as late as the first flowers of *Vanda coerulea*, which appear in later summer or early autumn, with some of the hand-made pollinations or sibling crosses showing a very irregular flowering period.

The flowers of both these vandas vary in size, with *Vanda coerulescens* about 5 or 6 centimetres across (2 to 2½ inches) and *Vanda denisoniana* about the same, although the whole flower tends to reflex. This characteristic may be bred out as exemplified by some of the later hybrid cross-pollinations.

There are many other species vandas for the fancier of the genus, but they usually fall into the 'one of' category, grown for their interest more than for their shape or beauty. In this group such things as *Vanda alpina,* with its neat habit and sparse flowers, match up very well with other semi-miniature species which are comparatively tame so far as the root system is concerned, an important factor in making decisions about the occupants of a mixed glass-house of orchids.

Moving away from the broad-leaf to the terete-leaf vandas brings in a completely different type of plant. Where the broad-leaf types have a robust main stem, the terete types have rather thin, wiry stems which may grow to great lengths; hence they need support, just like the creepers which grow and need support in the jungle. The word 'terete' means having a circular cross section or more commonly appearing pencil-like but tapered. Nearly all vandas and indeed most plants of this type, are naturally situated in bright habitats even in full sunlight, with the foliage evolved as a direct result of this exposure. It seldom burns or dehydrates as would the broad leaves of other types of vandas if exposed to the same conditions.

Some of the best examples of terete foliage occur in the Australian dendrobiums, with *Dendrobium beckleri, Dendrobium teretifolium, Dendrobium mortii* as prime examples. Although it may seem strange for a plant to have such foliage, it is one of the most primitive forms known. In vandas the term semi-terete is sometimes used, usually in reference to hybrids from the two types. It is part-way between the two, with deep channelling down the length of the leaves.

Vanda teres is widespread throughout Indo-Asia and has an untidy habit, with its long stems forming tangled masses like the epidendrums when untended. It grows in full sunlight and this was not allowed for in its early cultivated history, particularly in such climates as those of Britain and most of Europe. It was first collected in Sylhet Province, India, by Dr Wallich, taken to England by him about 1829 and finally flowered there about 1836. The flowers were presented to Princess (later Queen) Victoria.

The flowers of a pure white variety discovered about 1875 were sent to Reichenbach, the German botanist and taxonomist, and he was more pleased than surprised because he had predicted that many of the species would produce albino or pure-color forms. It is still rare as a naturally occurring species, although in the present century many clones of artificially raised pure-color forms have appeared on the market. There are several varieties of *Vanda teres,* all with the distinctively shaped flower of this species.

The principal difference between cultivating *Vanda terres* and other vandas is that the plants should be grown in almost full sunlight as far as possible, or if under glass the shading should be minimal. They would not mix readily with other orchids and are best left to outdoor tropical cultivation in warm climates.

Vanda hookerana is a terete companion to *Vanda teres*. It is a native of Borneo and other equatorial regions and it took some time after its introduction for cultivators to obtain flowers. The same problem of poor light plagued growers and it was not until 1882 that plants flowered in the collection of Lord Rothschild.

The habitat of this colorful vanda was thus described in *The Garden* in 1890: 'This district is thickly studded with marshes. These marshes are full of thick, low undergrowth and exposed to the full rays of the sun. In some of these marshes *Vanda hookerana* is found creeping over the undergrowth. The stems seem to rest on top of the bushes and the roots cling gently to them. The flower is always to be seen on the top of the bushes, away from all shade, in the blazing sun. I have passed through a marsh such as I have described, deep in mud and water, and seen the whole undergrowth covered with this orchid in bloom. . . So common is this flower in the district that it is called the "kinta weed". I have several plants growing in my garden on high, dry ground, well manured, also in wet, marshy ground. Thick common sticks are placed for them to climb up. In every case the plants are thriving wonderfully, the stems as thick as when in the jungle.'

Terete-stemmed vandas grow in cool climates as well as tropical. Vandas *amesiana* and *kimballiana* both originate at about 1200 to 1500 metres (3500 to 5000 feet) in Burma. This is a fairly high altitude, but the position of the area relative to the equator modifies the climate. *Vanda amesiana* was named after the American, F. L. Ames, who, like Albert Burrage, was an orchid enthusiast. *Vanda kimballiana* was discovered by Boxall in Upper Burma and one cannot but wonder that the other vanda escaped his notice. It is possible, however, that it was already known to him. He found great masses of it growing on bare rocks in open conditions, exposed to the sun for most of the day. It was named after the American, W.S. Kimball, a keen buyer for all types of Burmese orchids. A pure white form of *Vanda kimballiana* gained an Award of Merit for Mansell and Hatcher from the Royal Horticultural Society in 1911, but this form is still quite rare in naturally occurring plants.

The temperatures under which these two vandas grow so well in their habitat vary from 18 to 21 degrees Celsius (65 to 70 degrees Fahrenheit) by day to frequent falls to —18 degrees (zero) by night. The foliage has the added advantage in its terete form of withstanding frost as well as sunlight. During the course of the year there is a marked dry period during which there is sufficient dew at night to keep the plants in good condition, with the remainder of the year a wet period of monsoonal rains.

While many collectors did not note the origins of their plants very well, others such as David Burke whose history appears in *Growing Orchids — Book Two*, took an amount of time and trouble to note not only the habitat but to send detailed notes to such people as would publish them. Naturally, few of them, unless they were resident in the country, stayed long enough in one area to note its annual cycle.

Writing of these two vandas, David Burke noted: 'They grow mostly on rocks, sometimes on trees ... in very light shade, sometimes full sun. In the cold season the maximum temperature is 65 degees, minimum about 31; oftentimes the ground is quite white and sometimes icicles form in the morning, from 4 to 6 being the coldest time. Sometimes the plants are completely shrivelled, as the dew is not so heavy as that formed in countries close to the equator.' He found that in the southern Shan States of Burma at 1200 metres (about 3500 to 4000 feet) there was frost every night for about two months of the year, yet the orchids flourished in this climate.

Where do we go wrong? Haven't we all tried to grow those things and been defeated by just such conditions as he described? Well, orchids grow where orchids grow! Despite that, it is always best to try to get information on the background of the genera we fancy. There is one thing most of us neglect to provide and that is air flow over the plants, essential if they are to grow.

In general the terete vandas need a great deal more light than the broad-leafed types. While infrequently cultivated, the species of both kinds have a lot to offer if a mixed collection of non-hybrids is to be grown. It is a most uncomfortable program to take on, because only by combining the species from relative climates and altitudes can it be carried out with a hint of success. A collection of terete-leafed orchids of various genera is almost impossible to assemble, but the broad-leafed vandas may be grown as individual plants in a mixed collection as they take about the same degree of shade as cymbidiums and the foliage hardens well in strong yet filtered light.

Euanthe sanderana

The distinction of this orchid from the vanda family rests on one small detail: there is no spur on the base of the labellum. It was for very many years known as *Vanda sanderana* and because of involvement in *Sander's List of Orchid Hybrids* it is not easy to change the name completely or disregard the old one. It may appear both ways in this book. Similarly, the plants which should be known as vandanthes, the hybrids between *Euanthe sanderana* and other vandas, are referred to simply as vandas. Although it may be incorrect to say that it is the outstanding flower of its type, there is little doubt that its effect on the generations following introduction to plant breeding has been such that the claim is quite a good one.

Vanda sanderana was discovered by Sander's collector Roebelin in south-eastern Mindanao Island in the Philippines in 1881. Unlike *Vanda coerulea*, it is a lowland tropical orchid and Roebelin found it growing almost on the seashore in an area where the temperature seldom falls below 25 degrees Celsius (about 80 degrees Fahrenheit) day or night throughout the year. Other collectors including David Burke, the protégé of Charles Curtis, visited the region and sent consignments of plants to England, Europe and America. *Euanthe sanderana* first flowered in the collection of a grower named Lee in 1883 and little imagination is required to visualise his enchantment and perhaps wonder at first sight of so magnificent a flower.

The generic title euanthe is derived from a Greek word alluding to large, showy flowers. It is possibly the sole member of a genus created for it and perhaps it was an instance of taxonomy gone wrong, an opinion held by some of Schlechter's contemporaries.

Wonderful stories have been woven around the discovery of this orchid, such as that appearing in *The Woodlands Orchids*, published in 1901. But let us stick to the bare, plain facts and leave the romance of orchids to the picture books. Roebelin describes his discovery thus: 'I had collected a few plants which bore no flowers, but which revealed a novelty by their habit and remains of old flower spikes still remaining on the plants... We landed in the evening on a small clearing by a stream which we had traversed and there it was that I saw at the top of a tree some flowers which appeared to my vision glorious and some minutes afterwards, in spite of huge ants and other vermin in swarms, I held in my hand the beautiful *Vanda sanderiana*. All my miseries, all my fatigues were at that moment forgotten.'

For all its paucity of detail, the story holds a wonderful picture for orchid growers who know *Euanthe sanderana*. John Dominy, Veitch's innovative hybridiser, remarked of the orchid: 'Thank goodness I have lived to see this marvel among vandas.'

Hugh Low & Co.'s collector Curnow sent a large consignment of plants of *Euanthe sanderana* to England shortly after Roebelin's find and it was from these plants that Lee's first flowering came. Further flowerings brought to light the beautiful color variations and different shapes in this species and soon many named varieties were listed. Some very large plants were collected, with up to twenty and even thirty branches from the main monopodial stem. Thousands of fine plants were lost by collection, packing and despatch at the incorrect time of the year and finally the habitat was so decimated that only poor plants and remnants were left.

Micholitz sent a beautiful plant to Sanders', which was a conglomerate of *Vanda* or *Euanthe sanderana* and *Aerides sanderanum* (syn. *A. lawrenceae*). It is illustrated in *The Orchid World* of July 1913, flowering at Sanders' nursery at St Albans. This mass was taken from a humid lowland swamp covered by almost impenetrable mangroves on the coast of Mindanao. Also on the record of fine examples of *Euanthe sanderana* is the plant produced by J. Gurney Fowler's orchid grower in 1896 with twelve spikes and 137 flowers. It should be remembered, however, that these plants came to the growers already specimens and did not represent cultivation other than the ability to make them flower well.

Originally most growers had difficulty with this species because it was the direct opposite of *Vanda coerulea* and seemed to miss the humid heat of its habitat. Despite the records showing magnificent flowerings of *Euanthe sanderana*, it was without doubt something built into the plants before they left the habitat. Such specimens were rare in cultivation in the period when this book was published and possibly will never be seen again. It is difficult to estimate the age of such plants as have been described, but it could not be less than the order of some fifty to a hundred years.

Euanthe sanderana belongs to the broad-leaf series and hybridises readily with most vandas including the terete-leaf species and their hybrids.

Monopodial orchids like vandas are usually slow to produce side shoots, almost the only way in which a duplicate of a special type can be produced. Although advertisements may feature chemical attacks as an alternative, such methods could well result in losing the clone before it has a chance to multiply. Once the main stem has been grown to a height and with sufficient root to use the system, a knife cut may be made in the stem with a sharp, thin-bladed tool to a depth of about half the diameter, preferably with root above and below the cut, slanting downward and not straight across.

1

The knife blade in position, showing the depth of the cut. It will be found that if a blunt knife is used the tough stem may fracture by use of too much pressure. A sawing motion, slowly and gently pushing the knife downward, is the easiest method. Care should be taken to keep the cut under control and no more than half-way. If the top is accidentally severed the end result will be the same, but it is far quicker and easier if the top is still fed by all the available root. It is too risky to attack propagation by this method if there is no root at all above the cut and it should not be attempted on short growth of young plants.

2

18

Once the knife has been embedded in the main stem a 'splint' should be tied firmly in place above and below the cut with three or four twisties or raffia. The 'splint' should be of durable wood or strong wire as it may be necessary to keep it there for two or three years. The upper portion of the plant, still fed by the lower roots although through only half the stem diameter, will continue to grow and flower as though nothing had been done and no particular care is necessary unless it starts to lose leaves, which may indicate a basic weakness before the operation.

3

This should be the end result. Some leaf has been lost from the stem below the cut, which is still visible just below the lowest leaf. The splint has been removed and there is some danger that the break may become complete unless it is returned. When this small plantlet at the base has grown roots it may be taken away. Meantime it is possible that another latent 'eye' may develop on the bare stem and another plantlet will result. It took two years for the first one to form, but at least there is one prospective duplicate of a nice vanda.

4

Rhyncostylis

This numerically small genus did not have much importance for orchid growers until it entered the miniature stage of hybridising in the vanda complex. The passion for small flowers began in much the same way as for cymbidiums and all the preceding projects. It seemed more than anything else a move into a line which would stimulate interest in orchids, but perhaps the orchid-growing section of horticulture was not as jaded as some imagined. Possibly it could all be put down to natural human curiosity and the end result could have far exceeded the expectations of the innovators.

Rhyncostylis retusa has a fairly long history, because the type form was found by Dr Blume in Java about 1823 and for most of the period since it was known as *Saccolabium blumei.* The origin of the name rhyncostylis is the Greek words *rhyncos* (a beak) and *stylis* (a column) and the saccolabiums take their title from the Latin words *saccus* (a bag) and *labium* (the lip), in reference to the bag-like shape of the labellum. The purists may well wince.

The prehistory of the type species *Rhyncostylis retusa* goes back to Linnaeus, who referred to it as *Epidendrum retusum,* so he must either have seen dried flowers or even a flowering plant. John Lindley later referred to it as *Sarcanthus guttata.* In his reference to this orchid he wrote in *The Botanical Register* of 1831 that he '. . . saw in 1820 in Sir Joseph Banks' library a specimen in full flower that had been sent from the Royal Gardens at Kew'. This probably was the first time it had flowered in Britain, but neither the origin of the plant nor the date of its importation seems to have been recorded. Its history before 1830 is something of a mystery, although it was certainly well known before that time, possibly in Europe because of its association with Linnaeus and where it was known as *Saccolabium guttatum.*

The first plants recorded as having reached Britain came from Dr Wallich through the East India Company for the Horticultural Society of London. Considering its wide distribution throughout Indo-Asia it varies little from the type form, although albino clones and special varieties are known. In Java the Dutch planted teak as shelter trees around and through their plantations and *Rhyncostylis retusa* plants colonised them as soon as they became mature enough. They covered the trees in thousands. From descriptions of its occurrence as a natural tropical lowland orchid it appears that the plants were seldom found so thickly covering an area, but rather that they were solitary, sometimes with great distances between specimens.

In describing the habitat graphically, even if a little floridly, one traveller-collector had this to say: 'In Malabar it mostly affects the jungle and marshy banks of sluggish-flowing rivers thick with trees of low stature and thorny undergrowth composed of Solanum ferox, spiny acacias and the like, where croak innumerable frogs, speaking eloquently of malaria, ague and fever, and where crawls the deadly cobra, and where other reptiles and insects of strange appearance are abundant. In the midst of such surroundings, pendent from the branches of trees may be seen the charming blooms of the saccolabium (rhyncostylis) spreading a fragrance around which compels the explorer to linger in the locality, even at the risk of subsequent attacks of jungle fever . . .'

Few glass-houses would have much affiliation with the set of conditions outlined in that paragraph. Nevertheless, provided a good warm home is found for *Rhyncostylis retusa* it will reward the grower with just such a display of flowers together with its attendant faint perfume in sunlight.

The climate is one of extremes of wet and dry. In the one the plant grows quickly, sending out thick, clinging roots and in the other it flowers usually at the onset of the dry season. The temperature rarely falls below 21 degrees Celsius (about 70 degrees Fahrenheit).

In the period when they were known as saccolabiums and *Rhyncostylis retusa* was *Saccolabium blumei* an albino form was discovered. It was not connected with that species and was known as *Saccolabium heathii*. This occurred about 1884 or 1885 and it was not noted again until Baron Schroder presented a spike to a meeting of the Royal Horticultural Society in 1887. Some perceptive people recognised it for what it really was and a sale of a plant of this albino form was made at 150 guineas, a sum which is impossible to translate into present-day values. However, it may be put succinctly as the wages for three years of a considerable part of the work force in those days.

An orchid grower and collector named Rimstad searched the known habitat of *Rhyncostylis retusa* in Java over several flowering seasons in the following years, but he found few plants of the rare albino form. Until cultivated from seed, in which process it breeds true, it has always been a rarity. Some forms of white-flowered *Rhyncostylis retusa* plants are not true albinos and show slight signs of color in the labellum as well as the faintest touches in other parts of the flower. Rimstad also devoted many years to searching for an albino form of *Vanda tricolor* var. *suavis*, but in this he was completely unsuccessful, and it is doubtful, on the basis of present information, that such a variety ever existed.

Sir Joseph Banks

Rhyncostylis coelestis

One of the most important of the rhyncostylis seems to have little history attached to it. The secret of its success was its color. *Rhyncostylis coelestis* has a blue component and it was this which brought it into the miniature range. The blue of this orchid, in conjunction with that of the inbred lines derived from *Vanda coerulea* has given some of the most attractive miniature hybrids possible.

Rhyncostylis coelestis was apparently discovered by the collector Roebelin in Thailand sometime in the 1870-80 period. It is totally epiphytic according to Reichenbach's description and has a color range which includes all the intermediates from white to azure blue. It grows in a warm lowland climate of a long wet season followed by a dry, hot period when the plants flower. Unlike *Rhyncostylis retusa*, the flower spikes are upright.

There seems to be an endless repetition of information about the orchid and apparently little was visualised for it as a possible hybridising medium. The color intensity of some of the smaller hybrids which it engendered is amazing, but it was only in the alliance of *Rhyncostylis coelestis* with *Vanda* Rothschildiana, bringing into the combination a second-generation strain of *Vanda coerulea*, that this small rhyncostylis entered into a fuller life in the hybrid list. *Rhyncovanda* Blue Angel, bred by the Hawaiian hybridist, Takakura, in the late 1950 period and registered in 1961, has brought into cultivation some of the most beautiful miniature vanda-type flowers possible to imagine.

Rhyncostylis coelestis was first described by Reichenbach in *The Gardeners' Chronicle* in 1885, but the best description of the plant and its habitat is that of

Sander's Reichenbachia, one of the beautifully illustrated publications produced in the late nineteenth century. It runs as follows:

'It is quite distinct from the majority of saccolabiums in bearing upright flower spikes. The largest number of species in this handsome genus carry pendulous, long racemes of densely packed blossoms, varying in color from white to rose, purple, violet, and orange-crimson, but no kinds with which we are acquainted bear such charming sapphire and azure-blue lipped blossoms as *Saccolabium coeleste,* with just enough white in the sepals and petals to make the flowers perfectly exquisite. In a large batch of plants there is an almost infinite variety in size, form and coloring, sometimes the white color preponderating, at other times the blue. It is, however, always a gem and never fails to command admiration; we should be glad to see this elegant genus more generally cultivated.

'Our collector describes this species as growing upon trees in Siam in hot, moist districts where the land is often under water for a considerable time in the rainy season, when the temperature is very high. The plants grow with marvellous rapidity, emitting from among the leaves new roots in abundance, which grow with great vigor and freedom, apparently absorbing the moisture of the air to great advantage. After a time the rain suddenly ceases and then sets in a scorching, dry heat, often attended by forest fires, in which epiphytic plants suffer first and most severely. These fires often extend for long distances, and destroy multitudes of noble trees and lovely plants, which a few short hours previously were laden with handsome foliage and beautiful blossoms.'

While apparently there were no conservationists at hand in those days, the local fire brigades had their hands full. Like most of the other vandaceous orchids *Rhyncostylis coelestis* flowers at the end of the growing season, which in artificial cultivation would be in the warmer months of the year and in the wet season in sub-tropical and tropical regions.

Rhyncostylis gigantea

This orchid is another lowland tropical species with a regular climatic change influencing its growing and flowering cycle. It occurs in much of Malaysia and Burma as an epiphyte and is slow growing. Introduced into Britain about 1860, it was first noted in the collection of the Bishop of Winchester and was scarce until Veitch's nursery introduced a large consignment from their Burma agent, General Benson. Some of the early plants brought into Britain were of considerable size, with up to ten and more stems in the one mass, and up to a metre high. In flower it is spectacular, but the plants noted in cultivation in the 1970-80 decade were usually small and less than 30 to 40 centimetres high (about 12 to 15 inches).

In its habitat the climate pattern is of a rainy season from June onward with temperatures in the 20 to 30 degrees Celsius range (about 70 to 85 degrees Fahrenheit), followed by flowering of the plants from August to October, then with a fairly dry period of some months until the rains recommence in the following year. However, in all seasons the temperature is fairly constant and the humidity high even in the 'coolest' months of the year.

Like most rhyncostylis, the root system of *Rhyncostylis gigantea* is relatively short and sparse but thick, the growth of the plants themselves slow, with some two or at most three leaves added each year.

As with so many orchids, it was known and described long before its advent as a flowering plant in glass-houses. John Lindley described and named it about 1832. The name has been constant, but some authorities give it as *Rhyncostylis giganteum.*

A white-flowered form was introduced about 1880 by Linden, the Belgian nurseryman and botanist, and it was also sent to the French grower Godefroy by the collector Regnier from Thailand. As usual, these albino forms caused sensation as they appeared, but once it was found they grew freely from seed when self-fertilised they became more common, although there are some masqueraders which have faint intrusions of color. Some of the Asian growers in the middle years of the century grew magnificent plants of these white rhyncostylis.

The role of *Rhyncostylis gigantea* in modern hybridising for miniature flowering plants is considerable and in some instances the plants produce upright spikes of flower, with the red variety producing brilliance in some cross-pollinations.

The vanda family is large and in turn is related to a much larger group of orchids which grow over a considerable area of the world. Some are very selective in habitat and this includes various surfaces to which the roots attach the plants. In this plant the roots are gnarled and unhealthy, not because of the nature of the mount, which is tree-fern, but principally because the temperature and general environment are wrong. Natural weather conditions affect such plants even when they are grown in controlled conditions, as variations as small as 4 or 5 degrees could be detrimental to some. *Vanda coerulea* is an example which exhibits identical root failures and is so selective that many growers find it too much of a problem, unlike the plant illustrated and described on page 57.

1

Aerangis mystacidii, a small African relative of the vandas, growing happily on a slab of natural cork. This material should be selected to suit a genus and rejected once the roots show no inclination to attach and proliferate. While it may suit some temperatures and some genera, there is little doubt that others would be happier on other hosts. Orchid growers habitually change to different growing mediums as they become popular, but frequently it is to the dis-advantage of their collections; plants of whatever genus which seem to be growing well should have continuity of the system. Cork is difficult to saturate and this is a serious disability in some instances.

2

24

Sarcochilus ceciliae, a small Australian relative of the vandas, is most particular about growing mediums. The roots seldom enter potting material of any type and in their natural habitat grow only on the surface of rocks which may be covered with moss and natural detritus. In cultivation this habit should be respected and their roots given some similar anchorage by using pieces of sandstone or quartzite bedded in moss and with thin layers of moss packing between the pieces. The roots may attach to these pieces of rock, but as a preliminary and to keep the plants firm it may be necessary to use thin wire or nylon fishing line to tie them down. Other orchids may also respond well to this form of treatment.

3

Throughout these books closed benches have been mentioned as cultivation features. They suit various orchids, some of which, like these vandas take over completely. Originally standing in pots with chunks of bark to support them, the roots commenced to outrun the pots and were allowed to proliferate on the benches, which were covered with more chunks and smaller pieces of casuarina bark, which is second to none for orchid growing in glass-house climates. The lifespan of orchids growing in such conditions would depend on the height of the roof, because that would be the limit, with a great amount of scope for pruning down before they reached the clear glass under which they were grown. Provided the benching stood up to the conditions, an expectancy of some ten to fifteen years could be put on bark durability and the ultimate natural weakening of the plants.

4

Aerides

This genus associated with vandas was founded by the botanist-monk Loureiro on the species *Aerides odoratum*, the name referring to the supposition that these plants, because they did not grow on the ground or in an apparent growing medium, were capable of absorbing all their nutriment and moisture from the air. The name is compounded from two Greek words, of which only one seems to have any relevance — *aer*, which is almost the same as its English equivalent 'air'.

The genus is easier to trace than the man who named it. Joao Loureiro was a Portuguese who apparently lived in the Indo-China area for some time before the year 1800. The aerides were early discoveries among the beautiful Asian orchids and the species *Aerides odoratum* was no exception, because it was sent or brought to the Kew Gardens in England about 1800 from what is now Thailand. It is also common to other parts of Indo-Asia and both Dr Wallich and Dr Roxburgh sent specimens to the Horticultural Society, the plants flowering in their glass-houses in 1831. It was introduced commercially to Britain and Europe by Low & Co. and other distributors.

The records of some of the plants flowered in England include one which had almost a world trip to splendor. It flowered in the collection of R. Le Doux in Liverpool after being sent to him from Para, Brazil. The plant was said to have come originally from the Philippines and when Le Doux flowered it the plant stood about 2 metres tall (over 6 feet).

Aerides odoratum, as its name suggests, is scented and deserves seeking and growing by more people than presently cultivate it. It has few hybrid connections.

Aerides lawrenceae (Reichenbach) was introduced into Britain by Sanders, their plants collected by Roebelin on Mindanao Island, in the Philippines. David Burke also collected this beautiful orchid for his connections, both of the gatherers sending the plants back in 1880. Coming from a lower elevation than *Aerides odoratum*, the species *Aerides lawrenceae* is a tropical lowland orchid growing in a temperature seldom altering much from the 20 to 30 degrees Celsius range (about 70 to 85 degrees Fahrenheit), with a definite wet season of growth followed by a semi-dry to dry period during which it flowers. It was dedicated to the wife of Sir Trevor Lawrence, who was for a long period president of the Royal Horticultural Society. His mother was one of the noted growers of an earlier era and Sir Trevor grew up with orchids.

Aerides quinquevulneram has flowers somewhat similar to those of *Aerides lawrenceae*, but the pendant spike is considerably longer and the flowers usually spotted with purple over all the segments. It was named by Lindley and has several synonyms. Discovered originally in the Philippines, it was later collected by Cuming and sent to Loddiges, possibly from Manila. Like *Aerides lawrenceae*, it is a tropical lowland orchid suited to warm glass-house cultivation or in open to semi-open shelters in sub-tropical or tropical areas. It would also grow very well as a tree-grown plant in such areas.

Although the aerides have the reputation of dropping their leaves as they age, it is no more common to the genus than to vandas, and leaves should be etained on plants for many years in good cultivation. The unsightly bare expanse of stem is more a cultural fault than natural and the roots from this barren stalk also lose vitality. Although *Aerides quinquevulneram* seems to be one of the 'leggy' type, use should be made of the bare stem to produce side shoots before it becomes too aged. This is done by partially severing the stem, staking it firmly and putting a light band of sphagnum moss just below the cut. It should be kept moist at all times and must not be too thick or a sappy shoot finally emerges which may be hard to rear. The system is illustrated on pages 18-19.

Sir Trevor Lawrence

Ascocentrums

The genus was known for more than a century before Schlechter gave them this title in 1913. It is derived from the Greek words *ascos* (a bag) and *kentron* (a spur) for the large spur which is part of the labellum. To John Lindley they were also known as saccolabiums and the title was used throughout, despite Lindley considering them as a section of the aerides. Ascocentrums may still have been relatively sparse in cultivation had it not been for their use in cross-pollinations with others of the vanda complex. Their success as progenitors of the 1970-80 ascocendas needs no qualification, as reference to the color photographs shows.

Ascocentrum ampullaceum, one of the smallest flowers in the genus, was originally collected by Dr Roxburgh and Dr Wallich in Sylhet province, India, where it grows at about 500 to 1750 metres (about 1500 to 3000 feet). The first plants to arrive in Britain came from the Khasia Hills in Assam, where they were collected by Gibson. It is a widespread species and Low & Co.'s collectors took it from other regions all the way from Burma to the further reaches of Indo-China. Although Roxburgh and Wallich knew it quite well as far back as 1814, its introduction before 1865 is indeterminate. The expert orchid cultivator Paxton was one of the first to grow it, sometime in the 1830-40 period. The origin of his plants was probably Roxburgh or Wallich, although Gibson is credited with this consignment. John Lindley's plate in *Sertum Orchidaceum* is a copy of a painting by an Indian artist, which came originally by way of the East India Company. The history of this company is tied firmly to orchids and their discovery because many of its employees and servants were horticulturally minded and made the most of their opportunities while in India and Burma. It was Low & Co. who first brought *Ascocentrum ampullaceum* to England in any considerable numbers and it was a most popular orchid.

Specimens have been grown at times in the history of the genus which had stems up to 5 metres tall (over 16 feet) and it could be supposed that they could go on lengthening indefinitely if nothing supervened. As roots are continually produced from the leafy part of the stem there is no reason why plants should not be cultivated for a considerable time. The production of side shoots is a natural process, but one which in artificial conditions never seems to follow as frequently as could be expected. If it does not happen naturally it should be induced in the way outlined above.

Ascocentrum curvifolium was also a find of Wallich in the very early years of the nineteenth century; the origin was the tropical section of the Himalayan foothills. It was introduced into Britain about 1850 and flowered in the Royal Gardens at Kew about 1862. Again it was Low & Co. who brought it into the country in quantity.

Both these ascocentrums are variable in their flowering period, but *Ascocentrum ampullaceum* usually flowers in late spring and *Ascocentrum curvifolium* follows some weeks later.

Ascocentrum miniatum was introduced about 1846 by James Veitch & Sons with plants collected by Thomas Lobb. Their nursery listed it as being from Java and this inaccurate information was passed on to John Lindley who even established an incorrect specimen as the type form. This could have been a mistake in the Veitch nursery in the inevitable confusion of unpacking crates and baskets of totally unfamiliar plants which had no flowers or anything else to identify them. The plant Lindley listed was, in fact, *Ascocentrum curvifolium* which as the name indicates, has distinctive curving foliage, while that of *Ascocentrum miniatum* is almost straight.

This ascocentrum was first flowered in Britain by Sigismund Rucker in 1847 on what was supposed to be a Javanese plant. Whether it was an involuntary error or simply a ruse to keep other collectors out of new plant territory is unknown.

These three ascocentrums are attractive miniatures of the vanda complex and as such offer a challenge to would-be growers who enjoy a challenge, particularly in species orchids. While the hybrids derived from these seem relatively easy to obtain and grow, ascocentrums usually are a little more selective in their demands.

The cultivation of ascocentrums, aerides and rhyncostylis is dealt with in general vanda type culture recommendations at the end of the series on these orchids.

Vandopsis

This generic title was applied by Pfitzer in 1888 to plants previously included under the name stauropsis. It stems from the Greek word, *opsis*, meaning resemblance, and the complete title vandopsis indicates a vanda-like habit and flower. Some plants have a notable resemblance to phalaenopsis. The flowers of most of the species, however, are thick and fleshy. It appears as though the whole family of stauropsis was broken up and redistributed among other genera.

Vandopsis parishii (Reichenbach f.) is possibly the most common species in cultivation. It has broad, thick leaves, usually carrying only three or four in cultivation, and a short, thick root system which is surface and not likely to grow well in a pot.

It came to light in Britain about 1880, but was originally found by The Rev. Parish in Moulmein, Burma, about 1862. Low & Co., who seemed to have a deal to do in the vandaceous orchids, imported plants about 1870, collected in the Salween River area of Burma. At first its boundaries of occurrence were unknown and R. Moore, the discoverer of *Paphio. charlesworthii*, identified the Lake Inle area in the Shan States as another habitat. It is also known to have come from other parts of Indo-Asia.

The first Englishman to flower *Vandopsis parishii* was Sir William Marriott and he also flowered the beautiful variety *marriottiana*, a chance plant in a collection of the species he had in his glass-houses. These two species are entries in the hybrid list, so they are included in the vanda section.

Vandopsis lissochiloides (Gaudichaud) has a background extending to 1750. The Dutch botanist, Rumphius, author of *Herbarium Amboinensis,* described the plant under the name *Angraecum quintum* from material he collected on the island of Amboina, at that time under Dutch colonisation. The Dutch were far-sighted in their colonisation and at that time thought nothing of inter-marrying with the native races. In this way they preserved a good deal of harmony where insular attitude may have caused massacre at any time. The history of this side of their colonisation period is most bloodthirsty in patches, particularly the early periods. However, we have been sidetracked.

This beautiful orchid was once again given a name change when the French botanist Gaudichaud recorded it in 1862 as *Fieldia lissochiloides* for its likeness to the lissochilus, an Afro-Madagascan genus of orchids. John Lindley subsequently remarked: 'What could possibly have led Gaudichaud to compare this epiphyte with the terrestrial lissochilus we are unable to imagine, for there is only the slenderest resemblance between the two.'

The collector Cuming sent the plants responsible for the comment from the Philippines and James Bateman was possibly the first man in Britain to flower this species. Dissatisfied with the taxonomy, Lindley renamed *Fieldia lissochiloides* as *Vanda batemani*. It remained so known for some time and both Reichenbach and Bentham interfered again, with Bentham compounding the genera fieldia and stauropsis. *Vanda batemani* then became known as *Stauropsis lissochiloides*, fortunately retaining its species name. Differences in the floral structure of the genus eventually caused another change and the plants were separated under Pfitzer's generic title of vandopsis. *Veitch* *Manual of Orchidaceous Plants* gives a good résumé.

Vandopsis lissochiloides has produced some very beautiful hybrids, one of which is featured in the illustrations. The species itself is not easy to cultivate in cool climates. It carries some ten to fifteen flowers, the red buds of which give a promise which is adequately fulfilled.

Vandopsis gigantea (Lindley) is an orchid which seemed to promise many things for the hybridist. It had broad, fleshy leaves of 30 centimetres (about 12 inches) or more in length and a flower spike carrying from ten to twenty or more flowers, the buds of which are dull purple and the flowers when open golden and speckled with dull purple-brown. It was originally found by Wallich in Moulmein, Burma, about 1826 and later by Griffith in the vicinity of Tenasserim River near the Thailand border, growing on lagerstroemia trees. It was the collector Thomas Lobb, however, who sent the first consignment of plants to Veitch & Sons.

About 1858 Robert Warner became the first recorded grower to flower this new species in England and it was flowered about the same time in Europe. Both John Lindley and Reichenbach remarked on it, but the expectations of the fanciers were not fulfilled, as they had hoped for something rather larger in the way of flowers from such a plant. Interest in *Vandopsis gigantea* lapsed over the following years.

The orchid was not misnamed, however, as Bartle Grant, a British army captain in Burma in the 1890 period describes it thus: 'It forms masses of extraordinary size. One plant I found on the Shan border was a great deal more than I could have packed on an elephant. It is apparently a very local plant, but abundant in some places, viz., in the shady jungle about Tavoy...' The flowers are up to 5 or 6 centimetres across. His description recalls some of the plants I came across in the islands during service in the 1939-45 war. Their tangled masses would have comfortably filled a 1 tonne utility truck. Unfortunately I did not stay in any of the locations long enough to identify them, see them flower or name them.

Rapee Sagarik, one of the eminent hybridisers of the 1960-80 period, cross-pollinated the species vandopsis *parishii* and *gigantea* and in 1973 the resultant grex was named after him. The possibilities of this alliance may take many years to assess in following hybrids, but as the usual process in raising new orchids is long term, eventually something outstanding must flow from such work.

The genus had been cross-pollinated with various other genera as outlined in the list of such work at the end of the vanda section.

Although *Vandopsis parishii* has been removed from the genus and allotted the generic title hygrochilus, hybridism and the registration of names in *Sander's List of Orchid Hybrids* ensures that it will be known by the original title for some time to come.

Renanthera

This genus was named by Joao Loureiro in 1790 with a hybrid word beginning with the Latin word, *renes* (kidney) and the Greek word, *anthera* (anther). It alludes to the shape of the pollinia of the species *Renanthera coccinea*, with which Loureiro came into contact. As the name indicates it is predominantly red, the flowers produced in branching racemes from a growth system remarkably like that of the epidendrums, but growing taller and much more supine if unsupported. The flower spike emerges from the side of the lengthening stem, unlike the terminal inflorescence of epidendrums, and the leaves are also slightly different, being somewhat broad, blunt, short and fleshy.

It was one of the first orchids with which James Bateman came into contact and started him on a path which had many strange plants and notable people on it throughout his eighty-six years. But let him tell his own story: 'I was devoted to orchids long before I knew what an orchid was; indeed, the word itself was quite strange to me when I heard my mother apply it to a beautiful plant with spotted leaves and speckled flowers which I had gathered in a country lane and regarded with great admiration. "That," she said, "is an orchis." (*0. muscula.*) I must have been then about eight years old, but I was more than eighteen when, the scene being shifted to Oxford, I stepped into a nursery situated where Keble College now stands and kept by the veteran Fairburn, who had been gardener to Prince Leopold and Sir Joseph Banks. This sealed my fate! Presently Mr Fairburn drew my attention to a curious plant with leathery leaves and several stout roots feeling their way amongst a number of small pieces of wood to which it was expected they would become permanently attached. "Here," he said, "is a piece of the famous Chinese air plant (*Renanthera coccinea*) which flowered under my care when gardener to H.R.H. Prince Leopold at Bushey Park; Would you like to see a drawing of it?" "As you please." It was certainly a vision of beauty that Mr Fairburn, opening a volume of *The Botanical Magazine,*, t. 2997-2998, showed me, for here was a perfect portrait of the Chinese air plant, full size and correctly colored. Of course I fell in love at first sight and as Mr F. only asked a guinea for his plant (high prices were not yet in vogue) it soon changed hands and travelled with me to Knypersley when the Christmas holidays began. I had caught my orchid, but how to treat it I knew not.'

That was the beginning of the famous orchid collection of James Bateman at Knypersley Hall and part of his life story is given below.

John Lindley remarked of *Renanthera coccinea*: 'The work of the missionary Loureiro, published in 1790, a drawing in the possession of the Horticultural Society of London and the reports of some travellers who have visited China have been, up to the present time, the only evidence to Europeans of the existence of this truly magnificent plant, the beauty of whose blossoms surpasses everything known in the vegetable world. That the Chinese suspend in baskets from the ceilings of their rooms several of the tribe to which this belongs, some for the sake of their flowers and some on account of their delightful fragrance, is familiar to everyone.'

We have in the above an account of another era in orchid growing in an indoor cultivation environment within a house or dwelling and for how long it had been so we have no means of guessing. Of course Lindley's assessment of the beauty of those flowers was to be eclipsed many times later in his experience.

Sir Trevor Lawrence in 1911 possessed a plant of *Renanthera coccinea* which had been brought from China (?) about 1815 and owned by several other growers before coming into his hands. But again we have been sidetracked into history and perhaps we could stay there with Bateman, for whom association with renantheras meant so much to his future way of life.

It is somewhat difficult to place people in affiliations after a time lapse such as that which separates John Lindley from the 1980 decade, but the close association between John Lindley and James Bateman is quite evident. Bateman was born in 1811 and died in 1897, commencing an association with orchids early in his life and establishing at least three personal collections. History perhaps may judge him the lesser of the pair, and there is little doubt that Bateman was interested in the cultivation of the plants rather than their taxonomy. He was among the earliest to appreciate the difference between cultivation and the erroneous methods embarked on by the majority of growers.

Early in his career as a grower his father apparently financed his employment of a collector named Colley, who was despatched to Demarara (British Guiana, now Guyana) to collect orchids for him. Perhaps Bateman's own words are more expressive than a synopsis:

'It has been a great pleasure to me to revive memories of my first experience in orchid importing. I sent (with my father's permission) a man of the name of Colley to collect Orchids in Demarara. He was under the protection of two great Liverpool merchants, Moss and Horsfall, on whom he was authorised to draw to the extent of £200 or £300. Colley did his best and found an abundance of Orchids, i.e., of Catasetums and yellow-flowered Oncidiums, which were not worth their freight. The only new plant worthy of cultivation was a species of Rodriguezia or Burlingtonia with large white flowers, which flowered beautifully and then died. There is a beautiful white Catasetum in the Demarara woods, but Colley was not fortunate enough to meet with it; indeed, it has not been found until a very recent period. All this reads like a very poor speculation, but that was not the case. You have heard, no doubt, of *Oncidium Lanceanum,*, which Lance discovered in Surinam a year or two before Colley went to Demarara. He (Lance) only sent over two or three plants to England, which made Orchid collectors mad. It had never been found in Demarara, but Colley stumbled upon a solitary tree (about five days' sail up the Demarara River) covered from head to foot with this Oncidium. He immediately set to work and stripped the tree, determined not to give any others the chance! ... Anyhow, it retrieved the fortunes of my expedition, for when a large healthy cargo was known to have arrived, everyone (save the fortunate holders of Mr Lance's specimens) were prepared to go down on their knees for a bit, offering their greatest treasures in exchange. In this way (without any money passing) I became possessed of bits of all the then-known species which I cared to have. But for this unexpected find my expedition would have been a total loss and bitter vexation. We did not then know that good orchids are, as a rule, very rarely met with on the beautiful tidal tropical rivers, but must be sought on the nearest mountains, at an elevation of 3000 to 6000 feet.'

In his lifetime Bateman produced a number of beautiful books, although some are quite unknown to present growers. Most were illustrated by the noted artists of the period and were published at considerable expense because they were sold for ridiculous fractions of the cost of production and Bateman gave away a large number of each publication as it came from the presses.

Bateman did not realise in his lifetime what hybridists would eventually do to his beloved species. He detested the system of cross-pollinations which occurred in his lifetime and although he did not take this to a personal level with anyone, as another anecdote in this book reveals, the thought that species orchids could be subjected to such indignities was beyond him. It should not be imagined, however, that all his interest was centred on orchids, as he was an avid collector of plants, native and exotic, all his life.

The renantheras are morphologically alike, some with stouter stems than others, some with very long growths and the flowers carried in large numbers on the branching stems. I can close my eyes and see renantheras growing on dead trees in coastal areas of the islands in South-East Asia during the war years 1939-45 — in which all the other vegetation had been cut down with bombs, shells and rockets — flowering brilliantly in the morning sun and drenched in the afternoon rains.

Renanthera storiei is a native of the Philippine Islands and was originally sent to Hugh Low & Co. in England about 1880. J. G. Storie was the collector and when the plants flowered Reichenbach described this species as 'a new Philippines renanthera just matching or rather surpassing the celebrated *R. coccinea*.' It also is red, but mostly not as brilliant as its comparative plant. *Renanthera coccinea* is native to Thailand and southern China. So much of this region has been destroyed with herbicides and clearing of the country for farming and other uses that the species is endangered.

Renanthera imschootiana appeared in a collection of plants taken in hand by the Dutch grower A. van Imschoot. It was said to have come from Burma and grew in a climate where the temperature seldom fell below 15 to 18 degrees Celsius (about 60 to 65 degrees Fahrenheit) even in the coolest months of the year. It flowered in the dry season, which was considerably hotter though less humid. It is shorter than other species.

The renantheras were interbred along hybrid lines of some diversity, one of the first and most notable of the productions being *Renanthera* Brookie Chandler, raised by J. P. Russell, of Honolulu, in 1950, which is illustrated in the color photos. The flower spikes of this hybrid on well-grown plants may extend to more than a metre (over 3 feet) and branch into several side shoots.

The genus likes bright light, almost up to burning point for some which grow in full sunlight, and should be grown under clear glass or the minimum grade of shade-cloth in warm climates. In glass-house cultivation they should be grown in the brightest, warmest part of the glass-house and taken into shade when the flower spikes open, as they fade quickly if left in open sunlight or bright diffused light and their brilliance is lost.

Again their culture may be referred to at the end of the section, as their general habit and root system had much in common with the terete vandas.

Arachnis

The generic title was given by Blume, a Dutch botanist who lived for some time in Java. The Greek word *arachne*, for spider, denoted to him the strange resemblance which the flowers bore to those creatures. While it may seem surprising to attach any appearance of malevolence to orchids, the flowers of the genus, particularly the dark flowers of *insignis*, may seem so to some people. Perhaps it was this type which was originally found by Blume.

The species *Arachnis hookerana, Arachnis flos aeris* and *Arachnis maingay* are the three principal members and they have been interbred to provide an amazing range of flowers. Grown mostly by cultivators in the Indo-Asian region, these orchids are exported throughout the world. The climate of Indo-Asia suits the style of growing the plants in endless thousands in open conditions, where they can be trimmed back when they become too tall and wiry, so inducing side shoots which grow and flower in their turn.

In conjunction with vandas and renantheras and their derivatives, the arachnis have been hybridised to the point where they flower throughout the year, some clones almost continuously producing fresh spikes. The list of the vanda associates on pages 37, 38 gives some idea of the proliferation of the group and the compatibility of the various members.

Suited more to sub-tropical and tropical regions, where they are often almost a nuisance in orchid collections, most of the arachnis and various derivatives are considerably slower when cultivated in cooler climates and it is doubtful if the pruning techniques so nonchalantly carried out in the tropics would ever be needed in their lifetime. The wiry stems shed their leaves in natural or artificial conditions on the lower parts of the plants and provided some live root is still attached to these portions the top may be severed and the lower part soon sprouts. However, in cooler climates it may be better to try other means of getting the bare lower portions of plants to develop shoots, such as wrapping the stem in a thin layer of moist sphagnum moss after half severing the top portion and then tying it firmly to a stake to prevent the break becoming absolute. This also may take time.

Vanda Hybridising

The first hybrid vanda raised in Europe, from the cross-pollination of *Vanda teres* and *Vanda tricolor* var. *suavis*, was introduced by the nursery of Maron & Sons in France. It flowered in 1903 and was named Marguerite Maron. It gained an Award of Merit from the Royal Horticultural Society at one of the great flower shows of the period. From the description of the flower, all the spotting common to *Vanda tricolor* was lost and the petals and sepals were a pinky-rose color. The labellum, not a notable flower part in vandas, was the same deep rose-purple of the *Vanda tricolor* flower. A later reference gave the color as pale blush lilac. An illustration of the period indicates a type between the two parents.

An earlier hybrid was raised and named in 1893 from the cross-pollination of vandas *hookerana* and *teres*. It was named *Vanda* Miss Joaquim in honor of the originator of the cross-pollination and raiser of the seeds in Singapore. It was grown and flowered in Britain by Sir Trevor Lawrence, but the origin of the plant is indefinite. It must have been one of the seedlings raised by Miss Joaquim, as there appears to be no other record, and gained for Sir Trevor a First Class Certificate from the Royal Horticultural Society when flowering on a plant over 2 metres high (over 6 feet). The flower was light rose colored, fading almost to white as the spike aged.

W. van Deventer, who lived in Java for some twenty years, made the reverse cross-pollination for *Vanda* Marguerite Maron and took some of the plants back to Holland when he returned. His plants were eleven years old when he flowered them, as the seed was sown in 1908 and he had results in 1919. Van Deventer also made the cross-pollination of *Vanda tricolor* x *Vanda teres* and as the two were separate indentities in that period, they bore different names. This hybrid was named Emma van Deventer and it was one of the most influential hybrids in later work on the genus. The plants flowered in 1926 and when flowers were forwarded to the Royal Horticultural Society in England for assessment the plant was given an Award of Merit.

In *Vanda* Emma van Deventer the foliage resulting from the cross-pollination of broad-leaf vandas and terete foliage type first became apparent to growers. It is about intermediate between the two and allows cultivation in much brighter light than usual with broad-leaf vandas. This vanda has a tremendous increase in the type of growth common to most of the hybrids and may grow up to 2 metres (over 6 feet) before it flowers, with the final length of the monopodial stem as yet undetermined. Its influence on further hybrids is also quite startling, with some of the second generation almost pushing the glass out of the roof of houses up to 3½ metres (about 10 feet) at the peak of the gable.

Plants grown outdoors may be much shorter before they produce flowers and begin producing later plantlets from the main stem. *Vanda* Emma van Deventer is rose colored, with between six and ten flowers about 8 to 10 centimetres across (3 to 4 inches). Some clones have deeper speckling of rose-purple over the entire flower. A disadvantage of some of the Emma van Deventer hybrids is the habit of the petals to turn through 90 degrees and appear horizontal against the vertical plane of the flowers. It is possibe to breed this out, and it may come into the breeding lines through *Vanda coerulea* as well as the terete-leafed species.

On the other side of the family, the two broad-leaf vandas *sanderana* and *coerulea* were cross-pollinated rather later than could be supposed and the hybrid *Vanda* Rothschildiana resulting from the union surprised and delighted its raisers in 1931. This was the beginning of all the beautiful flowers of the 1970-80 period and the project may reach well into the future for as long as vandas are raised. The reticulations which are so pronounced a feature of two parents are brought forward into most generations since then. The standard of *Vanda* Rothschildiana flowers was improved by inbreeding the species and raising sibling of better shape for cross-pollinations.

The cross-pollinations in further moves with vandas Emma van Deventer, Rothschildiana and other hybrids and species such as *Vanda dearei*, together with the reworking of *Vanda tricolor* into the series, brought a certain amount of inbreeding. But they resulted in such notable grexes as *Vanda* Bill Sutton (*V. manila* x *V. sanderana*), *Vanda* Nellie Morley (*V.* Emma van Deventer x *V. sanderana*), one of the brightest additions to the genus, and *Vanda* Onomea (*V.* Rothschildiana x *V. sanderana*). The list is too complex to give in detail, but reference to *Sander's List of Orchid Hybrids* or a visit to the tropical and sub-tropical regions of Australia and other parts of the world in vanda flowering season, which seems to be perpetual, will soon convey an impression beyond mere description in a book.

It appeared at a late stage in the 1950 period that the hybridists had exhausted their imagination or become tired of hybridising or that the public turned away from the increasing numbers of the genus because of cultivation and accommodation problems and the hybridists turned to the smaller species to generate something new to catch the public interest. They turned toward the ascocentrums, aerides, rhyncostylis and vandopsis in quick succession. It was the ascocentrums which had the key to popularity because they interbred with such as *Vanda* Rothschildiana to produce plants which had miniature flowers of great beauty and which took up far less space than the orthodox vandas. The ascocendas, as the hybrids were named, produced most beautiful flowers, a few of which are illustrated.

The most important flowers in the vandaceous hybrids, irrespective of time and size were without doubt the two produced from the union of vandas *coerulea, sanderana, teres* and *tricolor,* with later contributions of experimental introductions helping things along. While many of these emanated from the Asiatic region, it is probably true that the bulk originated in the forty-ninth State of the United States of America, Hawaii. The color range is all the way through from the reds of *Vanda* Nellie Morley, the blue of *Vanda* Rothschildiana to whites and pinks such as *Vanda* William Oumae, also among the color pictures.

The arachnis, renantheras and rhyncostylis were introduced to the vandaceous hybrids in conjunction with the ascocentrums and aerides in the 1950-80 period and resulted in a maze of cross-pollinations and 'ara' hybrids, as the list which follows indicates.

Members of other genera were also combined in the groups, such as phalaenopsis, doritis, trichoglottis, sarcochilus and a few others, and recourse should be made to *Sander's List of Orchid Hybrids* to get a complete picture of the complex.

Mostly the resultant plants are vandaceous in character and culture. One constant is the temperatures under which they should be grown, for it is seldom that a temperate or cool-growing species has the capacity to influence the characteristics of the progeny and they revert in almost complete uniformity to the need for warm periods in cultivation, particularly at night.

The general characteristic of the root system is distinctly derived from the monopodials, with tips emerging at any point of the stem, at times in odd periods of the cultivation cycle. For this reason it is impossible to give a set of temperatures at which any hybrids may be grown. In most instances it will be trial and error, leading either to flowering and good growth or the next recommendation of discard as belonging to the 'too-hard' group.

There is a guide which may be used as a rough way of estimating the light requirements. In many of the vanda hybrids the foliage is semi-terete — that is, the leaves are midway between the broad-leaf type and the almost rounded, thin leaves of the terete species. Mostly this type of foliage is deeply channelled, but like the terete foliage it will withstand direct sunlight almost to the point of burning. If the plants are arachnis and renanthera-derived the short foliage is similarly burn resistant and the semi-terete or terete foliage more so. Generally, the broad-leafed hybrids retaining the *Euanthe sanderana* or *Vanda tricolor* type foliage are less durable in bright or open conditions. Some growers maintain that it is possible to grow these hybrids in bright outdoor conditions, but there is always that one unpredictable day which will do all the damage and a beautifully leafed plant or perhaps a number of them will be irretrievably ruined.

This is a list of the vanda complex as it stood at the end of 1975. Quite a number of others have been added since that year:

Vanda -

× Aerides	Aeridovanda
× Aerides × Arachnis	Burkillara
× Aerides × Arachnis × Ascocentrum	Lewisara
× Aerides × Ascocentrum	Christieara
× Aerides × Ascocentrum × Renanthera	Robinara
× Aerides × Neofinetia	Vandofinetia
× Aerides × Renanthera	Nobleara
× Aerides × Vandopsis	Maccoyara
× Arachnis	Aranda
× Arachnis × Ascocentrum	Mokara
× Arachnis × Ascocentrum × Renanthera	Yusofara
× Arachnis × Ascocentrum × Rhyncostylis	Bovornara
× Arachnis × Phalaenopsis	Trevorara
× Arachnis × Renanthera	Holttumara
× Arachnis × Vandopsis	Leeara
× Ascocentrum	Ascocenda
× Ascocentrum × Ascoglossum × Renanthera	Shigeurara
× Ascocentrum × Doritis	Ascovandoritis
× Ascocentrum × Doritis × Phalaenopsis	Vandewegheara
× Ascocentrum × Gastrochilus	Eastonara
× Ascocentrum × Luisia	Debruyneara
× Ascocentrum × Neofinetia	Nakamotoara
× Ascocentrum × Phalaenopsis	Devereuxara
× Ascocentrum × Phalaenopsis × Renanthera	Stamariaara
× Ascocentrum × Renanthera	Kagawara
× Ascocentrum × Rhyncostylis	Vascostylis
× Ascocentrum × Trichoglottis	Fujioara
× Ascocentrum × Vandopsis	Wilkinsara
× Doritis × Phalaenopsis	Hagerara

× Lusia	Luisanda
× Luisia × Rhyncostylis	Goffara
× Neofinetia	Vandofinetia
× Phalaenopsis	Vandaenopsis
× Phalaenopsis × Renanthera	Moirara
× Renanthera	Renantanda
× Renanthera × Rhyncostylis	Joannara
× Renanthera × Vandopsis	Hawaiiara
× Rhyncostylis	Rhyncovanda
× Trichoglottis	Trichovanda
× Vandopsis	Opsisanda

In addition to these it should be remembered that the various associates of the vandas given here have been combined between themselves to give an additional large register of hybrids which have flowered and been named in the same way as those above. For the purpose of all registrations the name vanda has been used even though in a large number of instances the species euanthe has been the one concerned. Obviously it would be too great a task to undo the list to make it conform to the wishes of the taxonomists and perhaps the day is not too far away when the generic name, vanda, will be recognised as the official one and that of euanthe relegated to the shadows from which it emerged to confuse growers and hybridists alike.

Cultivation — Vandas and Hybrids

Vandas in their habitat, wherever it might be, grow as easily on rock surfaces as on trees. With the type of root system they produce, the search for food is not as restricted as for the thinner rooted epiphytes like dendrobiums or odontoglossums. When growing on trees they may be found either on the vertical faces of the trunks or on the larger branches, at times even on thin parts of branches. Those growing on the vertical trunks grow close to the trunk with the roots becoming attachment points as soon as they leave the main stem. These roots may grow many metres long over the surface of the bark. Those plants on branches also grow vertically but after a time the stem of the vandas becomes too elongated to remain upright and the plants tend to bend over. Once this happens the plants send out side shoots which grow vertically in their turn. This habit may or may not be induced in artificial culture.

In tropical areas where coconuts are obtainable, the split husk is a very good container for the smaller members of the complex. When pot-grown, relatively large pots should be used considering the various sized plants, quite unlike the restrictions which are applied in cultivating many other epiphytic genera. As the whole of the root systems, aerial and those attached and pot-bound, feed the plants, they should all be treated with care and efforts made to keep them free from fractures in handling or potting.

When pots or other containers are used they should have adequate drainage holes in the bottom and preferably aerating holes in the sides if that is possible. The size of the material used for filling the pot, which in many instances is merely incidental, is anything which will not pass through a 1½ centimetre (½ inch) sieve; the coarser the better, within reason, always allowing smaller aggregates for smaller plants. Usually bark is used, but it may be combined with similar sized charcoal or even wood chips provided they are not from treated timbers, or raw pine or other woods containing aromatic oils.

Very little decay material need be used provided an adequate feeding program is arranged. If clean compost is available, not containing kitchen refuse, but clean leaf, twigs and grass clippings, it is an ideal addition. Animal manures, if used, should be hard old dry pieces from which normal watering may leach out the nutrients slowly so that the roots will not be overloaded in fertiliser. If poultry manure is blended (one part with three parts of wood chips or sawdust and allowed to mature for a whole year) it is an ideal additive, but fresh poultry manure or unblended manure is usually too strong for vandas.

Rockery-growing is an ideal way to cultivate some vandas in suitable warm areas. Much the same type of mix as for potted plants should be used with the same fertilisers, particularly decomposing vegetation. In either system it will be found that the vagaries of vanda roots are unpredictable and they will frequently avoid or even go in the opposite direction from a planned food source. On the other hand, provided the planned nutrients are what the plant is seeking, it is surprising how quickly the root system will travel in the right direction. When glass-house grown, allowances should be made for the roots to travel about and it is rare to find them conforming to a designed pattern which will have them all in the pot or container. They will grow on and cling to almost any surface which offers attachment and possibly traces of food.

In tropical climates neither pots nor other containers are really necessary. If the plants are grown in total enclosures they may be suspended from the roof by a tie around the main stem and the floor then covered with a thick layer of decay material blended with lumps of rock or broken brick. The roots soon find their way down into this and absorb all their growing needs from it. The only factor weighing against such a system is that the plants are a lot harder to take into shows or society meetings when in flower. An easy solution to this, however, is to sever the roots just above the surface of the feeding bed. The damage to them will be soon repaired by the plants on their return.

It will be noted, also, in tropical cultivation that potting material is entirely superfluous and that the plants, if stood in empty pots, particularly clay pots, will attach a network of roots to the inside of the pots and also the outside if given sufficient time. These roots may refuse to localise themselves in their own containers, but if a nutrient liquid spray pattern is worked out for them they tend to elaborate into a mass that will in time cover the surface of the pot. Most tropical-grown vandas look for support and some thought should be given to this when the plants are first attached to their containers. There is nothing worse than to detach a beautiful flowering plant and find that once it is removed from its surroundings it becomes top-heavy and refuses to remain upright. This is disastrous when the plant is flowering and the spike is disoriented, the flowers facing the wrong way or becoming inverted.

No part of cultural procedure is more important than following the annual cycle. Vandas, like most orchids, will rest or go partly dormant for a period even in tropical climates. The habits of the species are reflected in the growth of the plants in warmer and wetter months of the year in suitable climates. They will be better suited by climates, artificial or natural, which do not have marked peaks and troughs of temperature. Plants grown in glass-houses should have a minimum throughout the year of about 15 degrees Celsius (60 degrees Fahrenheit), with no reasonable upper limit, even visualising daytime temperatures of 40 degrees Celsius (100 degrees Fahrenheit).

The second part of the cycle, particularly flowering, is apt to be confused by the inclusion of species having different flowering seasons, so that in some instances plants will appear to be producing spikes in autumn as well as spring. The normal vanda hybrids adhere to a steady annual program once they have settled down in cultivation and can be relied on to give flowers within a week or so of a calendar date each year. When they seem to be slowing down, the root tips should be watched and if they seal off the green growing tip it is a sign that they are in the phase when they need less water and all nutrient feeding should be discontinued as long as they remain so. When reactivating, the approach to feeding should be slight and slow, gradually increasing the program as the plants show increased activity. In the dormant stage the plants should be conditioned more by increasing the humidity while decreasing the amount of water actually applied. The tips of the growths require particular attention to ensure that they do not fill with water or contain water, which may quickly rot out the complete head of the plant.

In outdoor cultivation seasonal rains play a big part in keeping the plants wet to damp and as this usually falls in the warm season of the year little harm will result. In glass-house cultivation the plants should be watered as they need it in the early part of the day during colder months of the year and changed over to evening watering in the summer months.

Day length has a considerable influence on glass-house-grown plants in latitudes below about 25 degrees south in Australia. This also has its minor effects in northern latitudes, whereas in tropical climates there is little difference throughout the year in day length. There is little to be done to compensate for this except paying more attention to cultural details.

Propagation is usually easier when vandas and their associates are climatically suited, because they will produce side shoots from the main stem which in turn grow roots and add to the plant bulk if not taken away. It is not a good idea to take these side shoots off too quickly and they should be either partially severed and tied back into position to force root growth or they may be wrapped in a loose ball of sphagnum moss to induce the same thing. From time to time chemical procedures are publicised for inducing the plants to produce these shoots but usually they are more adaptable to the environments in which they originated than to general use as cultural procedures. If vandas seem averse to producing shoots from the lower and barren half of the main stem another method of forcing the issue is illustrated on pages 18 and 19.

Although pot culture is adopted for most of the small members of the genera covered in this section, some are probably more at home in slat baskets. *Vandopsis parishii* and to a lesser extent the rhyncostylis are so slow growing that they are best left undisturbed for many years. This is possible when using coarse bark and charcoal, with the roots almost entirely apparent right through their period of occupancy of the wooden basket.

One of the points worth noting for culture of *Vanda coerulea* is that a topping of growing sphagnum moss placed on the surface of the pot or wooden basket at the commencement of the growing season is well worthwhile. The moss should be fresh and growing and not packed too tightly. This treatment could also be extended to the other plants grown in these containers, including the rhyncostylis and vandopsis.

One of the tricks played on renantheras and arachnis by some of their older cultivators was to tie a ball of sphagnum moss around the stem for a length of some centimetres on the part which should be expected to produce a flower spike. Naturally, this would be applied at the end of the growing season or the first thing to pop out would be a new root. If applied at the right time and kept moist it worked quite well provided the plants were given good light.

When any of the vanda alliance are grown in unsuitable conditions a number of symptoms become obvious. If full sunlight is allowed to fall on the leaves of those plants which burn, pale or light brown patches appear on the leaves at the point where they begin to bend and turn downward. If the tips of the leaves turn brown it may be taken as an indication of starvation or dehydration, conditions which are too cool or overfertilising. If black patches appear on the leaves it is also usually an indication that the conditions are too cold. If the leaves are cast on the lower part of the stem there may be a number of explanations, but the most probable is loss of roots. Overwatering, unsuitable potting material, overfertilising or even the conditions being too hot and dry may cause this. If the root system is intermittent and knobby it indicates too wide a fluctuation in temperature, particularly the difference between day and night temperatures. For good results a variation of no more than 2 or 3 degrees Celsius is best, which means that the conditions may not be so good for personal comfort but ideal for vandas.

The *Vanda coerulea* inheritance line for cool growing is mostly obliterated in hybrids which contain it, and those of the warmer growing species are dominant. A dominant leaf form is that of vandas *teres* and *hookerana* in most breeding lines and the plants are more light-tolerant than those with broad leaves inherited from vandas *tricolor, sanderana* and *coerulea*. But these plants suffer the same leaf symptoms from the same causes as the broad-leaf group.

The worst of the pests which attack the group are caterpillars or scale of various types, particularly if they infest the spikes. Fungus infections attacking the tips of the growths often have disastrous results if not checked with anti-fungus powders, solutions or sprays. Things which eat the root tips, such as slugs and snails and woodlice or slaters should be given something to attract and eradicate them. Ordinary slug and snail pellets are of little use against woodlice, but if the packet is emptied on to several sheets of newspaper, spread out and the contents sprayed with a strong solution of lindane they are most effective. They should be allowed to dry out after spraying then repacket-ed and put out of reach of children and animals. Contrary to popular opinion, birds will not eat them, although if fowls find them they may do so.

One of the worst pests to infest all orchids, not only vandas, in tropical and sub-tropical regions of Australia are the various beetles which attack green shoots or flower buds. Almost the only protection against them is total enclosure of the growing area after the fashion illustrated in the color section. Even when the green shoots or flower buds are protected by powders or sprays, the effect on beetles is delayed long enough for them to ruin a flower spike or tender part of plants.

Fertilisers for Vandaceous Orchids

Lacking the intense root ball or proliferation of such orchids as dendrobiums, fertilisers for vandas should be types which the roots may 'find'. They will, preferably, be allied to the containers so that continual watering after an application will release absorbed mineral salts, allowing the roots to pick them up in solutions. Absorptive containers may be of wood, ceramics or fern trunk. If this is seen as an opinion against the use of plastic pots this is true. When plastic pots are used a different system must be worked out so that the fertiliser is absorbed by the material in the container. This material may in itself be a fertiliser, such as animal manures, pine bark, wood chips or anything else which may absorb or attract the mineral salts so that additional watering will release a certain amount for the roots to absorb.

Decay material of vegetable origin such as leaves, wood, bark or even grass in compressed form are the sources of a considerable amount of plant food which vandas and their associates make use of in natural growing conditions. There is no better way of cultivating them than by trying to improvise the conditions of nature.

It should be noted in connection with fertilising that at certain periods in some climates the root tips will seal off and the plants appear inactive. Any fertilisers applied in this stage are useless and may cause more harm than good. In this period the plants may take up or leave absorbed residues from the materials with which the roots are associated.

The general growing conditions will control the plants and if they approach the ultimate, most vandas will continue growing and flowering right through the year instead of being seasonal. Fertilisers should be understood for what they will do in each individual's orchid collection and not for what the manufacturers say they will do in their information sheets or on the packets. It is always far better to err on the 'stingy' side than to overdo plant feeding, and once a nice moderate feeding program has been worked out which gives results no amount of persuasion from other growers should be heeded.

Where Did
Our Orchids
Come From?

Many orchids which grow in countries widely separated by sea are so much alike that they are provocative 'stirrers'. They have an obvious relationship, but the only way they may be connected is through a form of speculative linkage which depends on a 'way-out' yet not discredited theory known as continental drift. Although the use of satellites suggests that the hypothesis is worth following up, it may be a long time before confirmation or denial is available from photographic evidence.

In order to make the theory more real to anyone interested enough to read this, it is fairly common knowledge that the Earth has been reshaped and rearranged many times in the 4500-odd million years which are considered its age. If this supposed 'recent' rearrangement never occurred, it is logical to suppose that we would be aware of it from botanical evidence. This evidence is fairly reliable when plant distribution is considered and orchids play their part in the theory. The obvious age of some of these orchids is, by inference, a little beyond imagination. But failing some more reasonable explanation for the distribution of cymbidiums, as an example, they must be regarded as very ancient indeed. Introducing animals confuses and elaborates the theory, but of necessity they must enter an appearance.

It is fairly well understood that orchids have a habit of migrating and moving about the various countries where they grow in company with all the other vegetable components such as trees and shrubs and plants of all kinds, right down to the mosses. Although migration to another country is a completely different proposition, some orchids become international by this process. Their seed is designed by evolution to float on the wind and is produced in such numbers as to ensure that at least some of it survives and germinates and grows in suitable situations. Although birds have been mentioned in some contexts as possibly responsible by carrying the tiny seeds on their feathers, careful consideration of this brings conviction that for every such transfer hundreds from other methods would be more credible. Birds clean and preen too much and too often for foreign material to be present in their plumage. However, it cannot be dismissed out of hand.

Orchid seed scatter is a proved and reliable method of plant propagation, otherwise these plants would have disappeared long ago. While it may be a fruitless exercise to estimate the number of seeds in ratio which finally germinate and grow, two instances may be quoted, one from another country and one from personal experience.

That from another country concerned a plant which had been brought into an area and cultivated in a collection. It was pollinated by insects, setting several fruits which, when they burst, scattered literally millions of seeds on the wind. The search for seedlings some four years later revealed only two plants downwind from the scatter, germinated naturally on a host tree similar to that on which the orchid usually grew.

The personal experience is from plants of *Dendrobium kingianum* growing naturally on casuarina trees in southern Victoria, not the best place in which to look for natural germination of orchid seedlings. These plants set numerous fruit each year and scatter their seed some eight to ten weeks after development. This scatter would also be in the order of millions of seeds from the ripe capsules. Over a period of some five or six years, only four of these seeds lodged in suitable areas in the garden, germinated and grew into young plants. They were most vigorous.

These two instances are indicative of what could be reasonably expected of all orchids growing naturally and explains in part the necessity for the plants to have developed such large capsules and high seed numbers in order to survive. It is not a constant by which all orchids and all habitats should be judged, however, as I have also seen trees clothed from top to bottom with innumerable seedlings which have germinated and grown from seed scatter. The important thing about all this, from any standpoint, is the inability to express in numerals or decimal points the ratio between the number of seeds scattered and the development of orchid plants into adult form to further carry on the genus or species.

Other plants and trees move about in the same way and by similar means, but their movements are far more restricted than those of orchids, for obvious reasons, while still considering the ease with which they may grow when the seeds fall to the ground.

Nearly all orchids live on the decaying remnants of other plants which grow in the same ecological groupings and these groupings are vital factors in their survival. Although it is impossible to go very far into the subject in this section of the book, some instances of common origins from distant progenitors may be suggested to strengthen the hypothesis of continental drift and its effect on some of our orchid species. While it is almost impossible to prove the theory, it would be wrong to deny the probability; therefore we have an interesting exercise in make-believe.

If reference is made to the composite map of the southern hemisphere countries linked into one mass, it will be noted that the contour evidence seems to point to the fact that they all fit into a pattern which could form a land mass. At the projected time it is most unlikely that they were shaped as they are in the twentieth century, but in general they would have been similar. Perhaps it is just chance that the land masses fit into the jigsaw pattern we wish them to make, but the probability is just as strong that they really did so some 60-70 million years ago. (See page 52.)

So many other factors enter into the theory that it is impossible to explain them: the position of the land mass relative to the equator of that time and the south and north pole, the change in the position of the Earth in relation to its orbit on a line through the poles, the general instability of the land masses in both hemispheres in view of the tidal action of the oceans and the effect of volcanic activity.

It is supposed that when the land mass broke up, the various components drifted to what is now the north, India colliding with the Asiatic land mass and forcing up the immense barrier of the Himalayas and other mountain ranges, Africa colliding with the Asian-European section and South America attaching itself to the North American continent to form the land masses as we understand them.

The Australian continental mass is supposed to have been shaped like the second map and formed what has long been known as Gondwanaland. Much of it has been lost and it will be noted that several regions which are now separated are believed to have been attached to it. Islands like Niugini have been completely inundated at some time in their history. Australia itself is believed to be still moving northward at about 5 centimetres a year; and if the mathematics of the whole project are loosely worked out it is obvious that it as travelled some 3200 kilometres (about 2000 miles) in the 60-70 million years of its journeying. In that period it also has had its ups and downs. It may be impossible to have any idea of the climates through which Australia has passed in its history; but although the records are brief, it is believed to be still changing.

However, it is possible to relate some trees and plants to the whole period and some of the implications which emerge may be almost unbelievable for some people while credible for the thoughtful with vision beyond the yardstick of their seventy years. There are also some signposts which may hopefully lead us a little way along the road.

The first of these is almost a notice-board reading 'It All Began Here' on an island which could little be expected to have any orchid flora at all. On Macquarie Island in the 1970-80 decade a most momentous discovery was made of a flowering orchid plant — a corybas. Its presence could be explained in several ways — the chance arrival of a seed on the plumage of birds; in the clothing of visitors to the island, which was once a temporary home for seal hunters; it may have been included in the cargo taken to the island; and so on. Perhaps more importantly its presence could be explained by the original clothing of the island with a flora much more heterogeneous than that of the twentieth century.

Macquarie Island, some 1700 kilometres (about 1000 miles) south-south-east of Tasmania, is part of the land mass already referred to as Gondwanaland if the theory is good enough, left behind in the continental drift or the remnant of a larger mass. At least the signpost indicates that in the past it was associated with Australia and New Zealand, which have the only significant populations of corybas in the world. Although it is a cold-country orchid there is some reservation about whether seed carried by chance would germinate and proliferate on such an inhospitable land surface. It is better suited to ease of recognition as an original item of the island flora and as it suits the theory it fits into a pattern. It could be claimed at worst as something worth investigating on geological terms and at best as proving the existence of the great southern land mass of the period referred to as 60-70 million years ago.

A simple yet momentous question, of course, remains: Is the genus all that old? If it is, then the Australian terrestrial orchids would appear to be among the fundamental developments in world orchid flora following the older order, of which there are few surviving remnants.

The second signpost bears scarcely discernible words, but two stand out fairly clearly — *Dendrobium speciosum*. This orchid grows on the eastern coastline of Australia almost from its northern extremity to the southernmost point. It changes morphologically over the complete distance, from a dwarf form in the north where it approaches the tropics to a semi-dwarf form at its southernmost habitat. This appears to indicate that it was not a northern migrant from the direction of the equator nor that it came from the south, although some logical inferences could point in that direction. Instead we must look for a west to east migration pattern and this fits in with the Gondwanaland theory.

The natural affiliates of *Dendrobium speciosum* are the Indo-Asian members of the genus. One in particular is morphologically similar, although less robust than the fully developed forms of this orchid. *Dendrobium chrysotoxum* bears more than a passing resemblance to *Dendrobium ruppianum*, although we are not looking for an extension of that fact into the theory except through *Dendrobium speciosum*. It could be put forward that originally *Dendrobium speciosum* came from the land junction area between what is now modern India and Gondwanaland. It followed a west to east migration pattern, reaching its full development in the central Australian region when it was more fertile and finally migrating to the east coast of Australia when that strip stabilised following the intense volcanic activity of many millions of years ago. Some work has been done on the rise and fall of the Australian land mass as we know it and the inference from it leads to belief that the hypothesis is well based but scarcely provable. The Indian connection must be looked at for the origin of this orchid rather than other areas where dendrobiums grow and we cannot look at a southern migration pattern from that part of Asia because of the Wallace Line. (See map, page 52.)

So the signpost, although faint in outline and not altogether reliable, at least makes another link in the chain of circumstantial evidence advanced by orchids in particular.

Another orchid, perhaps more ancient than *Dendrobium speciosum*, is its fellow-Australian *Dendrobium falcorostrum*. This orchid is insular in its habitat, growing almost solely on the rain-forest beech *Nothofagus moorei*. Beech trees, possibly including this species, are known to have existed for at least 130 million years. The Australian representative of the genus is slowly dying out in Australia for two reasons — first the slow movement of the continent toward the now warmer region of the Earth's surface and second *the more likely extermination of this species by vandalism even up to legislative levels within the near future*. It is a cold-country tree, growing on Australia's east coast mountains at about 1000 metres (about 3000 feet) in small surviving pockets. It is logical to assume, as in the instance of *Dendrobium speciosum*, that the association of *Dendrobium falcorostrum* with this host tree is of long standing, however much the orchid may have modified or changed over the period. It is such a stable, monotypic species that it is not idle to suggest that they have had a symbiotic relationship over many millions of years. Perhaps not a signpost, but at the very least a legendary guideline.

The clearest of the signposts is embodied in the Australian cymbidiums. It is perhaps too overwhelmingly simple to be believable. The only way our members of the genus may be related to the other Indo-Asian members is through the pre-Gondwanaland theory embodied in the composite map of the proposed location of the various continents in conjunction on some point of the Earth totally unrelated to the position of Antarctica at the present time.

The cymbidiums appear to have morphological similarity in both continents in the twentieth century. This may be approached in two ways, the first of which is the least desirable if considering the Gondwanaland theory. It is that they had a common origin in the northern hemisphere and that the Australian species migrated southward. Assuming that in company with most plants and trees they had to be modified by time to conform to climatic patterns, it would be surprising to see identical phases of development bringing them to their present morphological state, one in Indo-Asia, the other in Australia, with no real linkage between them, plus the existence of the Wallace Line. The second approach is to consider them as separate developments from a monotype generated in the pre-Gondwanaland period on the land mass existing between modern Australia and modern India when they were in conjunction.

The Indian section of the genus developed into a series of species which have obvious affiliations and possibly a common ancestor; they have large flowers induced by the kind of climate in which they grow and they have spread in a west to east direction in a fairly narrow band of highland habitats. Only one of the present-day species is in any degree warm-growing and that is *Cymbidium insigne*, from Vietnam.

The Australian section has also developed in a pattern which could be expected from the habitat, and they are worth examining in detail and separately. *Cymbidium madidum* is the most luxuriant in growth, some clones when fully developed weighing almost a quarter of a tonne. One of the best habitats for this orchid is in the dead butts of enormous stag and elkhorn ferns. The flower spikes are long and pendant like most of the Indian species, but the flowers themselves are almost diminutive, possibly as the result of climatic enforcement in a country afflicted with severe droughts and prolonged dry seasons. Nature may be very economical at times with results as good as from a more luxuriant morphology. It should be noted that neither the diminutive nor tropical type cymbidiums enter into the hypothesis at all so far as this section of the book is concerned.

The second of the three members of the genus in Australia, *Cymbidium canaliculatum*, has the aspect of a true hard-country orchid. The leaves are thick and deeply channelled, the pseudo-bulbs small and closely enfolded in the leaf bases and the whole plant a most economical unit. The flower spikes are produced profusely and the flowers are most numerous. On a clone of some three or four flowering pseudo-bulbs there may be up to eight or nine horizontal spikes, each bearing fifty or more small flowers. The color of all three cymbidiums is reminiscent in general of the Indian species *Cymbidium lowianum*, but one variety of *Cymbidium canaliculatum* has red-purple flowers.

The third member is *Cymbidium suave,* which has a morphological affinity with *Cymbidium eburneum*. It has a pseudo-bulb system which extends in the same way as that cymbidium, continually producing new leaves from the apex of the growth. It is reasonable to allocate relativity to these two cymbidiums because of this. *Cymbidium suave* flowers again and again from the same pseudo-bulbs, in contrast to its two Australian associates. It also has another distinction in growing only in the butt ends of broken branches and holes in the trunks of trees where its roots may reach the decaying interior of eucalypts, very rarely in other places. Of the three, *Cymbidium suave* appears to be the archaic form of the genus and in this regard could be considered one of the progenitors of it as a whole.

It may be asked why the genus could not have originated in the Indonesia-Philippines-China area and migrated to Australia through the recognised routes by which some of the dendrobiums came. We can recognise all these 'interlopers', as I prefer to name them, and they are quite distinct from the Australian section as a whole. So far as it is possible to tell, the only orchid which broke the Wallace Line within 'recent' ages is *Phalaenopsis amabilis*, with all the other migrants into Australia originating in the nearer islands which were probably at one time part of the land mass Gondwanaland.

There are many other possible viewpoints and hypotheses just as tenable as the one outlined above, and the signposts read from a different direction would, of course, provide alternatives. These alternatives, however, would need not only to appear better but also to offer some explanation of the relationships set out in the previous paragraphs. There seems to be only one line of attack when looking for answers and that is to try working backwards with the material at hand. It could reasonably be asked, for example, why, if the American and African continents were once in conjunction, there are no cattleyas in Africa, no laelias nor any of the other orchids common in this century to the Brazilian catalogue. The answer is fairly simple, but perhaps the readers may like to work it out for themselves.

An elaboration of the theory in relation to the Australian dendrobiums was published in a paper submitted to a meeting of the Australasian Native Orchid Society in 1981 and reprinted in their bulletin. Animals play their part in the hypothesis because it is generally conceded that there has been a completely separate development of all the species within the confines of the Wallace

Line, with no evidence that the animals of the Indo-Asian region were eve[r] present. The break occurred within the period when the prehistoric animal[s] such as dinosaurs were still alive and their fossilised remains are as commo[n] within the confines of the line as outside.

So many things in our world still remain mysteries, but most are capable o[f] solution if sufficient time and money are devoted to them. Perhaps most of u[s] could think of many better ways of spending the money which government[s] annex and although some may consider devoting any of it to orchids as trivia[l] squandering, the same could most certainly be said of the bulk of the vast sum[s] involved.

The maps appended are simply guidelines to a theory, with no positive intention to suggest that they are authoritative or even reliable. It is possibly unreal to have even the theory accepted unchallenged, and the thought and research behind the idea and the maps are to stimulate others to think along similar lines. Contrary to the expressed opinions of perhaps recognised and unrecognised authorities, I believe that our orchids are among the oldest of the 'modern' plants.

In this brief review of possible origins for the Australian orchids no recognition is given to other countries. However, in the true Australasian sense New Zealand, as another remnant of the original land masses, has a dendrobium which is difficult to relate to most Australian species. But it is possible to relate it to some members of the genus which have not entered into the theory at all, and reference to Dockrill's *Indigenous Orchids of Australia* certainly provides food for thought along this line.

For the other orchids, particularly the South American genera, *Orchidaceae Brasilienses*, by Pabst and Dungs, gives a very clear outline of what they considered the migration routes taken by the orchids as they followed the changing environments of that continent. An extension of the theories of plant migration may be related even to the deserts of the world, which once, even the Sahara, possibly had their moments of glory with orchid populations just as numerous and varied as clothe other parts of the world in the closing stages of the second millenium of our calendar. As a calendar it is a travesty and a minute portion of 'time' when exposed in the same context as the world orchid populations.

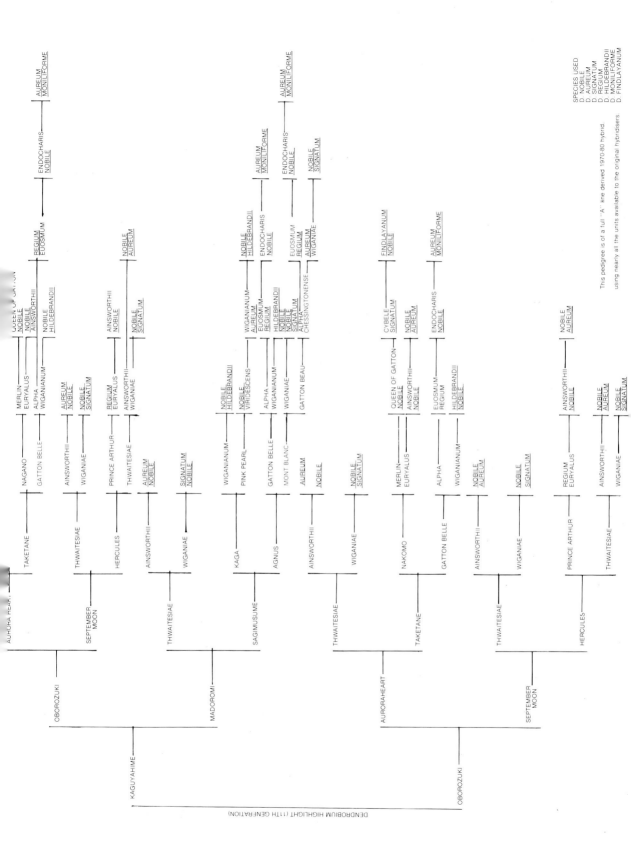

DENDROBIUM HIGHLIGHT (11TH GENERATION)

SPECIES USED
D NOBILE
D AUREUM
D SIGNATUM
D REGIUM
D HILDEBRANDII
D MONILIFORME
D FINDLAYANUM

This pedigree is of a full "A" line derived 1970-80 hybrid,

using nearly all the units available to the original hybridisers.

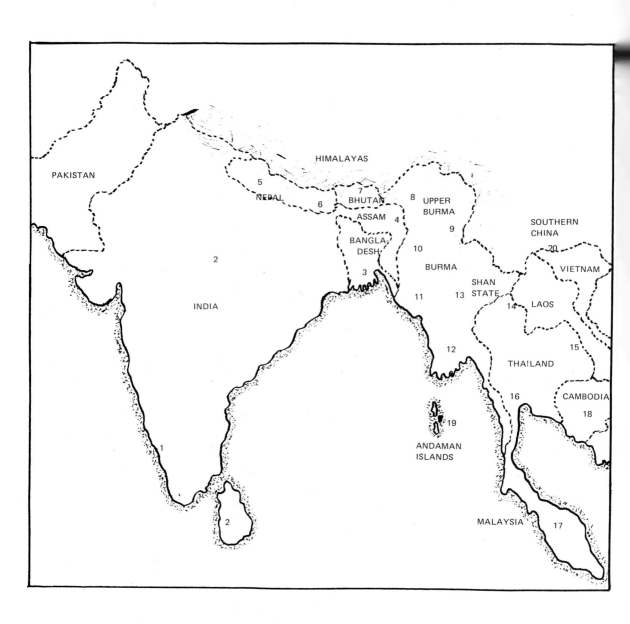

PAKISTAN

HIMALAYAS

5
NEPAL 6 BHUTAN 7 8 UPPER
BURMA

SOUTHERN
CHINA

ASSAM 4 9
2 BANGLA- 10 20
DESH VIETNAM
INDIA 3 BURMA
11 SHAN
STATE 13 14 LAOS
15
12 THAILAND
16 CAMBODIA
18
19 ANDAMAN
ISLANDS
1

2
MALAYSIA 17

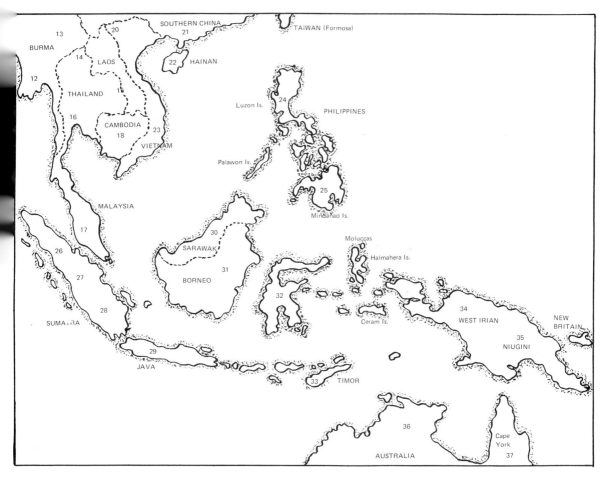

VANDAS
ALPINA 10
AMESIANA 10 16 18 23
BENSONII 11 12 13
BRUNNEA 14 15 16
COERULEA 4 10 11 13 14
COERULESCENS 13 14
CRISTATA 5 6 7
DENISONIANA 10 13
HOOKERANA 17 26 27 28 30 31
HINDSII 35
LAMELLATA 24 25
LUZONICA 24
MERRILLII 24
SANDERANA 25
TERES 11 12 16
TESSELLATA 1 2 4 5 6 7 8
TRICOLOR 29 33 36(?)
   var. SUAVIS 29 33 36(?)
WHITEI 37(?)

ASCOCENTRUMS
AMPULLACEUM 7 8 9 10 13
CURVIFOLIUM 10 11 12 13 14 15 16
MINIATUM 8 9 10 11 12 16 17 29 30 31

RHYNCOSTYLIS
GIGANTEA 10 13 14 15
COELESTIS 14 15 16
RETUSA 1 2 11 12 15 16 17 18 23 24 25 26 27 28 29 30 31

AERIDES
ODORATUM 4 6 7 8 9 10 13 14 15 16 17 18 23 25 30 31 32 34
FALCATUM 4 10 11 12 14 15
LAWRENCEAE 25

DENDROBIUMS
AGGREGATUM 12 13 14 15 20 21
ANOSMUM 15 17 18 23 26 28 29 30 31 32 33 34
BENSONIAE 4 10 13 14
BIGIBBUM 37
CRASSINODE 13 14
CREPIDATUM 4 5 6 7 9 10 13 14 15
CHRYSANTHUM 4 6 7 8 9 13 14 15
CHRYSOTOXUM 10 13 14 15
CRUMENATUM 30 31 32 33 34
CRUENTUM 12 16 17
CRYSTALLINUM 11 12 13 14 15
DEAREI 24 25
FARMERI 4 6 7 8 9 13 14 15
FIMBRIATUM 4 6 7 10 13 14
FORMOSUM 6 7 8 9 11 12 16 19
FINDLAYANUM 13 14 15 16
FRIEDRICKSIANUM 13 14 15 16
HETEROCARPUM 1 2 4 5 6 8 9 10 13 14 15 24 25
HILDEBRANDII 10 13 14 15
INFUNDIBULUM 4 10 13 14
LITUIFLORUM 4 10 13 14
LODDIGESII 21 22
MOSCHATUM 4 6 7 8 9 10
NOBILE 4 5 6 7 8 9 20
PARISHII 4 10 13 14 15
PHALAENOPSIS 33 34 35
PULCHELLUM 4 6 7 10 13 14 15 16
REGIUM 2(?) 4 (?) 20 21
SANDERAE 24 25
SCHULERI 34
SPECIOSUM 37
SIGNATUM 10 13
THYRSIFLORUM 4 6 10 13 14 15
WARDIANUM 4 10 11 13 14 15

51

In the beginning ... The land
masses as we now recognise them
were not necessarily so shaped and
this aggregation of the southern hemisphere continents is used only to
illustrate the possibility before they
began to drift away from each other.

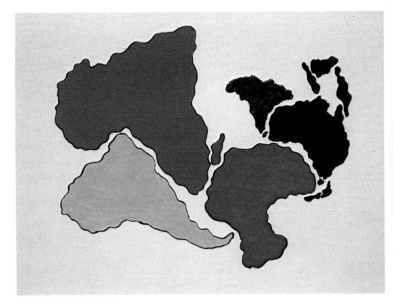

**The Possible origin of the Australian
orchids.**

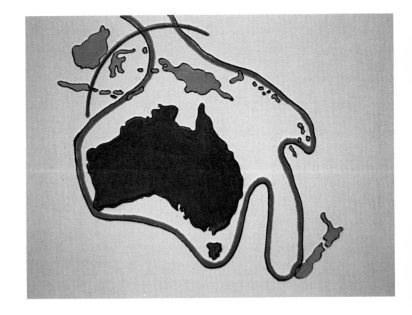

The Gondwanaland theory is part of
the original hypothesis. This illustration is only an attempt to give
some form to a vague imaginary
continent, the nucleus of which was
the remnant now known as Australia, plus other hypothetical attachments now separated, such as
Niugini and the Solomon Islands.
  The Wallace line is a hypothetical
boundary between Asia and
Australasia. In theory it has existed
since the formation of the original
continents and accounts for the
separate evolutionary development
of the fauna and flora of the two
land masses. (See also page 163.)

CALANTHE MASUCA, from the Himalayan foothills of northern India, is the matriarch of hybrid orchids. One of the parents of the first known man-made orchid hybrid, a member of the non-deciduous group, it may be grown in moderate conditions and in what could be considered the general mix associated with all semi-terrestrial orchids. The flowering head is elongated and the individual flowers continue to open and fade as long as the season lasts. The foliage is liable to deteriorate if C. masuca is grown in unsuitable conditions. It was named Bletia masuca by the botanist D. Don and later Calanthe masuca by Lindley.

CALANTHE TRIPLICATA, a widespread species, is similar to C. furcata, the other parent of C. Dominyi, as the first hybrid was named. C. triplicata, with aspidistra-shaped leaves, is native to many countries, mostly found as a base plant in rather dense forest areas and flowering about Christmas in Australia. Its origin is obscure, but the first plant in Australia was probably a migrant or interloper from Asian sources. It was named by Robert Brown.

CALANTHE VESTITA (Lindley) comprises many varieties, some with small flowers, others up to 6 centimetres long (about 2½ inches) varying from white to deep pink or rose. Wallich brought it to the notice of horticulture, finding it in northern India about 1826. C. vestita was later found to be extensively Indo-Asian.

CALANTHE VEITCHII (*C. rosea* x *C. vestita*), 1860, was among the earliest of the deciduous hybrids. It was raised in the Veitch nursery and later found as a natural plant by the collector Boxall. It is fairly typical of the main hybrid line, bearing spikes up to a metre tall which remain in flower for many weeks during winter.

CALANTHE HEXHAM GEM (*C. Angela* x *C. Bryan*) was raised by Cookson and named in 1925, which indicates how long the genus remained in cultivation. Perhaps it was an example of how difficult old habits are to change, some growers persisting with orchids they like long after they have 'gone out of fashion'. *C.* Hexham Gem is among the more richly colored hybrids.

CALANTHE RUBY 'Occulata' bears out the supposition about Cookson, because he produced it in 1893 and apparently his love for the genus never faltered. Its parentage was *C. Sedenii* x *C. vestita*. The genus throughout suffered from a small species family with insufficient material to give a cattleya-like hybridism, so calanthes became very much inbred.

54

PHAIUS TANKERVILLIAE (Aiton), synonym P. grandifolius (Lindley) and many others. Essentially a swamp orchid, it has spread throughout the world in the sub-tropical band where such orchids proliferate. It is allied to calanthes and similar orchids and over its range has developed many variations, some of which are known by specific names. It is one of the few orchids which will grow with 'wet feet.'

PHAIOCYMBIDIUM CHARD-WARENSE (Cymbidium giganteum x Phaius grandifolius). No one has ever been really satisfied about the authenticity of the orchid. Rolfe in particular cast doubt on the parent-age and maintained that it was almost identical with Phaius Ashworthianus (P. maculatis x P. wallichii). In habit it is typically phaius and its culture the same as for that genus.

BLETIA CATENULATA (Ruiz and Pavon), the species on which the genus was founded in 1794 in honor of Luis Blet. This is a Peruvian and Brazilian species in a family allied to phaius and spathoglottis. Bletias are principally American orchids but the origin of the genus was probably Asia. The pastel reproduction is from Margaret Skilbeck, a gifted young artist.

55

VANDA TESSELLATA (Roxburgh). It is probably better known by its synonym *Vanda Roxburghii* (R. Brown). The variations from plant to plant are remarkable, with some forms almost unrecognisable as the same species. This pastel reproduction by Joan Skilbeck is from an early lithograph, one of the few forms of color printing at one time, which gave great scope and licence to artists, occasionally with results devastating to botany and taxonomy.

VANDA TESSELLATA in another of its many colored forms, almost totally devoid of the feature responsible for its name. It is frequently disconcerting to read descriptions of orchids which fail to tally with names on labels, but it should be remembered that these descriptions are frequently the type or recognised form on which the species is based and all the variants cannot be described in full. *V. tessellata* is one of the oldest known and cultivated species in the genus.

VANDA SANDERANA (Reichenbach f.). Schlechter created the generic name *euanthe* for it in 1914. This orchid is one of the outstanding species of all genera, varying from greenish-white with deeper green reticulations to the deepest red-brown tonings with the darker reticulations prominent in all varieties. This example is a hand-pollinated sibling bred exclusively for further hybridising and selected for rounded outline. Some of the species are almost as good as this, although many fine varieties in early collections have been lost.

EUANTHE SANDERANA flowering habit is frequently close set and crowded, the flowers overlapping at the head of the spike, but the tendency lessened by hybridism with other species such as V. coerulea. In most instances the synonym Vanda sanderana is used throughout the book and until a total revision of Sander's List of Orchid Hybrids is made it will be referred to as a vanda in respect to hybrids stemming from it.

VANDA COERULEA (Griffith, ex Lindley) is the equal of E. sanderana in all aspects of orchid growing. Originally growing as a widespread native of the Indo-Burma region, predation has stripped many of its previously known habitats. Its con-tribution to hybridism has been equal to that of E. sanderana and perhaps it could be said that theirs was an exceedingly happy marriage. leading to a race of orchids for tropical areas in particular which is second to none. V. coerulea color varies from white into pink tones as well as the familiar blue, which may be without tesselations.

Orchids and trees. Vanda coerulea growing on the butt of a tree in a Grafton, NSW, garden. Originally ejected from a sheltered area to provide room for some other orchids, it was stood against the base of the tree. The tree later died, but the roots attached to the stump and the plant flowered profusely every year with no shade in the summer and no particular cul-tivation. Perhaps we treat some of our difficult species orchids too kindly. (See page 10.)

57

VANDA TRICOLOR (Lindley) is
typical for the broad-leafed section
of the genus, the flower stems
emerging from the axils of the
leaves. It is the third member of the
group most strongly represented in
the hybrid lists and although the
flower habit of twisting the petals is
sometimes visible in modern vandas
its color contribution outweighs the
fault.

VANDA DENISONIANA VAR.
HEBRAICA (Benson and
Reichenbach f.). Discovered in the
Arracan Mountains in Burma by
Benson, it was introduced to
growers by Veitch in 1868. The type
form is cream colored, but the
illustrated variety is much brighter.
It is a very strong-growing species
and added to color in some of the
inter-generic hybrids.

VANDA TERES (Roxburgh) (Lindley).
This is the variety andersoni, from
which a large number of hybrids
also get their color. This orchid
comes from the terete or channelled
foliage group and is the source of
the semi-terete foliage visible in
some of the other transparencies.
This foliage is sun-resistant to a
remarkable degree.

Vandas on transportable pipe
frames. Mobility is an asset where
vandas or similar orchids may be
grown entirely outdoors or for part
of the year. Some type of container
at the base of the frame should be
part of the design so that a rich
mixture can be offered to the roots.
They will quickly find it if attractive
blends are used, preferably containing some form of organic
fertiliser.

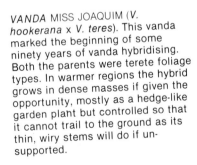

VANDA MISS JOAQUIM (V.
hookerana x V. teres). This vanda
marked the beginning of some
ninety years of vanda hybridising.
Both the parents were terete foliage
types. In warmer regions the hybrid
grows in dense masses if given the
opportunity, mostly as a hedge-like
garden plant but controlled so that
it cannot trail to the ground as its
thin, wiry stems will do if unsupported.

VANDA TERES VAR. ALBA. As in
most genera, vandas also have their
share of albino forms. Although V.
teres in both forms has few flowers,
most hybrids carry the same
number of blooms as V. sanderana,
which seems to set the pace. The
white forms of most vandas are
useful in hybridising because it is
so easy to superimpose desired
colors over the white factor.

VANDA ROTHSCHILDIANA (V.
coerulea x E. sanderana). Early
cross-pollinations for this hybrid
were of much poorer shape than
those bred from garden-raised
sibling species which came into pro-
minence after 1945. While it may be
wrong to give credit to one section
over another, the Hawaiian and
American hybridists appeared to be
first to bring out the best primary
hybrids such as this.

58

VANDA ROTHSCHILDIANA. Deeper color than this is rare.

Vanda flower tesselations come from the species vandas *sanderana* and *coerulea*. In this hybrid, V. Alexander Bowman x V. Blue Boy, only one other species enters, the Philippine orchid V. *lamellata* (Lindley), a vanda which on appearance and general size would scarcely recommend itself to hybridists.

VANDA ONOMEA x V. KAREN ONO, an unnamed hybrid when this book was printed, has the blue of V. *coerulea* developed to its most intense shade. Although other vandas appear in the breeding lines of the two parents, *Euanthe sanderana* and the blue species are most apparent in such hybrids and their influence is overwhelming.

VANDA NELLIE MORLEY (*V.* Emma van Deventer x *E. sanderana*) represents the move toward the other end of the spectrum in the color range. It was bred and named in the years following 1945, bringing into the mainline the species *V. teres* and *V. tricolor.* However, *V.* Nellie Morley did not have the impact of *V.* Rothschildiana and one or two other hybrids.

VANDA MADAME RATTANA (*V.* Sun Tan x *V.* Mem. Madame Pranern) follows the ultimate development of the red genetic influence of *Vanda* or *Euanthe sanderana.* It is a typical "A" line development, for an explanation of which *Growing Orchids — Book Two* should be consulted.

VANDA WALTER OUMAE (*V.* Mevr. L. Velthius x *V. sanderana*) indicates the outstanding influence of vandas *teres* and *hookerana* on the color and other characteristics of vandas. They have obliterated the tessellations, despite two infusions of the dominant species *V. sanderana.*

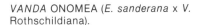

VANDA ONOMEA (*E. sanderana* x *V.* Rothschildiana).

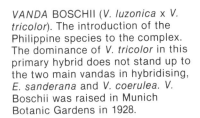

VANDA BOSCHII (*V. luzonica* x *V. tricolor*). The introduction of the Philippine species to the complex. The dominance of *V. tricolor* in this primary hybrid does not stand up to the two main vandas in hybridising, *E. sanderana* and *V. coerulea*. *V.* Boschii was raised in Munich Botanic Gardens in 1928.

VANDA hybrid Thananchai x Boonchoke, an unnamed grex. This represents the complete rounded outline which seems to dominate the outlook of some judging systems. It has its disabilities, including the notch in the petal and the dorsal sepal, which overlap to such a degree that entanglements occur in bud formation. The same thing is also obvious in many other hybrid flowers, from cymbidiums to vuylstekearas. Although the fault may not affect all the flowers on spikes, undiscerning judges blame slugs or caterpillars for what is just a little breeding fault in genera taken too far toward the ultimate, super-"A" line unnatural flowers.

VANDA TAN CHAY YAN (*V. dearei* x *V.* Josephine van Brero) is dominated by the Borneo species *V. dearei* (Reichenbach f.), the flowers of which are about 6 or 7 centimetres across (about 2½ to 3 inches), creamy yellow tipped with rosy brown. It was named about 1886 and was one of the orchids collected by Micholitz and sent to Sanders, establishing another color range in vanda hybrids.

VANDA THANANCHAI x *V. AURAWON* is the ultimate development of the *V. dearei* strain, possibly reached with all "A" line flowers. Despite this, the essential character of the species *V. dearei* remains in the flower color with only the faintest hint of *V. sanderana.* As *V. dearei* flowers almost continuously in its habitat, hybrids with this strain may be most variable in their flowering. The parent *V.* Thananchai is a notable breeding grex, with colored as well as monotone descendants.

VANDA BOONCHOO (*V.* Lenavat x *V.* Sun Tan) is the complete "A" line hybrid, with a little of everything coming through in its coloration. A strong-growing orchid, this flower was one of a head of some ten on a quite vigorous plant. Although shape has been a driving force in vanda hybridising, when it is allied to color such as this no complaint can be made about the methods used in cross-pollinations. For an explanation of "A" line breeding see *Growing Orchids — Book Two.*

There is much to be said for selecting orchids to suit climates in which people live. Lister Arrowsmith of Townsville, Queensland, grows vandas this way in a garden bed. His counterpart in cooler climates grows cymbidiums the same way, completely outdoors. Others less fortunate must grow their orchids completely enclosed in glasshouses. In every instance, however, the outdoor, fresh-air system is best for the plants.

No problems are so great that they cannot be overcome. In another part of this book these plants are illustrated and described. Here they are flowering in the autumn in southern Australia, all *Vanda* Nellie Morley and grown under clear glass right through the year. A constant stream of fresh air is blown into the glasshouse. See page 25.

The further north in Australia one travels the more hungry and numerous the pests become. Orchids must be grown in total enclosures if the best is to be had from them. This well designed and built enclosure is in Innisfail; the people talking about it are Karen, daughter of Kevin McFarlane, and her husband with Neville Ludwig and his wife, the latter from Townsville and interested in phalaenopsis. The basics of such a structure are shade-cloth walls, a partly opaque roof of mixed cloudy fibreglass sheets with corrugated aluminium or galvanised iron and complete sealing of openings which would allow entry for pests of any type, the quality and life of the flowers and plants depending on thoroughness of construction.

RHYNCOSTYLIS RETUSA
(Linnaeus). In suitable conditions
the plant proliferates into multiple
offshoots, but this is seldom
reached in cultivation except in
open situations in suitable climates.
Well-established plants flower
freely, with an attractive overall
effect. At times this species has
been known as the 'foxbrush
orchid'.

RHYNCOSTYLIS GIGANTEA
(Lindley). There are several beautiful
varieties of this species, with an
amount of personal choice associated with the popularity of one
over another.

RHYNCOSTYLIS GIGANTEA VAR.
RUBRA. The red form has been used
considerably in recent hybridising
programs aimed at color. In most
instances it is dominant and the
resultant inter-generic pollinations
are bright at times.

RHYNCOSTYLIS GIGANTEA VAR.
ALBA. Once rare, self-pollinations
produced many thousands of
replicas. It is a true albino, with
good color-carrying propensity when
cross-pollinated with colored
associates.

SARTYLIS BLUE NOB (*Sarcochilus hartmanni* var. *blue nob* x *Rhyncostylis retusa*). The cross-pollination is the product of Bill and Jean Cannons, of New South Wales and Queensland, who were notable innovators in many directions in orchid breeding. Despite the great difference in appearance of the two parents, their indirect relativity as members of the vandaceous group set up a good combination for an inter-generic hybrid.

RHYNCOVANDA KAUHANA (*V. teres* x *Rhyncostylis gigantea*). The combination is comparatively recent, with the first one registered in 1958. Most following cross-pollinations were from Asian sources, some very attractive. The terete-foliage group has the advantage of being free-flowering, well suiting the commercial flower export trade.

AERIDES FALCATA (Lindley). The genus is closely related to vandas, and this species is widespread over much of Indo-Asia. While some growers expect such plants to flower regularly at a certain period of the year, different growers in different countries will find that they are most variable, but usually in flower in spring or summer. *Aerides falcata* is most fragrant but unsuitable for cool cultivation.

AERIDES VANDARUM (Reichenbach f.). Sometimes sparse flowering, this species is from the cooler climates of southern China and the Himalayan foothills country. The foliage is terete and the flowers white, indicating a bright-light habitat, the root system unsuited for pot culture and much preferring a surface on which to cling, as a glance at its flat profile indicates.

AERIDES ODORATUM (Poiret, Loureiro). One of the commonest of the genus, its range extending even into Niugini according to some authorities. With plants from such widespread habitats, it is much better to know their origin so that a selection can be made in artificial cultivation. If borderline, it is some-times surprising to find how plants may conform to an artificial climate more moderate than the habitat after two or three years of ac-climatising treatment.

AERIDES JAPONICUM (Reichenbach f.). One of the smallest of the species, this attractive little orchid will thrive in cool to moderate con-ditions. First introduced to Europe by Linden of Brussels about 1862, its flowers, principally white, appear in late spring to summer. During cooler weather the plant should be watched carefully to note that the centre remains clean and free of water.

68

AERIDES LAWRENCEAE
(Reichenbach f.). One of the strongest members of the genus, closely allied to *Aerides quinquevulneram* (Lindley) and both from the Philippine Islands. The similarity of the flowers is such as to cause confusion. Very little hybridising was carried out within the genus, most of the work occurring in relation to inter-generic hybridising with vandas, ascocentrums and other minor species.

ASOCENTRUM AMPULLACEUM
(Lindley). The genus was separated out and named by Schlechter, before which they were known variously as saccolabiums or aerides. A small flowered family, these beautiful orchids became popular only through their association in cross-pollination to fulfil the mid-century craze for miniature orchids. *Asco. ampullaceum* is common in the Burma-Thailand area, growing thickly in some places like the sarcochilus in Australia — if one knows where to find those orchids. Free-flowering and miniatures morphologically, these small orchids are good subjects for those with a premium on space.

ASCOCENTRUM CURVIFOLIUM
(Lindley) was popular with hybridists for its color contribution. Like *Asco. ampullaceum,* it is free-flowering and needs warm conditions. Although the hybrids with vandas seem to thrive in semi-tropical and tropical conditions, occasionally a cross-pollination will prove most difficult to grow in these climates and seems to prefer cooler cultivation, probably because the variety used originated in the Burmese section of the Himalayan region.

69

ASCOCENTRUM MINIATUM
(Lindley). Native to the Javanese-Borneo section of the Asian complex and other places, this neat plant with its stiff, straight foliage also had the color attraction for hybridists. The free-flowering habits of this small genus were not always transferred to the inter-generic hybrids.

VANDOPSIS GIGANTEA (Lindley). The strongest growing member of the genus, although the plants seldom grow tall, branching considerably and forming shortish masses of epiphytic growth. The flowers are of heavy substance and on appearance would hold promise for cross-pollinations which do not seem to be borne out in the production line. It is a most attractive orchid, flowering variably but mostly in the warmer periods of the year. A native of the Burma-Thailand area.

VANDOPSIS PARISHII (Reichenbach f.). On appearances more like a phalaenopsis plant than a vanda, to which both are related, if only distantly. The genus as a whole carries few flowers but they are long lasting. This orchid is now correctly named *Hygrochilus parishii* in *Sander's List of Orchid Hybrids* but so far as most growers are concerned it will remain a synonym.

VANDOPSIS PARISHII VAR. *MARRIOTTIANA.* This is perhaps the most colorful of the genus, the startlingly white centre of the flower, including the column, showing starkly against the brown-purple of the flower.

VANDOPSIS LISSOCHILOIDES (Gaudichaud-Beaupre). The Philippines' representative of the genus. As the lengthening of the spike reveals, the buds are usually a purple-red color, leading growers to expect the interior color to be the same. A warm-growing species.

RENANTHERA IMSCHOOTIANA (Rolfe). The plant is typical for the genus as a whole, with rather short, stubby leaves. In some forms of culture the roots also are typically short. The flower spikes lengthen and branch like some of the oncidiums. The genus extends considerably more than some taxonomists and authorities credit. *Renanthera imschootiana* is Indo-Asian, its habitat usually hot. In cultivation it may flower variably, but usually in the warmest and driest part of the year.

71

RENANTHERA STORIEI (Reichenbach f.). This orchid is a typical tropical lowland species, thriving in a climate which is hot and humid for the whole of the year. While such orchids certainly present a challenge to growers in cooler climates, unless they are matched up with plants from similar climates a satisfactory collection may not be built up.

RENANTHERA BROOKIE CHANDLER (*R. monachica* (Ames) x *R. storiei*). One of the most fascinating of all orchids, it is a strong grower and produces branching spikes of flame-colored flowers. Some find it shy-flowering, but this hybrid and others similar are worth persevering with. The individual flowers of all renantheras are comparatively small, but their numbers and color on the spikes make them outstanding.

ARACHNIS CLARKII (Reichenbach f.), after Johann Joseph Smith. At various periods known as an arachnanthe and an esmeralda, the last name given by R.A. Rolfe, as he was dissatisfied with its affiliation. The plant form is typically vandaceous like the renantheras, the flowers sparse and rather bizarre, also quite variable.

ARACHNIS FLOS-AERIS (Linnaeus). These Malaysian orchids are tremendously varied and common in certain areas. They are tropical plants in the true sense of the word, almost constantly in flower and for this reason favored as export crops. There is scarcely one country in the world to which they are not sent.

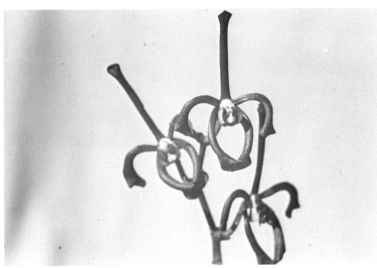

One of the few black orchids and not at all romantic; in fact almost sinister. This is probably *Archnis insignis.*

ASCOCENDA MEDA ARNOLD (*Ascocentrum curvifolium* x *Vanda* Rothschildiana). One of the first and, even after the lapse of some thirty years to 1980, still one of the best of this inter-generic pattern. These 'mini-vandas' were part of a world-wide change in orchid breeding. Instead of the desire for larger and larger flowers, orchid growers began to realise their limitations for space and started buying smaller plants.

ASCOCENDA MEDASAND
(Ascocenda Meda Arnold x *Vanda*
(Euanthe) sanderana). The return to
the species brought back the reticulations which are so much a part
of the vandas generally. The same
neat plant habit and smaller flowers
persisted in this hybrid, together
with a coppery color which shows
up so well in all lights.

ASCOCENDA RAKPAIBULSOMBAT
(Vanda coerulea x *Asco.* Medasand).
No orchid ever deserved a name like
this. Most fanciers of these small
vanda-type hybrids consider the
best of them are the blues. The
dominance of the blue from the
species *V. coerulea* is never less
than astonishing, but it is frequently
intensified by other species.

ASCOCENDA COPPERTONE *(Vanda
sanderana* x *Asco.* Red Gem).

74

ASCOCENDA ARAYA (*Vanda* Onomea x *Ascocenda* Yip Sum Wah). *Vanda* Onomea (*Euanthe sanderana* x *Vanda* Rothschildiana), although inbred, produced some particularly beautiful clones and they were used extensively all over the world in further hybridising.

ASCOCENDA MADAME NOK (*Vanda* Hilo Blue x *Ascocenda* Yip Sum Wah). Something very different in the ascocendas with its attractive spotting and good shape.

ASCOCENDA 50TH STATE BEAUTY (*Asco.* Yip Sum Wah x *Asco.* Meda Arnold). The cross-pollination of two outstanding ascocendas and the result reflected in the color and spike habit of the plant.

RHYNCOVANDA WONG YOKE SIM (*Vanda* Rothschildiana x *Rhyncovanda* Blue Angel). The color is all inherited from the second infusion of the vanda and the original color of *Rhyncostylis coelestis.* Some clones of this hybrid are almost violet-blue. The rhyncostylis was introduced with the same aim as the ascocendas, to get compact plants which produced medium-sized flowers.

MOKARA ENA LING (*Arachnis hookerana* x *Ascocenda* Yip Sum Wah). These inter-generic hybrids have a winter-flowering season at times and as such are useful additions to collections with only summer or autumn flowers. They are very much arachnis-type orchids, with that genus dominant to a great degree. As an inter-generic hybrid, however, the possibilities for future generations appear good for essentially tropical climate orchids.

NEOFINETIA FALCATA (Thunberg), related to the angraecums, obvious from at least one part of the flower, the spur. Also related to the vandas. It was first brought to cultivation about 160 years ago, since when the taxonomists have had their field days with this single-species genus. It was originally featured in *The Botanical Magazine* (England) as *Limadorum falcatum,* the first plants of which were sent to a grower in that country by Roxburgh. It is native to Japan and Korea and other lesser areas and in the nature of being a miniature.

76

ASCOFINETIA CHERRY BLOSSOM (*Neofinetia falcata* x *Ascocentrum ampullaceum*). A delightful combination which produced a free-flowering hybrid with some of the color of the ascocentrum and all the charm of the neofinetia.

OPSISANDA KAENA (*Vandopsis lissochiloides* x *Vanda tricolor* var. *suavis*). Not the type of flower to suit all tastes, but outstandingly attractive in an orchid collection and with a fairly long spike of flowers, the red outer coloring transferred to the interior in the form of spots. It was brought into being by the hybridist Kirsch, of Hawaii, in 1952.

OPSISANDA JULIET KIMBALL (*Vandopsis gigantea* x *Euanthe sanderana*). This hybrid is produced from entirely different lines and the influence of *Vanda sanderana* is subdued but still there. It was also a Hawaiian production from about the same period. The series appeared to cease there and perhaps a promising line was crossed off the list.

77

LYCASTE VIRGINALIS (Scheidweiler), perhaps better known as
Lycaste skinneri (Lindley), a Central
American native and one of the
most beautiful orchids in the world.
It flowers variably in winter to
spring, this plant grown by the
author and carrying thirty-two
flowers on a comparatively small
group of pseudo-bulbs. Each
flowering bulb is capable of producing up to six blooms, sometimes
more.

LYCASTE VIRGINALIS VAR. ALBA.
Pure white varieties do not occur
freely in lycastes generally, but their
rarity has been lessened by self-
pollinating them and raising
seedlings. Even by these means, the
white strains show poor vitality and
losses are high.

LYCASTE DEPPEI (Loddiges). This
orchid is among the hardy species
and is here photographed growing
in the branching butt of a casuarina
tree in the author's garden. Flowering in summer on the new growth, a
pattern which suits cooler climates,
it produces the blooms as freely
outdoors as when glass-house
grown.

LYCASTE DEPPEI, scented on a sunny day, is unsuited for warmer climates as are nearly all the genus. Although *L. virginalis* varies considerably in color and shape, *L. deppei* shows little of this characteristic and is commonly like this flower.

LYCASTE MACROPHYLLA (Poeppig and Endlicher). Lindley is more usually accorded the distinction for having named this species and opinion on this is divided. It does have tall foliage, as the name indicates, the flowers are variable in color and it is infrequently seen in cultivation. The influence on hybrids is extensive, particularly in the coppery tones of some of the primary hybrid flowers.

LYCASTE AROMATICA (Graham) ex Hooker. Again Lindley is credited with allocating the name by a number of publications. This orchid is one of the most delightful of all the lycastes. It grows its leaves then casts them, or nearly all of them, and produces its flowers in profusion from the bare pseudo-bulbs as well as new pseudo-bulbs in many instances. The size of the flowers varies from clone to clone, but the scent remains. Like most of the yellow lycastes, it flowers usually in summer but is neither a tropical nor cold climate subject.

LYCASTE CRUENTA (Lindley). Identification of most orchids from printed descriptions is always difficult and in the lycastes this is a common problem with all growers except with their own national plants. *L. cruenta* is often confused with other species which are sold under that name. It is one of the larger of the yellow-green deciduous types and produces its flowers freely when suited by conditions.

LYCASTE CILIATA (Ruiz and Pavon), Lindley ex Reichenbach f. Again a most confused species. Although this plant was brought into Australia under the name *Lycaste horichii,* which is a rather indefinite synonym attached to *L. tricolor* (Klotzsch), it is fairly recognisable as *L. ciliata.* The flowers have tall stems and the foliage is very tall for a lycaste.

LYCASTE LOCUSTA (Reichenbach f.). Green orchids seem to appeal to orchid growers' eyes more than other colors. This is no exception. It is one of the most attractive of the genus and while hybridists are carried away by the possibilities of *L. virginalis* and its hybrids they are neglecting a most worthwhile Peruvian species.

LYCASTE LASIOGLOSSA (Reichenbach f.). One of the Central American members of the genus, introduced into British cultivation by Veitch about 1870.

LYCASTE SCHILLERANA (Reichenbach f.), a Colombian representative, entered orchid history in the collection of G.W. Schiller in Hamburg about 1850, although how it came into his possession is not known or at least not freely recorded and it remained an isolated cultivated specimen for some twenty-five years. It is variable in color and never seems a robust species like some of the others. Schiller may have got it from Linden of Brussels whose collectors worked extensively in South and Central America.

LYCASTE POWELLI (Schlechter), a Panamanian species, J.A. Fowlie remarks in his book *The Genus Lycaste*: 'This plant was originally published by Schlechter . . . in 1922. It was found on the hills near Panama City and it is a little difficult to explain why prior botanists had not made note of it earlier.' As a native of Panama it should be one member of the genus which could survive sub-tropical cultivation and also could be the source of hybrids between other species which may also sustain such climates.

LYCASTE BALLIAE (*L. macrophylla* x *L. skinneri*), raised in 1896 by Sanders, is one of the keys to the success of hybridisers in the 1960-80 period. A great amount of scope for the genus was missed by following through an inbreeding pattern instead of introducing other species into the line. Nevertheless, orchid growers have good reason to be satisfied with the 1980 type of hybrids.

LYCASTE AUBURN (*L.* Balliae x *L.* Sunrise) is a follower along the same lines as *L.* Balliae but with the added introduction of the species *L. cruenta*, some influence of which is still visible in hybrids considerably removed from this step.

LYCASTE KOOLENA (*L.* Auburn x *L. skinneri*) continued the inbreeding program. The grex was raised by Wondabah Orchids of New South Wales and rekindled immense interest in the genus. Many forms of *L.* Koolena are known, some of award quality, and decorative clones such as this are worth comment and appreciation. A point worth noting is the absence of foliage on the plant, not usually a *L. skinneri* feature.

LYCASTE SHOALHAVEN (*L. skinneri* x *L.* Koolena). Returning to *L. skinneri* in selected clones for both parents, particularly with reference to non-reflexing petals and sepals, it shows a gain in shape for some clones of this grex, although it was not consistent right through. Inbreeding the *L.* Shoalhaven line produced some outstanding new colors which were not generally known when *Growing Orchids—Book Three* was published.

LYCASTE KOOLENA. An inbred "A" line cross-pollination using two selected varieties which produced remarkable color variations in the 1981 first flowerings.

ANGULOCASTE OLYMPUS (*Angulocaste* Apollo x *Lycaste* Sunrise) is an interesting hybrid because it has a strain of *Anguloa clowesii* and *Lycaste* Imschootiana running through the breeding. It is a beautiful, large flower, almost pure white, which may prompt some speculation about its authenticity. It was raised by Wyld Court Orchids in England in 1959, a nursery noted for several such inter-generic hybrids.

LYCASTERIA DARIUS (*L. skinneri* x *Bifrenaria harrisoniae*) appears to follow the pattern of flowering difficulty shown by *Bifrenaria harrisoniae*. This orchid, however, has its years of plenty, which seems to indicate that our cultural habits are at fault and cannot all be caused by the bifrenaria. *L.* Darius is seldom noted in flower and has been passed over by many growers. It was raised in 1954.

DENDROBIUM SPECIOSUM (Sir James Smith). The largest of the genus, some clones developing into masses which would weigh up to 500 kilograms and more (about half a ton). This Australian orchid is spectacular in flower in cultivation as well as in the wild. This is a plant of the variety *hilli* growing in the author's garden attached to a casuarina tree, the flower spikes about 40 centimetres long (about 15 inches) each carrying sixty-odd flowers.

DENDROBIUM FALCOROSTRUM (FitzGerald). A spectacular orchid like *D. speciosum* but with a more limited habitat and tolerance. Where possible it should be cultivated outdoors as it dislikes confinement in glass-houses, showing this by poorer flower size as well as quantity. This plant is also growing attached to a casuarina tree in the author's garden in southern Victoria, although usually it is selective in its host tree. The individual flowers are about 4½ to 5 centimetres across (1¾ to 2 inches).

84

DENDROBIUM KINGIANUM (John Carne Bidwell). It is no exaggeration to say that it would be possible to collect a hundred different varieties of this dendrobium. When suitable and amenable clones such as this are grown in temperate to warm conditions they are in miniature what dendrobiums *speciosum* and *falcorostrum* achieve in their size. The flowers vary in color and size but would average about 2 centimetres across (¾ inch), and few to a stem. It forms the third member of a notable trio.

DENDROBIUM BIGIBBUM (Lindley). The State emblem of Queensland, in the northern part of which this dendrobium grows. It is what could be termed a migrant and not one of the original Australian members of the genus. This flower is fairly typical of the species as a whole, one most difficult to tame and flower in glass-house climates in the southern part of the continent where even an interior weather pattern cannot be developed to suit it all the time. It carries ten to twelve flowers.

DENDROBIUM BIGIBBUM VAR. *COMPACTUM.* This dwarf variety of the species is much easier to cultivate, although the flowers, deeper in color and better in form, are usually a little smaller than the type form. The pseudo-bulbs of the variety *compactum* are only about one-third the length of the average of the type form, which may grow up to 60 centimetres (24 inches) high. *D. bigibbum* var. *compactum* may carry up to twenty flowers.

85

DENDROBIUM DICUPHUM (Baron Sir Ferdinand von Mueller). This dendrobium is most probably a development from the migrant form of *D. bigibbum*. It grows in the Northern Territory, found usually in the vicinity of water and on melaleucas or paperbarks, as they are commonly known. The flowers are about half the size of *D. phalaenopsis* and usually pallid shadows of that orchid.

DENDROBIUM SCHRODERANUM or *PHALAENOPSIS* VAR. *BICOLOR*. FitzGerald gave it the name *D. phalaenopsis,* but confusion over the names remains despite various attempts to sort out the varieties. The original *D. schroderianum* was sent by Forbes to the Royal Botanic Gardens at Kew about 1857 and its source remained obscure. The collector Micholitz later found it in Niugini. In recent years, if the name remains valid, it became *D. schroderanum* with the elimination of the letter 'i'. It is half again as large as *D. bigibbum* and is native to several areas other than Niugini It is still an Australasian orchid, however, and the probable progenitor of its Australian relative.

DENROBIUM TUCKURIMBA (*D.* Lady Fay x *D.* Lowana Red). A hybrid from the Cannons' nursery at Port Macquarie, derived from *D. phalaenopsis* in stages to this delightful red. The flowers are about 7 to 8 centimetres across (over 3 inches).

DENDROBIUM KULTANA (*D. American Beauty* x *D. Gold Flush*). Working toward the other end of the rainbow from *D.* Tuckurimba, this blue-tinted dendrobium was raised in Thailand. Most common in this type of dendrobium are the purple-reds, of which some very large flowers have been raised, some up to 9½ centimetres across (about 4 inches). Again this is typical "A" line hybridising, but quite successful in developing new colors and size. Nothing is yet known about the stamina of the plants or the number of flowers, although *D.* Kultana carries few.

DENDROBIUM PEEWEE (*D. bigibbum* x *D. tetragonum*). This is a breakthrough in creating a dendrobium type which could be further developed into the Australian dendrobiums to produce eventually a *D. bigibbum* type orchid which may be grown in moderate climates. *D. tetragonum* also held other surprises in Australian-raised hybrids and work on it in 1982 was about the midway stage to full development.

DENDROBIUM AUSTRALIAN BEAUTY (*D. speciosum* x *D. Meadie*). This was a spectacular breakthrough for Kevin McFarlane of Cairns. The spike, typically *D. speciosum* in production, carried almost as many flowers as that species. It is not a simple dendrobium, because locked up in its chromosomes are the species dendrobiums *aries, schulleri, phalaenopsis, stratiotes, tokai, veratrifolium, violaceo-flavens, taurinum* and finally *D. speciosum* — in all nine different dendrobiums, some most distantly related.

DENDROBIUM DISCOLOR (Lindley), also known by its synonym *D. undulatum.* This is close to the type form. In tropical climates this dendrobium may grow to 2 metres and more tall, flowers freely and is most widespread through the Australasian area in its northern confines. The variety *D. discolor* var. *broomfieldii* is bright golden to canary yellow and although the species has been subdivided into varieties and forms it is just as variable as most dendrobiums and the types most difficult for growers to identify.

DENDROBIUM SCHULLERI (J. J. Smith). This Niugini native was exploited considerably in the 1960-80 period for its color and robustness. The shape is typical of many Niugini dendrobiums and quite different from the usual open form of the Indo-Asian dendrobiums and the Australian types.

DENDROBIUM CUNNINGHAMII (Lindley). This isolated southernmost member of the genus grows prolifically in parts of New Zealand. The wiry stems — they could scarcely be termed pseudo-bulbs — grow and branch almost up to a metre long, trailing from the trees in an easily recognisable manner. It is rather shy-flowering in cultivation.

No garden plant is more decorative than *Dendrobium speciosum* in moderate climates. Some forms will not grow in southern Australia, but most are readily amenable to cultivation in Australia where the weather is not too harsh. It will grow in various containers or on hosts, with this plant in a tree-fern pot or cup.

DENDROBIUM NOBILE (Carl Peter Thunberg). The matriarch and the progenitor of nearly all the soft-cane dendrobium hybrids. Native to much of Indo-Asia including southern China and as far east as Formosa according to some authorities, this dendrobium has influenced the evolution of these orchids for a very long period. The form illustrated here is a sibling cross-pollination selected from the batch for further hybridising.

DENDROBIUM NOBILE VAR. *VIRGINALE.* This orchid is not as robust as the type form or various clones of the colored *D. nobile.* It was first found as a chance albino, but considering the Indo-Asian genus as a whole, it could have been a mistake to call it *D. nobile* in the first place. Think it over!

89

DENDROBIUM HETEROCARPUM
(Wallich), syn. *Dendrobium aureum*
(Lindley). This orchid should
possibly rank equal with *D. nobile*
as a prime selection. There are
several forms and only in the
Philippines' type are they as tall-
growing as *D. nobile.* The flowering
habit of no more than three or four
nodes producing blooms is in part
responsible for reducing the free-
flowering habits of *D. nobile* in
many late-generation cross-
pollinations.

DENDROBIUM FINDLAYANUM
(Parish and Reichenbach). One of
the most decorative of the soft-cane
species, also with great influence
on the labellum color of hybrids.

DENDROBIUM SIGNATUM (Reichenbach f.). A mystery still, with several
descriptions to guide or confuse.
The major opinion is that it is a
form of *D. bensoniae,* others that it
was a natural hybrid involving such
species as *D. friedricksianum, D.
tortile* and *D. bensoniae.* But there
is no certainty that the various
opinions were generated by the
same orchid. The form used by Sir
Jeremiah Colman and others was
stated to be canary yellow to
sulphur colored and from the base
of the various opinions pastel artist
Joan Skilbeck has reconstructed
this composite colored reproduction. Considering its use and impact
on the complex, it is surprising that
a so much used orchid could
disappear so completely as *D.
signatum.*

DENDROBIUM HILDEBRANDII
(Rolfe). A dendrobium with a
physical structure midway between
the soft-cane species like *D. nobile*
and the hard-canes such as *D. thyrsiflorum.*

DENDROBIUM REGIUM (Prain). This
reproduction may be a little
overdrawn regarding the lining of
the petals and sepals. It appeared in
a gardening magazine in the early
part of the century and it may be
that the color would be more
uniform and the lining less obvious
in many of the clones. It is not
apparent in any of the hybrids
generated from it.

DENDROBIUM AINSWORTHII (*D. nobile* x *D. aureum*). This is an
illustration which appeared in a
catalogue of a release of divisions
of first-class orchids from the
Walton Grange collection in 1898,
most of which were odontoglossums. It was known as *Dendrobium
splendidissimum* 'Grandiflora',
Thompson's variety. This primary
hybrid marked the beginning of a
line which continued until this book
was published and an example of
which is noted in the pedigree on
page 49. It also appears in
Sander's List of Orchid Hybrids
from the days when the varieties
used in cross-pollinations were
sometimes given.

91

DENDROBIUM CYBELE (*D. find-layanum* x *D. nobile*). A primary hybrid, like its contemporaries, which was taken to extraordinary development over a period of about a hundred years.

DENDROBIUM THWAITESIAE (*D.* Ainsworthii x *D.* Wiganiae). Little of *D. nobile* is obvious, as it had the influences of dendrobiums *aureum* and *signatum* to overcome. Seldom recessive for long, the *D. nobile* influence is always paramount and obvious in the 1980 decade hybrids from all sources.

DENDROBIUM WIGANIAE (*D. nobile* x *D. signatum*). Another of the influential primaries, most bred from *D. nobile* var. *nobilius.* Like *D. signatum*, this last-named orchid is very hard to locate, although once grown extensively.

92

DENDROBIUM EURYALUS (*D.* Ainsworthii x *D. nobile*), among the free-flowering early hybrids, flowering easily from the smallest propagations and excelling when cultivated into specimens such as this. While quality may be lacking, flower numbers counter this deficiency.

DENDROBIUM PLUMPTONENSE (syn. *D.* Model) (*D.* Cybele x *D. nobile*). The form of *D. nobile* used to produce most clones of *D.* Model (or Plumptonense) known in the 1900 era was the variety *nobilius* and this accounts for their shapeliness. A classic example of inbreeding or "A" line development, they were so finely proportioned that they have outlasted countless thousands of their contemporaries and equal the quality of many finer clones of late period hybrids from the Japanese and others.

DENDROBIUM UTOPIA (*D.* Glorious Rainbow x *D.* Orion) is typical of the so-called Yamamoto hybrids. It has size, color and basic shape and represents the follow-up of Japanese breeders along the lines so well laid down early in the century.

DENDROBIUM AKATUKI (*D.* Permos x *D.* Konan). Another of the Yamamoto hybrids. If the flower in the lower corner of the picture is studied it reveals the faults which show up in dendrobiums that are raised as mericlones. While it may be a basic natural failing with many hybrids to exhibit such faults in seedlings, the process is accentuated by mericloning and spoils an otherwise perfect umbel of flowers. It could be caused by "A" line breeding.

DENDROBIUM YORK (*D. regium* x *D. nobile*). Primary hybrids such as this are far easier to cultivate into multiflowered specimen plants than the more complex clones of six and more generations. While it is impossible to illustrate all the noteworthy primary hybrids in the section in a book of this size, most of the important primaries are included.

DENDROBIUM SUNBURST 'Tain' (*D.* Merlin x *D.* Thwaitesiae). The characteristics imparted to dendrobium hybrids by the species remain fairly constant and may sometimes be recognised, like the cream and gold of the interior of the labellum in this dendrobium. It came from the species *D. findlayanum*.

94

DENDROBIUM MONTROSE (*D. Ainsworthii* x *D.* Thwaitesiae). The evidence of participation of the mystery species *D. signatum* is plain in the labellum of this second generation hybrid. *D.* Montrose may flower variably in cool climates, but in the warmth of the southern Australian summer of 1980-81 it prepared for its best flowering ever. This was the tip of a pseudo-bulb with as many flowers again on the lower section.

DENDROBIUM GOLDEN BLOSSOM (*D.* Golden Eagle x *D.* Dream). Among other influences, possibly *D. nobile* var. *virginale* and *D. signatum* were the strong source of yellow in these beautiful clear yellow flowers.

DENDROBIUM ANNE MARIE (*D.* Montrose x *D.* Winifred Fortescue). A German-raised hybrid from the middle of the century, possibly marking the resurrection of the genus from the disuse into which it fell and producing some robust clones of very large flowers and strength in breeding.

DENDROBIUM HIGHLIGHT (*D. Kaguyahime* x *D. Oborozuki*), an eleventh generation hybrid. The background to this dendrobium consists of thirty-five infusions of *D. nobile,* fifteen of *D. heterocarpum,* ten of *D. signatum,* six of *D. regium,* five of *D. hildebrandii,* four of *D. moniliforme* and one of *D. findlayanum.* It is typical of the soft-cane dendrobiums of the later years of the twentieth century and the lower echelon of "A" line flowers. The proportion of super-"A" line flowers in the cross-pollination would probably be the usual ratio of one good one to every hundred or so of flowered clones. It is impossible to estimate the number of germinated seedlings which would fail to prosper in such a cross-pollination, but it would probably be high, principally from attenuated breeding lines and lack of stabilising genetic material from the "B" and "C" lines. See *Growing Orchids — Book Two,* for further information on this. For pedigree line-out see page 49.

DENDROBIUM HIGHLIGHT. Another seedling from the same cross-pollination, similar yet different. Considering the number of species involved, it is surprising how dominant one or two of them become. A glance back to those illustrated will indicate this.

DENDROBIUM WARDIANUM (Warner). This warm-climate orchid grows naturally right across the upper portion of the Indo-Asian area and down into Thailand, but it is not a tropical species. Although cultivators try to grow it erect, its natural habit is to be totally or almost pendant. One of the most beautifully colored of the species, it did not transfer any characteristics in this direction to future generations and fell into disuse.

DENDROBIUM LITUIFLORUM
(Lindley). A minor species after the fashion of *D. nobile* and could be regarded as an offshoot from that general line. It is Indo-Asian, pendulous and variable in color, growing at some 2000 metres (over 5000 feet). The climate in this region is not subject to sudden changes of temperature and this is one of the cultural necessities for most of the soft-cane dendrobiums.

DENDROBIUM CRYSTALLINUM
(Reichenbach f.). An orchid with a flower similar to *D. falconeri* (Hooker), one of the most demanding of the genus. Both are pendant orchids, but would-be growers may be better off trying to grow *D. crystallinum* than *D. falconeri*. There are quite a number of the soft-cane dendrobiums with flowers similar to this.

DENDROBIUM VICTORIA-REGINAE
(Loher). This beautiful Philippine Island dendrobium from the high country of the Baguio province on the island of Luzon has been known and cultivated since 1897 when it was introduced and named in honor of Queen Victoria for her jubilee year of reign in Britain. No one quite believed first reports, perhaps with some 'sour grapes' about it all; but this cool-growing dendrobium withstands the onslaughts of all but the most devastating of growers. It is a pendulous type, growing freely from the lower parts of the pseudo-bulbs as well as the 'eyes' near the rhizome.

97

DENDROBIUM ANOSMUM (Lindley).
Sometimes scented, sometimes not,
a dendrobium widespread through
Malaysia and repuledly down into
Niugini, or West Irian. Niugini as a
whole is a very large island, incom-
pletely explored and far from
catalogued in its orchids. *D.
anosmum* is pendulous, varies from
white right through to deeper
lavender colors and is sometimes
known by its synonym *D. superbum.*
Some authorities quote the two as
separate species.

DENDROBIUM CREPIDATUM
(Lindley). A beautiful miniature
introduced to English glass-houses
about 1849, from Assam, north-
eastern India. It was subsequently
found to be widespread through
Indo-Asia, some varieties auto-
gamous or self-pollinating before
fully opening the flowers. Mostly it
is an erect soft-cane type which
thrives in moderate to mildly warm
conditions.

DENDROBIUM PARISHII (Reichenbach f.) is a similar miniature,
varying considerably in color and
form. Originally sent from Burma to
Low & Co. in England by The Rev.
Parish, mentioned in connection
with other orchids from lower and
upper Burma, about 1863. Little was
noted about it in contemporary literature other than its scent, which
some authorities considered
offensive. It is slightly reminiscent
of rhubarb.

DENDROBIUM LODDIGESII (Rolfe). This miniature dendrobium was a puzzle for many years following its discovery and introduction to orchid growers by Loddiges about 1832. Originally the habitat was given as India, which is a large place to indicate as a habitat. Subsequently it was known to have come from the island of Hainan and also grew in southern China. Not an easy orchid to cultivate, if it finds a happy home it proliferates into a tufted mass of short pseudo-bulbs and aerial growths from nodes over their length. If well suited it remains in leaf for some time and will flower profusely and brilliantly in late spring to early summer. It grows in moderate warmth with some varieties seeming to like cooler conditions.

DENDROBIUM CRUMENATUM (Rumphius). A Malaysian orchid with thin, bamboo-like pseudo-bulbs which straggle freely. It grows in a warm climate with a rainfall which is spread over most of the year. Like most orchids which grow in such climates, this dendrobium may hold its buds at opening stage until conditions are precisely right. In such climates orchids of various types are in flower throughout the year and *D. crumenatum* may thus flower variably according to the program adopted by individual growers. It is a decorative small plant.

DENDROBIUM MONILIFORME (Swartz). This rather insignificant dendrobium from the eastern Asian area including Japan, is one of the fragrant species which, unless taken into consideration because of involvement in the basic pedigrees of many modern hybrids, would pass almost unnoticed in orchid collections. It is a warm-growing orchid and was used by the Chinese in their medications long before the advent of the European races in what was once known as the Far East.

DENDROBIUM PULCHELLUM

(Roxburgh). Common to the northern Indian area and across to Malaya. It was found by Roxburgh about 1030. Gibson found it growing in the Botanical Gardens at Calcutta and sent it to Chatsworth collection about 1837. Dr Wallich had also found it in northern India about the same time and named it *D. Dalhousieanum* after the Countess of Dalhousie and this became its proper name for a considerable period. It is now the synonym. A tropical climate orchid, its rightful place is in warmer regions where it grows and flowers profusely. The pseudo-bulbs are well-leafed, hard-cane type and grow up to about 1½ metres (about 5 feet) or more.

DENDROBIUM MOSCHATUM

(Willdenow). Common in variety to a considerable amount of the Indo-Asian area, it is similar morphologically to *D. pulchellum*. It was first brought into cultivation from lower Burma about 1825 and flowers variably in spring to early summer, depending, like *D. pulchellum*, on the climate or system in which it is grown. Glass-house grown plants are prone to differ in season. Both these dendrobiums are ideal outdoor epiphytes in sub-tropical conditions.

DENDROBIUM SANDERAE (Rolfe).

Typical well-leafed hard-cane dendrobium, similar to *D. moschatum* and *D. pulchellum*, but bearing only short spikes of flowers where the other two have longer racemes. It was originally said to have come from Niugini, its real habitat subsequently proving to be Luzon Island in the Philippine Islands, overlooked by collectors until about 1905. *D. sanderae* grows as tall as other dendrobiums of this type and, as the illustration shows, may flower all the way up the pseudo-bulbs or patchily from them.

DENDROBIUM SANDERAE flowers are about 5 centimetres across (2 inches), the inner labellum marked with purple stripes on a green ground. The plant Sanders' exhibited at an RHS show in 1909 gained a First Class Certificate.

DENDROBIUM DEAREI (Reichenbach f.). Directly related to *D. sanderae* and similar in appearance, but the flowers are pure white with just a tint of green. First taken into cultivation after discovery in the Philippine Islands about 1882, it is a warm-growing dendrobium which needs a fast summer growth period to produce and mature the tall pseudo-bulbs.

DENDROBIUM THYRSIFLORUM (Reichenbach f.). More commonly thought of as a Burmese orchid, this dendrobium was discovered by The Rev. Parish about 1860 and sent by him to Low & Co., with whom he seemed to have a connection. The unopened flowers, covered by enclosing bracts, form a beautiful pale-colored cone and this is the origin of the name. It differs slightly in pseudo-bulbs from its close affiliate *D. densiflorum,* which are slightly more squarish and often shorter, the flowers more colorful. It is now regarded as a variety of *D. thyrsiflorum.* Both should flower in late spring but are frequently variable, depending on the climate in which they are grown, as they are temperate-zone orchids.

DENDROBIUM FARMERI (Paxton). Common to the Indo-Asian area, slightly warmer growing than *D. thyrsiflorum* which it resembles. The slightly squarish outline of the pseudo-bulbs may be noted. First found in Moulmein, Burma, in 1847 and flowered by W.G. Farmer after whom it was named. The petals on opening are a pale mauve which later fades to almost white.

101

DENDROBIUM MOUSMEE (*D. bronckartii* x *D. thyrsiflorum*). Raised by Sir Jeremiah Colman and named in 1907. A hybrid raised from the *D. thyrsiflorum* complex, one of the few and very colorful. *D. bronckartii* was introduced early in this century and is allied to *D. farmeri*.

DENDROBIUM CHRYSOTOXUM (Lindley). There are several types, noticeable in the pseudo-bulbs more than the flowers. This dendrobium was first imported into Britain about 1847, principally through the collector Boxall, who found it in upper Burma where it grows mostly about the 1000 metres mark (about 3250 feet). It flowers from both old and new growths, at times from leafless pseudo-bulbs, thriving best in fairly bright light, but it is intolerant of tropical conditions of high temperatures and high humidity.

DENDROBIUM AGGREGATUM (Roxburgh). An Asian orchid, obviously related to *D. chrysotoxum* but a little more difficult to grow in glass-house conditions. Most of these dendrobiums need a fairly prolonged dry period in which both temperature and humidity are critical. Many growers are able to overcome such disabilities by transferring plants to the higher parts of a glass-house and preventing the worst of shrivelling stages by careful watering control.

DENDROBIUM GATTON SUNRAY
(*D. pulchellum* x *D. illustre*).
Another Colman triumph from 1919.
The form of *D. pulchellum* used was
golden yellow, but the distinct 'eyes'
are still a prominent feature. *D.
illustre* was the combination of *D.
chrysotoxum* and *D. pulchellum*
raised by Veitch in 1899. *D.* Gatton
Sunray is a much easier and better
producer of flowers in sub-tropical
climates, those grown in cooler
climates occasionally proving
stubborn in growth and maturing
stages.

DENDROBIUM FIMBRIATUM VAR.
OCCULATUM (Hooker). A Burmese
orchid of singular beauty, one of the
shorter-growing fully-leafed hard-
cane group, it flowers from leafless
as well as fully-leafed pseudo-bulbs.
The nurseryman Loddiges flowered
a specimen with over 800 flowers in
1840, noted in *Paxton's Magazine of
Botany* for the period. Wallich found
the plain-flowered type in Nepal
about 1820 and Gibson the variety
occulatum more than a decade later
in the Khasia Hills in upper India.
As Veitch remarked, plants with
over 1200 flowers were known in
those early importations. Moderate-
to warm-growing.

DENDROBIUM FLAVIFLORUM (Hay).
A Formosan representative of the
hard-cane section, by far the most
beautifully perfumed of the group.
Warm-growing, possibly best in
milder sub-tropical climates.
Formosa is now known as Taiwan.

103

DENDROBIUM CRUENTUM
(Reichenbach f.). One of the
prettiest dendrobiums in the genus.
A member of the nigrohirsute range,
it is not an easy orchid to cultivate
unless suited by natural conditions
in an area where it may be grown
outdoors, preferably in a tropical
climate. Native to Malaysia, it is
mostly found as a lowland epiphyte.

DENDROBIUM FORMOSUM (Roxburgh). It was cultivated as early as
1811 in India and introduced to
Britain and Europe about 1837 from
the Khasia Hills, northern India. It is
also native to one or two other
Burmese locations. Like many of the
lowland species, as indicated by the
color of the flowers, it should be
grown in strong light to almost open
sunlight for most of the day.

DENDROBIUM INFUNDIBULUM
(Lindley). A close relative of *D.
formosum*, it occasionally goes
under the name of *D. jamesianum*. A
little easier to cultivate in cooler
climates than *D. formosum*,
principally because of its source at
higher altitudes, this dendrobium
should still be grown in fairly bright
light and with warmth if grown in
climates with natural low winter
temperatures. The nigrohirsute
series particularly have always been
difficult to grow in artificial
conditions.

DENDROBIUM LAWESII (Lawes). A Niugini orchid of considerable charm. It grows in a country which is mainly mountainous and tropical and in which the orchids are still an unknown group. Although many are known, dendrobium knowledge, apart from a few enthusiasts familiar with them, is scant. This typically shaped flower of many of the genus in Niugini, is unlike most of the Indo-Asian dendrobiums and in this species may be any color from light yellow to deep red. The juvenile pseudo-bulbs are usually fully leafed like D. moschatum, but they are quickly shed. Mostly found at a high altitude, it should still be regarded as a tropical orchid.

DENDROBIUM BRACTEOSUM (Reichenbach f.). Two distinct varieties of a Niugini species, illustrating the great differences in color which may be found within a species. It has the peculiar shape common to many Niugini dendrobium flowers and thrives in moderate to warm temperatures despite being almost an equatorial species. It grows at fairly high altitudes, where the weather may be quite cold at night and even in the daytime in certain seasons.

CATASETUM PILEATUM VAR. AUREUM (Reichenbach f.). One of the most beautiful and spectacular of the Colombian orchids, growing in a wooden slat basket, the type of suitable container for the genus. This is the male flower of the species, the synonym of which is C. bungerothii (Brown).

105

CATASETUM PILEATUM. The female flower. This, in a measure indicates the confusion which the genus caused in the first days of its cultivation. A pastel reproduction by Joan Skilbeck, to whom the author is indebted for illustrations of flowers important to the text and unavailable for photography.

CATASETUM CERNUUM (Lindley). This Brazilian orchid grows in widespread areas and the color is fairly consistent throughout. It is more spidery than others of the genus, which is still one of the puzzles of the orchid world. The plants grow principally on trees, alive or dead, subsisting on the food the roots may absorb from these barren surfaces. The transpiration of plant foods from the bark and interior of trees to subsequently feed epiphytes is an unknown province but it is undoubtedly a bountiful source of mineral salts and moisture available to the epiphytes without their roots parasitising the host. This is a typical well-grown plant, the foliage annual, the flower spike issuing from the base of the pseudo-bulb.

CATASETUM CERNUUM. The female form of many catasetums is similar to this, the flowers mostly appearing with the hood uppermost, but variable in this regard.

106

CATASETUM SACCATUM VAR. *CHRISTYANUM* (Lindley). An extraordinarily variable species over its range, which is widely South American. This is a very bright form. While some of the catasetums have this bag-like cavity in the flowers, others are devoid of it. None, however, has the flat profile of other orchids.

Catasetum hybrid. This plant was imported into Australia as an unknown species, collected in the field, growing in the same general area as catasetums *pileatum* and *trulla*. The first named is obviously one of the parents of this beautiful natural hybrid, with *C. trulla* as a possible pollinator or seed parent. It has also been suggested that *C. macrocarpum* is the other parent, which would mean that it is *C. splendens*.

CATASETUM TRULLA (Lindley). Catalogued mostly as a purely Brazilian species, but possible native of other South American regions.

CATASETUM GNOMUS (Lindley and Reichenbach f.). A Brazilian species which would defy analysis by a tyro. One may well ask where is the labellum and which part of the flower it is in this example. *C. gnomus* varies considerably in color.

CATASETUM VIRIDIFLAVUM (Hooker). A Central American species. The labellum is uppermost and the spike most attractive when fully opened. The column is the small round object at the base of the opening.

CATASETUM FIMBRIATUM (Lindley). A Brazilian species, varying in color. This is one of the most attractive of the varieties, pink and green, the flowers lasting, as with most of the genus, a matter of days or even a week or two, largely depending on the climate in which they mature. Once opened they should be kept cool but not cold.

CATASETUM FIMBRIATUM root system when grown in a wooden slat basket. A notable feature of this plant, however, is the appearance of small plantlets on the roots themselves. They are not chance seeds, which may also grow in this fashion, but are budded from the roots in the same way as extensions of the root system form. It is not a common form of plant propagation and is rarely noted.

CATASETUM INTERGERRINUM (Hooker). Although the flowers of this species do not last very long, they already look half-dead by the time they open. A Venezuelan native, it is also found in Central American regions.

Root system of Catasetum intergerrinum. Many orchids produce such root systems, which are literally food traps for the plants. Only in good growing conditions do such formations take place and in the instance of this species most of this is annual only and a new root growth takes its place, the older portion still acting as the trap.

CATASETUM (CLOWESIA) ROSEUM (Lindley), Reichenbach f. A native of various regions, relegated by some authorities to its original generic name. Its flowers combine both sexes and so far as is known no variation from this occurs. It is still known as a catasetum by a majority of growers and old habits die hard.

CYCNOCHES EGERTONIANUM (Bateman). This is the male flower, the racemes of which may be up to 2 metres long (over 6 feet), trailing away from the plant and borne in large numbers in suitable conditions. It has a pollen ejection mechanism which is triggered by the slightest contact.

CYCNOCHES EGERTONIANUM. The female flower, distinguished from various other cycnoches by the short column. Its resemblance to *C. ventricosum* is remarkable.

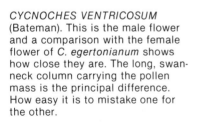

CYCNOCHES VENTRICOSUM (Bateman). This is the male flower and a comparison with the female flower of *C. egertonianum* shows how close they are. The long, swan-neck column carrying the pollen mass is the principal difference. How easy it is to mistake one for the other.

CYCNOCHES PENTADACTYLON (Lindley). This is a spectacular and beautiful orchid and like its relatives native to various parts of South America. Although seldom noted in orchid collections, they grow under the same conditions as catasetums, with a marked dormant period and swift growth and flowering stages in hot, humid conditions.

CATASETUM ORCHIDGLADE (*C. pileatum* x *C. expansum*). A 1974 naming, raised by the American nurserymen Jones and Scully. For those able to climb out of the rut of cultivating the orthodox and numerous hybrids available, such things as this beautiful orchid give years of satisfaction provided growers are able to accommodate all the inter-generic and outlandish combinations produced over the last thirty years. An appearance of female flowers would be interesting, as all types of flowers would be possible from such a hybrid.

CORYANTHES SPECIOSA (Hooker). A reproduction from an old lithograph of about 1880. The genus is described in the text. An extract in reference to the association of ants with the genus: 'Coryanthes usually occur as a conspicuous element in the unique arboreal myrmecophyllous gardens in the nests of ants of the genera camponotous and azteca ...' from Woodson and Schery's *Flora of Panama* and indicating just how far authors can distance themselves from the ordinary orchid grower.

PHALAENOPSIS AMABILIS
(Linnaeus). A widespread Malaysian-Australasian species, varying a little over its range, but consistently white. Plants of this species were collected in hundreds of thousands and in the ultimate phase of this business they were attached to short sticks by a shortened root system and allowed to stabilise in this way before they were packed and shipped. Before understanding came they were lost in enormous numbers.

PHALAENOPSIS SCHILLERANA
(Reichenbach f.). No orchid contributed more to the hybrids than this phalaenopsis. It also suffered in the same way as *P. amabilis* and a photograph of the ultimate successful method of importing them is shown on page 199. *P. schillerana* may carry multiple spikes and anything up to 300 or 400 flowers on the one plant when well cultivated.

PHALAENOPSIS LUEDDE-MANNIANA (Reichenbach f.). This is a particularly colorful form. The color varies considerably, but the usual combinations are brown, yellow and amethyst, the flowers varying in size from 3 to 5 centimetres (1¼ to 2 inches).

112

PHALAENOPSIS EQUESTRIS
(Reichenbach f.), synonym *P. rosea*
(Lindley). This lovely miniature
species had something the
hybridists turned to when the cross-
pollinations of the white and pink
hybrids stalled in repetition. The red
labellum was a dominant feature,
even if the flower itself is small.

PHALAENOPSIS VIOLACEA
(Teijsman). While morphologically
gross, the flowers of this species
are sparse, at most two or three
being common. This is a reproduction of a lithograph and while
the foliage appears striped, this is
rare in natural leaves. A sign of the
times, the artists of those days had
no photographs to guide them and
were at the mercy of verbal descriptions, both accurate and
inaccurate. *P. violacea* is a
Sumatran species, also found in
other parts of Malaysia.

PHALAENOPSIS SUMATRANA
(Korthals and Reichenbach f.). In
some ways similar to the species *P.
lueddemanniana,* with the ground
color and hieroglyphic patterning in
brownish red. It was found about
1840, its introduction to the glass-
houses of Europe delayed for some
twenty or more years. Like many of
the genus, it grew in close contact
with river systems, overhanging
water in its prime positions. John
Day, the artist-grower, was the first
Briton to flower it.

113

PHALAENOPSIS FASCIATA and *P. lueddemanniana* are regarded as conspecific and this flower is a cross-pollination of the two. It gives a good representation of the commoner form of *P. lueddemanniana*. Despite its rather bizarre patterned segments, hybridists look to it to provide a break from the pink and white monotony of the *P. schillerana-amabilis* complex.

PHALAENOPSIS DORIS (*P. Elisabethae* x *P. Katherine Siegwart*). A noted progenitor of the white hybrids of the late 1900 era. Selection and reselection and "A" line hybridising have broadened the segments of the flower until the sepals are barely visible behind the enormous petals of some of the later hybrids.

PHALAENOPSIS hybrid (*P. Pueblo Jewel* x *P. Lois Jansen*). This orchid combines two of the features which broke the general run of hybrids, first the striping which hybridists seek to eliminate in other genera and then the red labellum of the small species *P. equestris*. Unnamed when *Growing Orchids—Book Three* was published, the hybrid was indicative of the trend of the 1980 decade.

PHALAENOPSIS ABENDROT (*P. Lippezauber* x *P. Lippstadt*). Typical of the ultimate development of the pink series from *P. schillerana.* A very large phalaenopsis at 10 centimetres (about 4 inches), it naturally carries only a few flowers and some growers have difficulty in getting enough on a spike to qualify under some of the judging standards levelled at the genus.

DORITIS PULCHERRIMA (Lindley). John Lindley also named the genus, which has close affiliation with phalaenopsis. The plant is similar to a phalaenopsis in most ways, the flower a little smaller than the general run of those orchids but most acceptable because of its bright color. Orchid growers first seeing this orchid are charmed by it for life, some trying to grow it and succeeding if they have the qualifications, others failing and never really appreciating its true beauty in their own glass-houses.

DORITAENOPSIS RENEE KLEIN FREED (*Dtps.* Mem. Clarence Schubert x *Dtps.* Malibu Pink). The beautiful color of *D. pulcherrima* with much of the size of phalaenopsis. There is no difference in the culture of these hybrids from that of phalaenopsis or doritis, but this last named species does have a slightly different cycle from phalaenopsis and may need special treatment at times during that cycle.

SARCOCHILUS FALCATUS (Robert Brown). This small Australian orchid is related, although distantly, to phalaenopsis and other Malaysian orchids. The term Malaysian is applied to the total island area between the continent of Asia and Australia, a naturally rich area for orchids but not necessarily the source of the evolutionary elements in such places as Australia.

SARCOCHILUS HARTMANNI (Ferdinand von Mueller). The strongest growing of the genus in Australia and the inspiration of W. and J. Cannons when they sought to amalgamate it into the phalaenopsis and its allies. There are several varieties of *S. hartmanni,* some growers considering the variety *blue nob* the best.

SARCANOPSIS MACQUARIE LILAC (*S. hartmanni* x *Phalaenopsis* Federal Monarch). This orchid was a triumph for insight and perseverance. As a development toward a cooler-growing series of orchids in a diverse family it may prove successful. As an orchid hybrid in its own right it grows vigorously like most primary hybrids and has been proved to flower in southern Victoria as a garden plant attached to a casuarina tree in the author's garden, although it does much better in a moderately warm glass-house.

116

SARCANOPSIS MACQUARIE SUNSET (*S. hartmanni* x *Phalaenopsis* Aristocrat). This was the best of a series of three cross-pollinations which flowered. Perhaps a little more difficult to cultivate than *Srnps*. Macquarie Lilac, it never reached the easy proliferation of growths shown by that orchid. The Cannons nursery at Port Macquarie was the birthplace of the successful sarcanopsis cross-pollinations.

COELOGYNE CRISTATA (Lindley). Not the easiest of orchids to grow. To produce a plant such as this needs considerable patience and attention to detail.

COELOGYNE SPECIOSA (Blume). Despite origins in the Malaysian region, this orchid may be grown in mildly warm conditions, as it is generally found at about 1000 to 2000 metres (about 3000 to 6000 feet). Although many varieties were noted originally, there is little more uniformity in the species than in most other orchids and varietal distinctions are superfluous.

117

COELOGYNE MASSANGEANA
(Reichenbach f.). Although there is a
certain drabness about the color of
flowers of this species, the long
trailing racemes create a very
attractive plant. It grows best in
warm conditions in fairly bright
light.

COELOGYNE OVALIS (Lindley). An
awkward orchid to accommodate
because of length of rhizome
between pseudo-bulbs. It is best
grown on a stick of tree-fern which
gives it scope to climb and branch.
A warm-growing species, although it
occurs in foothill Himalayan
habitats as well as parts of Thailand
and other minor sectors.

COELOGYNE PANDURATA (Lindley).
A tropical member of the genus,
suited best for tropical cultivation
but needing a little careful growing
in early shoots so that they do not
become waterlogged and rot. The
spikes may carry up to twenty and
more flowers.

118

COELOGYNE MOOREANA (Sander).
In early notes on this coelogyne it
appears that either the variety or
the culture was not up to the
standard of later specimens
because it was held that the flowers
were smaller than those of C.
cristata. In fact, the flowers of C.
mooreana are among the largest of
the white group. Unlike C. cristata,
its habit is erect and not straggling
over potting material in the mass
which is responsible for the show of
flower produced by that orchid.

COELOGYNE MEM. W. MICHOLITZ
(C. lawrenceana x C. mooreana).
Both these coelogynes are natives
of Thailand and both were
discovered and collected by
Micholitz, whose biography is briefly
related in Growing Orchids—Book
Two. Few hybrids have been created
within the genus and there is
material on which amateur or pro-
fessional hybridists could work.

ANGRAECUM SESQUIPIDALE
(Thouars), the plant and the flower.
While some orchid plants look
delicate — and this includes some
of the vandas — most of the
angraecums have a 'tough'
appearance and tolerate light to a
degree which would burn most
genera.

119

ANGRAECUM EBURNEUM (Bory). The inversion of the flowers is a habit followed by many orchids. Although this orchid and *A. sesquipidale* grow and flower well in glass-house culture, they are better suited by the partly open cultivation systems of semi-tropical and tropical areas. High humidity marks the flowers and may encourage disease in the heads of the growth.

ANGRAECUM INFUNDIBULARE (Lindley). This species is unusual because of its arachnis-like growths. A West African orchid, it was a feature in the Rothschild collection at the beginning of the twentieth century. This collection was one of the few which specialised in African orchids of all types. *A. infundibulare* is a semi-tropical species and like most of the genus has a rambling, tough aerial root system.

ANGRAECUM VEITCHII (*A. eburneum* x *A. sesquipidale*). Raised by Veitch in 1899. This is one of the strangest orchids because the flowers are held at all angles on the stem. The parents have flowers which are positioned normally with the spur downward in most instances, but *A. Veitchii* has them frequently pointing upward.

ANGRAECUM COMPACTUM. One of the low-growing dwarf species from Madagascar. The flowering habits of the genus vary, some producing racemes, others single or two flowers on a stem like this species. It also has another point of difference in originating at altitudes of 800 to 2000 metres (about 2500 to 6000 feet), making it an ideal orchid for moderate warmth and a small glass-house.

ANGRAECUM PHILIPPINENSE. At one time a threatened species, this miniature has been protected at glass-house level by seed-raising, but its continued existence as a wild orchid is uncertain.

ANGRAECUM DISTICHUM (Lindley). This miniature flowered species is one of the peculiarities of the orchid world and in good moderate conditions proliferates into a most attractive plant which at times may be covered with flowers.

121

AERANGIS MYSTACIDII (Reichenbach f.). One of the fairly common epiphytes of southern Africa, this beautiful miniature of the angraecums grows at medium to low altitudes in a number of situations from dry areas to the banks of streams. In cultivation it is free-growing on cork or wood sections, seasonal in activity, with new leaves appearing in early to mid summer and the flowers following in autumn. The spur is about 5 or 6 centimetres long (about 2 to 2½ inches) and the flowers should be kept dry. Most of these orchids will stand very bright light, but some of the softer leafed species should be given moderate shade. In dormancy the roots seal off and the plants should be given little water. Unfortunately, many of the South African angraecoids are neither freely available nor much cultivated in Australian collections.

MAXILLARIA PORPHYROSTELE (Reichenbach f.). One of the hardiest of the genus. This plant was photographed growing in the author's garden, atttached to a casuarina tree to which the roots, after only one season of establishment, clung so firmly that the maxillaria could not be removed. Winter to spring flowering.

MAXILLARIA NIGRESCENS (Lindley) growing in the same way as *M. porphyrostele*. It is very strongly scented, flowering usually in autumn to early spring. Most of the genus prefer growing as epiphytes rather than as pot plants, flowering more freely and maintaining a better root system in such conditions.

MAXILLARIA SANDERANA (Reichenbach f.). The largest of the species, growing in a moss-lined wire basket, the flower spikes spearing through the sides. If incorrectly grown, the flowers, which are about 10 centimetres across (about 4 inches), discolor quickly, the labellums discoloring first and then the base color of the petals turning yellow.

MAXILLARIA PICTA (Hooker). A hardy species preferring slightly warmer conditions than *M. porphyrostele*. This wire basket was lined with the husk of stag or elk fern and filled with a rough mixture based on coarse cymbidium aggregate and left undisturbed for many years. *M. picta* is bright canary yellow on the interior surfaces and blotched with red to red-brown or purple on the outside of petals and sepals.

MAXILLARIA VARIABILIS (Bateman) ex Lindley. A Central American orchid with a different inflorescence from the single flowers from the base of the new bulbs which are common to the other species. It is warm-growing yet not tropical. If grown in tropical conditions some maxillarias may fit into collections but need a little protection in the wet season.

MAXILLARIA RUFESCENS VAR. *FLAVIDA* (Lindley). This species is one of the most widespread of the maxillarias. Like so many of the genus, it is single-flowered, the blooms opening soon after the pseudo-bulbs mature. In southern hemisphere climates that would be in early winter. While some of the hardy species are unharmed by cold, others are severely affected and the buds may brown off before opening.

MASDEVALLIA COCCINEA (Lindley). No more colorful addition may be made to an orchid collection than a few plants of this lovely semi-epiphyte. This group was photographed in the author's glass-house about 1965.

MASDEVALLIA VEITCHIANA (Reichenbach f.). If ever an orchid distributor was honored in a name it was Veitch and as much through this orchid as another. Although quite variable, the usual characteristic of purple velvety overlay on a unique contrasting color is a prominent feature of the whole species. The reaction of the flower to changing light intensities is startling and unique in the orchid world.

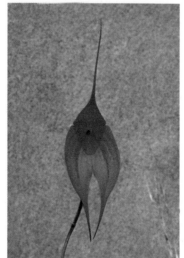

MASDEVALLIA COCCINEA almost rivals *M. veitchiana* for color because the prevailing light at any moment when it is viewed so changes the fluorescent lower sepals that they would be difficult to identify even with a recognised color chart.

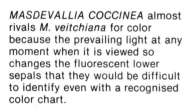

MASDEVALLIA TOVARENSIS (Reichenbach f.). Although this species is the only all-white masdevallia, pure white or albino forms of several others were known and grown in the early history of the genus.

124

MASDEVALLIA SCHROEDERANA (Sander). It seems impossible that an orchid could be taken into cultivation without anything or at least very little being known about it, but this happened with *M. schroederana*. It was first noted in 1890, a Peruvian species, growing at a high altitude.

MASDEVALLIA MILITARIS (Reichenbach f.), synonym *M. ignea*. Josef Warscewicz found this masdevallia growing at about 2500 metres (about 8000 feet) in Colombia in 1850 and sent it to Europe. The upper sepal never lifts, but the brilliant color stands out in orchid collections.

MASDEVALLIA ROLFEAE (?). This small unidentified species is one of the dwarfs of the genus, the leaves about 4 to 5 centimetres long (about 2 inches), the flowers, produced most freely, nestled down among them. It was photographed growing quite cold as an epiphyte on a casuarina tree in the author's garden, a situation also occupied by *M. coccinea*.

125

MASDEVALLIA BOCKING HYBRID
(*M. cucullata* x *M. veitchiana*). One
of the few surviving members of a
cross-pollination phase in the genus
which did not last. *M.* Bocking
Hybrid was raised in the collection
of Sydney Courtauld in 1899. Like
most of the genus, it must be suited
by general conditions or the foliage
marks badly, a condition usually
caused by stagnant air as much as
humidity.

BULBOPHYLLUM ROBUSTUM
(Rolfe). This Niugini orchid is a
member of a very numerous genus,
over 300 of which are to be found in
Niugini and Irian Jaya. It is one of
the largest of the genus, the flower
panicle measuring over 15
centimetres across (about 6 inches)
on well-grown plants. A warm-
growing species, it was first found
about 1890, flowered in Britain in
1895 and gained a rare distinction
for a species orchid, a First Class
Certificate from the RHS.

BULBOPHYLLUM GLOBULIFORME
(Nicholls). From the largest to the
smallest. This orchid is possibly the
tiniest in the world. Its companion,
B. minutissimum, also grows in New
South Wales. It was once common
around the Rushcutters Bay area of
Sydney harbor as noted by an 1880
orchidophile. The pseudo-bulbs are
about the size of a pinhead or a
little larger.

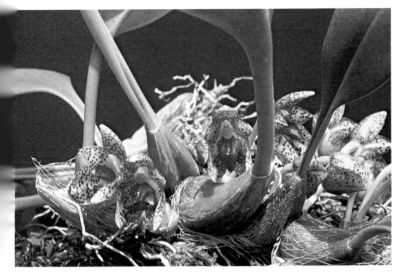

BULBOPHYLLUM LEOPARDINUM (Lindley). This north Indian species is one of the most decorative and least grown of the genus. It is a surface-growing orchid and is best suited in a flat dish or pan. Although there are points against this type of receptacle, the genus as a whole dislikes deep pots of material and the root system, mostly surface on natural-growing plants, should be given something similar to work on. The potting material in these shallow dishes may be any of the better-known bark mixes, not forgetting to allow a few holes for drainage in the dish itself and to simplify tying the plant down for security.

DISA UNIFLORA (Bergius). The genus and species were named by the same man. This South African orchid is one of the most admired and one of the most difficult to grow. The genus is mostly marshland and moist habitat inclined and until some study of this technique is made little success is possible. New Zealand growers in particular have been successful and although their methods are too involved for a description here, they are based on moist culture seed-raising and growing techniques. (Photo courtesy of George Fuller of New Plymouth, NZ)

ANCISTROCHILUS THOM-SONIANUS (Reichenbach f.). This tropical African orchid was first found by the collector Kalbreyer. It is one of the most attractive of the African orchids and may be cultivated in similar fashion to the bulbophyllums. It was named *Pachystoma thomsoniana* by Reichenbach but was subsequently removed from that genus and given a new name by Rolfe. The peculiar squashed-looking pseudo-bulbs are among the curiosities of the orchid world, the flowers lovely and freely borne, up to about 7 or 9 centimetres across (3 to 3½ inches).

127

CHYSIS AUREA (Lindley), synonym
C. bractescens. The typical form of
most collections. Native of Central
America, the weather pattern is
rather harsh in some seasons and
right up to flowering stage,
following which the new growths
slowly expand and mature. From
about May to the next flowering
phase in southern hemisphere
climates the plants should receive
little or no water, despite shrivelling.
Chysis bractescens was originally
found in Venezuela.

CHYSIS AUREA (Lindley). One of the
many beautiful variations in the
species. It is difficult to choose
between them, some preferring the
glistening white or cream flowers,
others the beautiful shaded pinks
and tawny colors.

CHYSIS LAEVIS (Lindley). Again
Central American in origin, this
species sometimes flowers later
than C. aurea and is not as
frequently noted in collections. The
root systems of chysis should be
vigorous and extensive in growth
stages and until they reactivate in
the growth stage following
flowering, little moisture should be
given, relying on humidity and
benching of the plants in moist
surroundings.

128

BIFRENARIA HARRISONIAE (Hooker). The cymbidium-like flowers of this species are among the handsomest of all orchids, the stems always short and the flowers prone to mark easily if splashed with water. An orchid which does not object to extremes of pot binding, it is affected by the natural seasons, regardless of glass-house care and heed to temperature. Although appearances may count with some growers, burnt-looking hard foliage is frequently the precurser to free flowering.

STANHOPEA TIGRINA (Bateman). Although this orchid has been renamed *Stanhopea hernandezii* (Kunth) by Schlechter, the old name has become difficult to dislodge from books and the minds of orchid growers. It is among the best known of the species, the flowers extraordinary in all contexts, the scent first almost pleasant then becoming objectionable in the later stages of flower life, which is relatively short for orchids.

STANHOPEA WARDII (Loddiges). The extraordinary flowers of the genus almost defy description but are clear when examined, with the sepals flung back to expose the peculiar column and labellum. Even this, when examined in detail, becomes clear also when the various parts are understood.

STANHOPEA ECORNUTA (Lemaire). The downward pointing column over the peculiar labellum is quite clear in this profile. As insects crawl past the column the sharp backward tip of the column is dislodged, the pollen released and glued to the body of the insect just behind its head in a very businesslike arrangement.

A hybrid. *Stanhopea ecornuta* x *S. costaricensis,* syn. *S. graveolens.* The habit of stanhopeas of folding back the petals and sepals is obvious in this photograph. It could be imagined that there is enough variation and peculiarity in the species flowers to satisfy orchid growers, without the necessity to hybridise or cross-pollinate. Note also the backward pointing tip on the column of the right-hand flower.

STANHOPEA LEITZII growing in a wooden slat basket. Whatever the container, there must be allowance for the downward-moving flower stems of the genus. The mesh of wire baskets or the distance between the slats should be gauged to allow room for this. Stanhopeas are among the most awkward plants to move about or exhibit because of this flowering habit.

GONGORA ARMENIACA. Although the stanhopea flowers may seem complex and peculiar, the impression created by some of the gongoras is that they commenced where the stanhopeas ended their development of confusing flower parts. Lindley and Paxton named the illustrated species, but the genus was named by Ruiz and Pavon. *G. armeniaca* is a Central American member of a genus which extends into South America.

ARPOPHYLLUM SPICATUM (La Llave and Lexarza). A warm-growing orchid from Central America to Colombia. The collector Bernard Roezl gathered plants of this orchid which he saw in flower, some of them bearing up to twenty-five or more spikes of bloom. The plants grew prolifically on the upper branches of tall trees in bright light, as their foliage would indicate. The generic name loosely translated means 'sword-leaf'. Hartweg first found it about 1830 but despite its beauty few people cultivate it.

SPATHOGLOTTIS PRIMROSE hybrid. Karl Blume named this widespread Asian genus in 1825. The habitat extends to the northern Pacific region and as far south as Australia. Better considered as a tropical genus, it dropped out of cultivation soon after introduction to the larger collections, yet most of the hybridising occurred from about 1920 onward. Allied to the calanthes, its appearance is similar to that genus and as a semi-terrestrial it could be grown in the same way as those orchids.

THUNIA MARSHALLIANA (Reichenbach f.), the genus named by the
same man. This Asian orchid with
bamboo-like pseudo-bulbs, from the
new growth of which the flowers
emerge, should be cultivated in
similar fashion to calanthes, with a
fast warm-growing period in
enriched coarse loamy compost.
The growths are usually about 45 to
60 centimetres tall, (18 to 24 inches),
well leafed and annual only. The
plants go into a marked dormant
phase and as the new growths show
roots plants should be repotted into
new compost. The flowers are about
7 to 10 centimetres across (about 3
to 4 inches) and not long-lasting.

SOBRALIA MACRANTHA (Lindley).
The genus was named by Ruiz and
Pavon and consists of several
species, mostly Central American
but extending into South America.
Sobralias are almost purely
terrestrial orchids which prefer
undisturbed cultivation for years in
rather heavy potting mixtures but
with sufficient alternation between
wet and a little on the dry side in
the non-growing season. The stems
or pseudo-bulbs are thin and wiry
and flowering plants look better if
they are tied erect.

SOBARALIA XANTHOLEUCA
(Williams). Plants of this species
may grow up to 2 metres high
(about 6 feet). Like *S. macrantha*, it
is Central American in origin and
the flowering head produces blooms
in succession as long as the season
lasts. The flowers of both species
may be over 12 centimetres across
(about 5 to 6 inches). As a group the
sobralias had fewer synonyms than
most orchids and originally were
neglected for the more exciting
epiphytes of the period 1820 to
1900.

132

LUDISIA DISCOLOR (Achille Richard), synonym *Haemaria discolor* (Lindley). One of the orchids grown more for its foliage than flowers. This Asiatic orchid is partly tolerant but better grown in warmer climates below the subtropical zones, prefers humidity to dryness and is subject to many pests which attack the foliage. The best plants are those cultivated from a small offshoot which over a period builds up into a plant such as this. Potting material should be rich in humus and light in texture. They are rightly named 'Jewel Orchids'.

ANOECTOCHILUS YATESAE (F. M. Bailey). This beautiful miniature grows in moist conditions on rocks and decaying forest detritus along the banks of creeks in Cape York areas of northern Queensland. It is difficult to cultivate, most growers losing the leaves quickly once deterioration sets in. One of the puzzling things about all orchid growing is the inability to produce a set of conditions which is rough enough while suitable for such delicate things to survive. The author managed it for only two years, growing in moss and as well protected as possible.

PLEUROTHALLIS ORNATA. A member of the largest family of orchids in the Americas, this small flower is about 2½ centimetres long (1 inch), the tendrils pendant from the lower parts thin and waxy and very delicate. No doubt evolution has decreed some role for these filaments, which break off at the lightest touch. There are more than a hundred species in Peru alone and many pleurothallis are yet to be found and identified and named.

PLEUROTHALLIS MINUTISSIMUM.
The genus was named by Robert
Brown, but it is very difficult to find
the nominators of many of the
species. This small plant is only
some 3 centimetres high (1 ¼
inches). Such orchids are very
attractive in collections, many of
them fairly easy to grow in a
moderate glass-house and subjects
of animated conversation when
exhibited.

PLEUROTHALLIS FLORIBUNDA
(Poeppig and Endlicher). It is
satisfactory to be able to put a
name to an orchid, but there is
always the probability that someone
will be able to say it is incorrect.
This Peruvian pleurothallis is the
subject of disputed identity, but it
indicates the flowering capability of
the genus. The usual reasons of
multiple cataloguing are responsible
for most of the mistaken identities
and endless synonyms.

PLEUROTHALLIS APHTOSA
(Lindley). A widespread Brazilian
orchid with petals which are almost
non-existent. The extraordinary
variation of the flowers is equalled
by the morphology of the genus,
which is most diverse. It is not like
looking at the recognisable things
like cattleya or dendrobium
pseudo-bulbs. Almost the total
genus is warm-growing, suited to
cattleya conditions or enclosures
where such orchids may be
protected from the weather in
tropical climates.

DENDROCHILUM COBBIANUM
(Reichenbach f.), synonym
Platyclinis cobbiana. The genus was
named by Karl Blume, it is
widespread through the Philippines
to Sumatra area and the inflorescence of all the species somewhat similar. An easy orchid to grow
in moderate conditions, it is subject
to all the usual restrictions and
dormant periods of most epiphytes,
although in some sub-tropical
regions it may be in movement all
through the year in growth or
flowering.

VANILLA PLANIFOLIA (Andrews).
The genus was named by Swartz
and this species is almost a tropical
parallel for *Phaius tankervilliae* in
its widespread occurrence, both as
a cultivated commercial crop plant
and as an escapee at times into
tropical areas. It could almost be
classed as a vine, considering its
morphology, but the flowers are all
'orchid' and almost continuously
produced in natural conditions. It is
not an obliging plant in glass-house
cultivation and likes the outdoors.

HUNTLEYA MELEAGRIS (Lindley).
One of the most widespread orchids
in Brazil, its range is up into
Venezuela and Central America.
This orchid is allied to a number of
genera throughout the area, most of
them with few members. Normally a
tropical type, its cultivation is based
on that for vandas and similar
genera, although it is allied to the
zygopetalums and some authorities
regard it as a cool to intermediate
growing species. Quite spectacular
in flower, the color of which may
vary from plant to plant.

GALEANDRA DEVONIANA (Lindley).
This orchid has an amazing habitat
in general where for some months
of the year the plants may be
almost totally submerged beneath
water and in the alternating phase
may be dry for some weeks or
months. Not unlike a dendrobium in
habit, G. devoniana is a possible
link extending some considerable
millions of years into the past, a
warm-growing orchid from a
numerous genus, and credited to
Schomburgk by a number of
authorities. He found it in northern
Brazil, Guyana and Venezuela, with
pseudo-bulbs up to 2 metres tall
(about 6 feet), always growing in
high humidity or very near water.

EPIGENEIUM LYONII (Ames),
synonyms Dendrobium lyonii and
Sarcopodium lyonii. The genus was
named by Francois Gagnepain, its
range extending from southern
China to Niugini. This species is
seldom noted in cultivation and is a
beautiful addition to a warm-
growing orchid collection, has two
definite seasons of growth,
flowering and resting and is quickly
discouraged by either cold or poor
growing techniques. It is a
Philippines' species and cultivation
is much the same as for warmer
growing dendrobiums.

PLEIONE FORMOSANA (Hay). The
genus was named by George Don
and no other has more confusion of
names. This beautiful species is
native to the island of Formosa and
has close affiliates in much of Indo-
Asia. Some of the species grow in
cold, unheated conditions and temperatures as low as 5 or 6 degrees
Celsius (40 to 45 degrees
Fahrenheit) while others are
considered warm-growing.

PLEIONE FORMOSANA growing in an ideal container, a broad, flat dish which must have drainage perforations in the bottom. Most of these orchids propagate in the orthodox way by basal offshoots, others by forming cormlets on the tops of the bulbs as well. While some of the genus like annual repotting into a moist, fairly rich humus compost, others are best left until the dish is overcrowded before they are disturbed. While in growth and flowering they should be carefully and regularly watered until the foliage decays and they turn to dormancy, the process being repeated once signs of leaf and roots and flowers again occur.

ORCHIDS AND WOOD.
The association between orchids and wood, both dead and alive, is close and intimate. The wood takes many forms, from the bark used for potting material to sawn timber for fabricating containers. This photograph is self-explanatory. A chain saw being used to cut a blister from the trunk of a fallen dead tree. The blister is the remnant of a branch socket in a eucalypt which had decayed long before the tree fell.

The branch socket removed and showing how the hollow forms a 'pot' which may be used as a natural container. These containers suit certain subjects and may be suspended or benched like ordinary manufactured pots and containers.

137

With two steel spikes to support
and balance the blister, a section of
Dendrobium speciosum has been
planted in the hollow. In this 'pot' a
hole already existed in the bottom,
otherwise a perforation would have
been necessary. A piece of heavy
plastic mesh was nailed over this
hole with copper nails to keep pests
out of the bottom, and ordinary
potting bark and additives used to
bed the plant in.

Natural materials frequently induce
better growth than artificial
products. Although not freely
available, sections of hollow
branches like this hasten growth of
such things as seedling vandas. But
once attached to their host, nothing
can make them release their hold
and the next step is into a larger
container. Demonstrating the
natural pot is Selena Black
of Townsville and the vanda
seedling very much younger.

A natural wood container complete
with backing as it was split away
from a log. It is hollow and the
plant, in this instance an oncidium,
is very much at home with the wood
to grow on. This container was
suspended and the roots were both
aerial and firmly fixed to the
exterior.

A manufactured container. Slat baskets are frequently mentioned in these books. As may be noted, they are simply strips of suitable wood drilled at each end and wired together to form a loose framework. Stainless steel, copper, or aluminium wire should be used so that it does not corrode and undo all the good work. These containers are suitable only for coarse potting materials unless they are lined with stag or elk fern husk or similar material. Coconut fibre is also useful. The plant is *Chondrorhynca discolor* (Lindley), a Central American warm-growing orchid, the genus also named by Lindley.

DENDROBIUM AGROSTOPHYLLUM (F. Mueller). Whatever the form of wood used in artificial cultivation, it cannot equal the natural attachment between epiphytes and their hosts. This plant of *D. agrostophyllum,* from tropical Queensland at an altitude of about 1000 metres (about 3250 feet), is growing on a casuarina tree in the author's garden, firmly attached and some ten years from its introduction to the southern Victorian climate. As a glass-house grown plant or even attached to a piece of the same tree, would it have survived and prospered as well?

The beautiful flowers of *Dendrobium agrostophyllum*, an Australian species so far neglected in the hybridising applied to the genus in the 1950-80 period.

Catasetum pileatum var. *aurea*

Angraecums, Aeranthes, etc

This genus was named by Bory in 1804, the title stemming from the Malayan *angurek*, used by that race to denote plants of the vanda or aerides type. In conformity with taxonomic procedure the word has been Latinised.

Aeranthes were named by Lindley, the origin being two Greek words signifying air or mist flowers, from the aerial habit of the plants and the supposition that they lived solely on air and mist.

Aerangis, a genus of more than sixty species, were named by the younger Reichenbach with reference, again through Greek words, to the long spur or nectary. The separation of the last two genera is most obscure and together with the mystacidiums they offer little in the way of self-identification and are frequently misnamed and labelled wrongly. The mystacidiums were titled by Lindley and the main species of the genus, *Mystacidium capense* was named by the younger Linnaeus.

The climate and terrain of the African regions are totally different from equatorial and southern America, although there is a tropical section in which orchids grow. So far as can be traced they never approached in numbers and variety those of Central and South America. The orchids of Africa are so radically different from those of Asia and America that few parallels present themselves except in the instance of the vanda tribe. Not possessing an orchid population of consequence, the continent was not exploited in this way and the species were less known and cultivated over the orchid-growing epoch.

The history associated with its orchids is sparse and information mostly dispersed in such records as *The Orchid Review,* Alex Hawkes' *Encyclopaedia of Cultivated Orchids* and earlier books such as *Veitch's Manual of Orchidaceous Plants.* In the 1970-80 decade other informative books were added. The main epiphytic family has a vandaceous habit, some with heavy foliage, others with much lighter foliage like that of the sarcochilus in the smaller species. These orchids are divided into several genera and at times the nomenclature is far from unanimous in various publications.

One of the orchid collectors who worked in Africa for plant stock was Guillermo Kalbreyer. As agent for the Veitch nursery he travelled and collected through the tropical areas of Africa in 1876 and brought a consignment back to the nursery in 1877. Later Kalbreyer went to South America for Veitch and finally settled in Colombia where he established an orchid collecting and export business, also acting as a clearing house for many other plants. He died during 1912 in Colombia where he was then known as Wilhelm Kalbreyer, consul for one of the European States. He retained the same Christian name although spelling it differently. The English equivalent is William and doubtless he was known by that as well.

Angraecums and associated genera are common to eastern Africa from Kenya almost to the Cape of Good Hope and reaching eastward from the continent to the Seychelles Islands and Madagascar and its associated islands of Mauritius and Reunion. Some related genera extend across tropical Africa to the West coast.

It was always difficult to get angraecums into Australia, but when available they proved hardy and comparatively easy to cultivate. They belong, with the aeranthes, aerangis, mystacidiums, listrostachys and minor relatives, to the monopodials such as vandas and sarcochilus in the sarcanthinae.

There are some two hundred angraecum types native to the African regions, twenty-five or so aeranthes ('air flowers') and more than double that number of aerangis ('air vessel'). The spur from the base of the labellum, in proportion to the size of the flower, is a consistent feature.

Since the discovery and cataloguing of the various species, taxonomists have worked on the genera and rearranged them periodically. The process is still going on, with sometimes minute floral or morphological characteristics as the dividing lines. Principally, however, the genera are similar in many respects.

Mystacidiums were originally named by Lindley in 1836, although in 1781 the younger Linnaeus named a plant which originated in South Africa, *Epidendrum capense*. It was later named *Angraecum capense* until transferred to Lindley's new genus. The generic title derives from the Greek work *mystax* (moustache), which indicates the peculiar origins of some of these names. A part of the flower led to selection of the word.

Similarly, the aerangis were titled by Reichenbach in 1865 using the Greek word *angos* (a vessel), possibly in allusion to the long spur which contains nectar.

The differences on which the genera were founded were described in some detail by R.A. Rolfe in *The Orchid Review* in 1904, but many changes have intervened since then.

Angraecum sesquipidale has exercised a fascination over orchid lovers ever since its discovery by Du Petit Thouars. It is the largest of the genus and is a tribute to him from among the eighty-odd new orchids he described in the Madagascan group. His original reason for visiting these islands was, it is said, to search for La Perouse, who had some part to play in Australian history. La Perouse was believed to have lost his ship in the area. Du Petit Thouars ran into financial difficulties and joined the staff of one of the wealthy land owners on Mauritius. A skilful botanist, he was most useful to his employers and in the ten years of his stay made several excursions to other islands including Madagascar. In 1822 he published a history of his discoveries of orchids on Madagascar and its associated islands. Written in French, and with no known translation. *Histoire Des Plantes Orchidees* is nevertheless an admirable book for identification of the angraecums from its eighty-odd beautiful line drawings.

Whenever this orchid is placed in print a rather tired and overstressed story always appears with it and the actual beauty and size of the flowers misses out. In the words of the author of the story, however, it seems to gain more significance than when garbled:

'The *Angraecum sesquipidale,* of which the large six-rayed flowers, like stars formed of snow-white wax, have excited the admiration of travellers in Madagascar, must not be passed over. A green whip-like nectary of astonishing length hangs down beneath the labellum. In several flowers sent me by Dr Bateman I have found nectaries eleven and a half inches long [about 29 centimetres], with only the lower inch and a half filled with nectar. What can be the use, it may be asked, of a nectary of such disproportionate length? We shall, I think, see that the fertilisation of the plant depends on this length, and on nectar being contained only within the lower and attenuated extremity. It is, however, surprising that any insect should be able to reach the nectar. Our English sphinxes have proboscides as long as their bodies; but in Madagascar there must be moths with proboscides capable of extension to a length of between ten and eleven inches! This belief of mine has been ridiculed by some entomologists, but we now know from Fritz Muller that there is a sphinx-like moth in south Brazil which has a proboscis of nearly sufficient length, for when dried it is between ten and eleven inches long. When not protruded it is coiled up into a spiral of at least twenty windings.'

Those were the words of Charles Darwin in his book on the fertilisation of orchid flowers by insects. His words were prophetic and borne out by later fact. He correctly described the flowers, although in most experiences the flowers discolor to creamy tones after a few days. As would be expected from so large a flower, few are borne on a raceme, at most three, but a healthy plant may produce as many as four or five spikes of flower at a time. It is a difficult flower to photograph owing to the long spur and the color — one influencing the position of the plant and receptacle to get in the full length of the spur, the other the usual difficulties associated with getting detail into so white a flower.

It may seem strange that so beautiful an orchid was not introduced to English glass-houses for more than thirty years following its discovery. It was said that the opening of the Suez Canal in 1869 offered so much quicker transport that the plants travelled better than around the Cape of Good Hope, on which route plant losses were incredibly high. The credit for bringing it to England goes to The Rev. W. Ellis who took advantage of his love of orchids to collect and cultivate them when a missionary to the East African islands about 1850.

Angraecum sesquipidale was named by Du Petit Thouars. Literally translated, the word means 'a foot and a half', which is a slight stretch of imagination, but is no doubt in reference to the length of the spur.

Another genus with a spur of similar length is *Plectrelminthus caudata*, at one time known as an angraecum, from tropical West Africa where it is fairly widespread. The spur on these flowers is about 30 centimetres long and thus they must have a relative pollinator. The generic title was devised by Rafinesque-Schmaltz from the Greek words *plectron* (spur) and *minthion* (worm).

Angraecum sesquipidale is an extremely hardy orchid, growing in direct sunlight for most of the day in its habitat. It is not recommended that it be so treated under glass, however, as it would probably lose a lot of leaf and suffer burns to the remainder.

Most of us get carried away by our orchids, but it is unusual to find poetry dedicated to them. This effusion was possibly from some neophyte who could not sleep for thinking about his plants, particularly *Angraecum sesquipidale*:

Nun-like thou art, in snow-white vesture veiled,
With the sheer atmosphere of heaven regaled,
Thou art a gleam of heaven, a soul of light,
A star beyond thy bars of leafy night.
Lo, thy long spur full-deep with nectar blest,
That none may have for feast save bidden guest;
And he shall come and feast and drink the whole
Sweet passion-secret of thy fragrant soul.

Except for the fact that the females of the moth species apparently did not have tongues long enough to reach the nectar, the poet used his words economically and wisely in describing the beauty of the flowers of *Angraecum sesquipidale*. And I cannot resist the afterthought that at least he did have more metre and rhyme for his work than the poets so-called of the late years of this century.

There is good reason to believe that the French botanist Du Petit Thouars was the first European to discover *Angraecum eburneum*, but credit for its botanical description is allocated to Colonel Bory de St Vincent, another French traveller and botanist, usually referred to simply as Bory. It was named by him about 1822 despite the fact that Du Petit Thouars had found it so many years earlier and failed to register it with any of the contemporary herbariums.

Aubert-Aubert Du Petit Thouars, to give him his full name, contributed more knowledge of the orchids of Madagascar and its satellite islands than any other botanist or naturalist. Considered most eccentric, he devised his own system of classifying and cataloguing them and his artistry is apparent in one of his few surviving works, which is listed in the bibliography.

Bory found *Angraecum eburneum* on the tropical island of Reunion, to the east of Madagascar, some time between 1800 and 1804. Several varieties are known and the species is also common to Madagascar itself. It is probably the largest plant of the genus, almost entirely epiphytic, but unlike *Angraecum sesquipidale* it is occasionally found growing on rock surfaces. It remained rare in cultivation for many years, one of the few flowerings occurring in 1854 on a plant in the collection of the Rev. Clowes. Several varieties, generally localised forms from different sources, were collated into the single species from the various epithets by which they were known. The plants grow at times to a metre high and more, with leaves, broad and of heavy substance, up to 50 to 60 centimetres long.

An innovative and successful orchid grower named Forbes, who worked in the glass-houses of the Duke of Bedford, spent some time abroad collecting. During this time he found *Angraecum eburneum* on the island of Reunion, then known as the Isle de Bourbon, and sent a plant to the Horticultural Society in England where it flowered in 1832, the only known plant in European cultivation at that time.

The hybrid *Angraecum* Veitchii was raised by Messrs Veitch & Sons and exhibited at the Royal Horticultural Society in January 1899. It was awarded a First Class Certificate and the hybridiser Seden, author of so many novelties, was given a silver medal for his achievement. This lovely orchid is extensively grown in Australia and New Zealand, much of it propagated from a single plant brought into Australia many years ago. It is a tribute to the quality of *Angraecum* Veitchii that after so many years in which so many hybrid orchids have come and gone it is still eagerly sought by orchid growers for its beauty and free flowering habit.

Originally, the parents used in producing *Angraecum* Veitchii were given as *Angraecum sesquipidale* and *Angraecum superbum*, the latter still recognised as a separate species as late as 1922. John Lindley recognised it so many years before as *Angraecum eburneum*, but his opinion was challenged. He remarked of it in *The Botanical Register* of 1832: 'It was also met with at St. Mary's, Madagascar, by the unfortunate Forbes...'; but he did not mention the reason for so designating Forbes. Eventually, with the publication of *Sander's List of Orchid Hybrids, Angraecum* Veitchii was noted as the result of the cross-pollination of *Angraecum eburneum* and *Angraecum sesquipidale,* the first named the seed parent.

Angraecum superbum was also featured in *Lindenia* and *The Orchid Album* from a plant flowered by De Barri Crawshay. Ultimately, however, it was recognised as a form of *Angraecum eburneum*. Following this, the hybrid *Angraecum* Wolterianum, raised in Europe some years after *Angraecum* Veitchii, had to forgo its name and become *Angraecum* Veitchii. The raiser of

144

his hybrid had a long wait for his first flower from the 1909 pollination, because the seedlings did not flower until 1918. Considering the ease of culture and free flowering habits of *Angraecum* Veitchii, there must have been something wrong with the culture of its European counterpart.

Other hybrids of the genus are grown, but to the time this was published little work had been done on the related genera or within each genus and there appears to be so much promise in the material.

De Barri Crawshay

Cultivation of angraecums and nearly all the members of associated genera should have reference to their mostly epiphytic habit and the tropical or near tropical habitats. Temperatures should conform to a rather narrow limit and prolonged cultivation in too cold an environment leads to severe leaf marking, die-back of the leaf tips and blackened areas and occasionally the loss of the crown of the plants. Any of these indicators should be noticed and plants removed to warmer conditions.

Angraecum sesquipidale originated in the hot tropical lowlands of Madagascar and, as one of its earliest cultivators remarked: 'I did not see this plant in the higher and cooler regions of Madagascar, but only in the lower and hottest districts and there by no means so abundant as the *Angraecum superbum*, which is a splendid growing orchid. The *Angraecum sesquipidale* does not grow in the moist and thickly wooded parts of the island, but generally on the straggling trees along the edges of the forest, or in other parts where the trees are only thinly spread over the country. It seemed to grow most frequently in the driest parts of the trunks and branches of thinly leafed trees and though occasionally, yet seldom, seen near the ground. The largest plants were found about 12 or 20 feet from the ground and smaller ones were often seen higher up among the smaller branches. It seemed to grow more frequently where there was plenty of light and air.' The Rev. Ellis was not only observant, but also established a basis on which the growers in cold climates could grow plants under artificial conditions.

After establishing that the temperatures provided will suit angraecums, the next consideration would be potting materials. Even in the days of plentiful supplies of the various fibres, angraecums of the larger type were far more at home in the rough type of potting materials now used for vandas. If grown in pots at least one-third of the pot should be taken up with pieces of brick or charcoal or broken tile as drainage. The remainder of the pot should be filled with a mixture of large bark, charcoal and broken tile or brick or old pot shards. Clean humus which has not broken down too far or leaves from deciduous trees could be mixed with these — foliage, fresh from the fall and not decayed, of oak, maple, plane and other similar trees is suitable for orchid growing.

Like vandas, angraecums have an extensive, coarse root system, little of which seems inclined to enter potting mixes and most remains aerial. A topping of fresh sphagnum moss in late spring to early summer may attract the roots and promote branching tips on the older parts of the system. The plants should also produce new roots from the main stem during this period.

Shade will vary according to the climate, but most of the genera in the complex should be grown in fairly bright light in outdoor culture. Under glass they should have a minimum of 50 per cent. While the foliage is tough it is not sun resistant, particularly if the atmosphere is humid and condensation forms on the leaves. A good ventilation system is necessary and this could be met by air circulation in a glassed enclosure, preferably introduced from outside. In semi-tropical climates most of the genera are more at home when grown completely outside, bringing the plants into shelter and protection when they flower.

In general, to get the best from the angraceums in particular, temperatures

145

should not drop below about 15 degrees Celsius (about 60 degrees Fahrenheit) throughout the year. In such conditions the plants would be in some stage of growth throughout the year, but in fluctuating warmth and cold they may stagnate, leaves are not produced as freely and their texture is usualy dull and unhealthy looking. They may also drop, leaving bare expanses of stem, which is a most unhealthy state for any of the genera. The flowering season may be variable from one set of conditions to another, some species flowering in autumn, while others may flower in spring to early summer.

Watering these orchids should be very much an individual affair, sparingly applied unless good plant activity is noted. The plants, even when appearing dormant, should not be allowed to dehydrate and conditioning of the growing area is more important than actual plant watering. When in full growth, particularly in summer and when partly shaded, the plants may be soaked a couple of times a day with benefit, and if liquid fertilisers are used they should be applied after one of these drenchings and the plants left to think things over for a day or two — something of which they are quite capable. Natural humidity is one of the best conditions for angraecums and their associates to take up considerable amounts of moisture. In some respects they are almost xerophytes.

Flowers should be kept dry, particularly the spurs, which are such a feature of many of them. Do not let these spurs rest on either foliage or other surfaces or they will decay very quickly. Spotting of the flowers usually indicates that the temperature is too low or that condensation has formed on them through poor air circulation. In still conditions fungus spores may germinate on the petal surface and mar the flowers.

The various species have different annual flowering times and even these may vary from place to place. In tropical or semi-tropical climates it is possible to have plants of *Angraecum eburneum* and its affiliates flowering from autumn to spring, arranging their flowering habits to coincide with the reversal of weather conditions from the cycles common to cooler climates. Cultivation should be matched to these conditions and in the warmer areas where the plants will grow in open yet sheltered conditions a program should be worked out to suit them. In a pattern of summer rains these orchids will grow vigorously and flower at the conclusion of the wet period and then revert into a sluggish or dormant stage until the rains again affect them.

Fertiliser programs should be worked out to suit the morphology of the plants. With such a vanda-like structure, the larger members of the genera will be suited by solid nutrients applied to the potting medium for the roots which generate in the pots, while for those which remain aerial little can be done. Nutrient sprays which rely on leaf absorption are at best an unproven way of applying fertilisers to plants such as angraecums, although there is good reason to believe that such a program does have effect with their relatives the phalaenopsis. However, in all instances of attempts at foliage feeding, it can never be proved how much the process is affected by nutrients washing down to the root system from the upper parts of the plants.

Humus is a good way of supplying nutrients to pot-grown plants, while those on slabs of tree-fern, cork, wood or any other type of mount, should have a backing of some sort to encourage roots to penetrate to the mount. This backing, such as stag fibre, mosses of various types or fern-root fibres of all types may be impregnated with small amounts of blood and bone or hoof and horn meal to decay and so feed the root system. The smallest amounts of these fertilisers are effective, an oversupply tending to sour off the materials supposed to encourage the roots, and so sending them elsewhere seeking food.

Angraecums are not easy to propagate by methods applied to other genera and in this are similar to vandas. All monopodial orchids, or at least the greater number, usually develop side shoots from the main stem below the butts of flower spikes and rarely above the last flower spike unless the growing tip is damaged or destroyed, in which case the upper portion branches one or more new growths from just below the damaged tip and even lower down on the stem.

The method illustrated in the vanda section is a fairly sure way to obtain at least one side shoot. The partial severance activates the plant and accelerates reaction. *Angraecum* Veitchii is exceptional because it habitually produces side shoots. This must be an inherent factor from one or other of the species which has been intensified — fortunately for the owners of this beautiful orchid. These side shoots should not be removed until they have formed at least one root tip. If they seem slow to do this, the new growth should be partially severed at the point where it meets the main stem and then tied securely in place so that it cannot break away. This will induce it to produce a root. If by some mischance the shoot is either broken off accidentally or deliberately removed for some reason, the base should be wrapped in a ball of fairly loose sphagnum moss and stood in a pot in a moist atmosphere. The moss should be kept damp but not wet and although the plantlet may wait until the growing period in warmer weather to produce a root or roots, this is a better way to induce root growth than to pot it in the mix used for mature plants. Side shoots on any of the various genera should be treated in exactly the same way if they have no roots when they are removed or accidentally dislodged. A hot-box will speed up the process, regardless of the season.

Dendrobiums

This genus was named by Olaf Swartz, a Swedish botanist, in 1799. The derivation of the name is from two Greek words — *dendron* (a tree) and *bios* (life). Most dendrobiums are epiphytic — they live on trees but the roots do not penetrate after the manner of parasites.

Dendrobiums are possibly the most morphologically diverse of the orchid genera. Principally Indo-Asian in origin, they have habitats in an arc stretching through northern India, southern India and Sri Lanka, once called Ceylon, as far as some of the Pacific islands and New Zealand, which has only one member of the family, *Dendrobium Cunninghamii* (Lindley). Over this great area of the earth the genus varies so widely that a comparison, say, between *Dendrobium pulchellum* (Roxburgh) and *Dendrobium toressae* (F.M. Bailey), the first from the Himalayan region and the other from northern Australia, is hopeless if based on recognisable similarities. The genus as a whole has been sectionalised and sub-sectionalised to such a degree that it has become impossible to generalise on their culture or affinities. However, some system must be devised to advance cultural propositions and the only way this may be done is in the same simplicity as for mixed collections of orchids, in that they belong to types which need warm glass-house culture, those which need intermediate conditions and those which will tolerate cool conditions. There are few of the last-named group.

If an average had to be given for the altitude at which the genus thrives best it would be somewhere about 750 to 1000 metres (2500 to 4000 feet). The conditions at this altitude vary considerably as distance from the equator increases, but a bargain may be struck by exchanging this latitude for altitude. A plant originating in a tropical area at about 850 metres (about 3000 feet) would be a good subject for cultivation in a sub-tropical to temperate climate at sea level. This gives more scope to growers in countries like Australia to establish collections suited to their particular area, but the altitude at which they live must always be carefully considered.

In addition to being the most diverse, dendrobiums are probably the most numerous orchid species. It is doubtful if anyone has been sufficiently interested to count the number of species, but an educated guess could put the number at about 2000, perhaps higher. Many, particularly from the islands to the north of Australia, are yet to be correctly identified and named and doubtless there are quite a number which remain to be discovered, despite the way the region has been opened up in the years from 1940.

Dendrobium cultivation is a little different from that of cattleyas, particularly in the initial stages, as they cannot all be grouped under the same conditions as so-called cattleyas can. Using the two already quoted, while *Dendrobium pulchellum* may be a suitable subject for potting, *Dendrobium toressae* would be ill suited in such a container and would find a slab of wood, cork or fibre a much more suitable habitat.

It should be remembered that, as their name indicates, dendrobiums grow mostly on trees and occasionally on rocks with the greater part of the root systems exposed freely to air. While some of these root systems will adapt to pot cultivation, the risk of overwatering is constant and there is little way of gauging the amount of residual moisture at any given time following watering. While the materials used will not vary much from those used for other epiphytes, for dendrobiums they should combine to form a bed which will release excess water quickly while retaining enough to promote root activity at the relevant growing periods for the different species.

In the top line of priority is fresh air — it must flow over and about the plants in all seasons — allied with shade at the right time of the year and clear sun if necessary also at various seasons. Climatic origins should be understood by studying the plants of other growers or knowing the various altitudes at which they grow. The number of leaves on the pseudo-bulbs, their color and substance, the color of the flowers and even the general appearance of the various dendrobiums all convey something for observant growers.

Selecting two examples: *Dendrobium bigibbum* (Lindley) has slender yet tall pseudo-bulbs, relatively small pointed leaves and these only at the apex of the growths, which could be taken generally as indicating a plant which will tolerate quite bright light, almost direct sunlight. *Dendrobium nobile*, typical of all the soft-stemmed species, is almost the direct opposite. It has fleshy-looking, soft pseudo-bulbs, jointed in sections and with a leaf at each section of the pseudo-bulbs. The leaves are soft and light colored, glossy and giving the impression that they would not tolerate the same conditions. Nevertheless adequate light is necessary for the health of each, with a 50 per cent diffusion for *Dendrobium nobile* where *Dendrobium bigibbum* would be in full sunlight. Naturally, if grown together, one must die, so they should never be bought with the intention of growing them together. This may be extended over the whole range of dendrobiums, choosing compatible species or hybrids for combined cultivation.

In addition to this, they have diametrically opposite flowering habits. While *Dendrobium bigibbum* flowers from the apex of the new growth almost as it is maturing as well as from nodes near the apex of older pseudo-bulbs, *Dendrobium nobile* and hybrids derived from it usually flower on growths made some fifteen to eighteen months previously and usually after that growth has shed all or most of its leaves. These leafless pseudo-bulbs seldom flower again except from unflowered nodes at the tip of old growths which have not properly matured to produce all their flowers in their season.

These developments are environmentally controlled and are the result of plant evolution over considerable periods to adapt to the changes which have occurred, and if sufficient thought is given to this aspect a very clear picture emerges to account for the various growing and flowering habits of the species. Unlike cymbidiums or other singular genera, they cannot be generally classified and cultivated in a single set of conditions.

It may take a year or so for certain species to modify their programs slightly to suit, but they will do so, even if the ultimate results in flower may be a little less than expected from illustrations or the efforts of people with slightly better situations, climates or conditions.

The color of dendrobium flowers while not an inflallible guide, may frequently indicate the amount of light various species will tolerate. *Dendrobium chrysotoxum* (Lindley), with its stout, spindle-shaped pseudo-bulbs topped by three or four grey-green, hard-looking leaves, obviously is morphologically or physically formed by evolution to withstand fairly severe periods in its annual cycle. Its flowers are bright golden yellow and all indications are that, while it may thrive in comfortable glass-house conditions, both plant and flowers are well adapted to bright light. The combination of stout morphology and yellow flowers is apparent in several other dendrobiums, but should not be taken as an infallible guide. If found growing naturally, however, the odds are that for some time during their days the plants would be in direct sunlight, on the tops of trees or on rock faces.

Experience will give confidence after a time in predicting the type of plants to buy which will suit the conditions available. It will — or should — guide buyers into purchasing dendrobiums which will 'homologate', to use a word that may not be quite applicable but which describes the system of combining things for the best results.

Experience, too, should indicate when dendrobiums should be potted and when they should be mounted on slabs of wood, cork or tree-fern or the short section of a branch cut from a suitable tree, such as casuarina, oak, lillypilly, but never pine and seldom eucalypt because of the resins and saps they contain. Home-made cups or pots of tree-fern are occasionally used and they are most successful containers for soft-cane dendrobiums. If tree-fern is used in any way it should be weathered for about six months; frequently, when fresh it is far too acid for dendrobium roots. At least it is a safety precaution and not just a waste of time.

The Soft-Cane Group

In listing and describing the following dendrobiums no attempt has been made to establish them as more important than others, although a few deserve the honor. The criteria adopted for their appearance are in part due to their involvement in *Sander's List of Orchid Hybrids* as progenitors of the better known hybrids grown in collections. Species dendrobiums are probably grown in greater numbers than usual for a genus.

Dendrobium nobile must take pride of place as the most important species in the soft-cane section of a genus noted for beauty and variety. It passes to its hybrids lasting qualities and abundance of flowers.

It was first known in England from a Chinese drawing, commissioned by a traveller named Reeves, in the library of the Horticultural Society. Reeves later presented a plant to Loddiges' nursery where it flowered in 1837. John Lindley had the honor of naming it. A beautiful and accurate illustration drawn and colored by Miss Drake appears in his *Sertum Orchidaceum,* published in 1838.

This first plant came from southern China, probably near the Burmese border, and was bought by Reeves in a market at Macao. Later the habitat was found to be extensive and different varieties were credited by the Horticultural Society, including the beautiful albino form *Dendrobium nobile* var. *virginale.*

To growers accustomed to looking at the type of plant grown in our artificial conditions the sight of plants gathered in the habitat would be somewhat dismaying, as usually they are straggly and most unattractive.

One of the outstanding clones was *Dendrobium nobile* var. *nobilius* which is twice the size of the type form and a deep rose-purple almost totally. This outstanding form is still grown, but is rare in collections.

Lewis Castle, at one time employed at the Royal Botanic Gardens, Kew, England, had this to say of the variety *nobilius* in 1887: 'It was bought at Stevens' auction rooms in a bundle of plants for 12 shillings in 1876. It flowered in 1877, when it was exhibited at Kensington and afterwards sold for five guineas. The plant subsequently nearly died, but aerial growths sold for large sums. In 1877 small propagations sold for 10 guineas, larger ones for 40 to 50 pounds.'

Fortunately for posterity the plant survived through the habit of the soft-cane dendrobiums of producing aerial or adventitious growths and its influence survives in the Japanese hybrids of the later years of the twentieth century. It has been surmised that this variety is a tetraploid for valid reasons, but whether exhaustive tests have been made is an obscure question.

In Sikkim, northern India, *Dendrobium nobile* grows from about 800 metres to 2000 metres, in company with many other species including *Dendrobium aureum* (syn. *heterocarpum*). In the early stages of importing, natural hybrids of the two were frequently found when the plants flowered. In cultivation the man-made hybrid is known as *Dendrobium* Ainsworthii.

Naturally, these strangers caused much speculation at the time they appeared, but there were sufficient perceptive growers about at that time who understood just what they were and set out to prove it in the only possible way.

Many varieties of *Dendrobium nobile* were named and exhibited and like the so-called labiata cattleyas, the supply seemed endless. *Dendrobum nobile* var. *virginale* appeared in 1897. It was flowered by Thomas Rochford in the root system of a very large plant of the type form. It was only a small seedling and was apparently a pure white mutation after the fashion of the mutations which had appeared in the cattleyas, laelias and other orchids imported from the Americas.

After initial troubles with *Dendrobium nobile* and other dendrobiums of the area a cultural program was soon worked out. It consisted mainly of warm, moist conditions with plenty of fresh air, some successful growers even cultivating their plants outdoors in vine arbors over the summer months and flowering them well in consequence. Bright light was one of the necessities.

Dendrobium nobile var. *Sir Frederick Moore* was a garden production from the cross-pollination of *Dendrobium nobile* var. *nobilius* and *Dendrobium nobile* var. *elephant*. It was used successfully in the hybrid *Dendrobium* York, which had *Dendrobium regium* as its other parent.

Dendrobium regium (Prain) was a much later discovery from Lower Hindustan, northern India. It was first known about 1900 and brought into cultivation in the following decade.

It is basically different from *Dendrobium nobile*, although obviously closely related. It is almost completely self-colored pink to rose-purple, with a totally different cream to yellow-lemon labellum without the deep purple throat of *Dendrobium nobile*. It was first flowered in cultivation at the Royal Botanic Gardens, Calcutta in 1901.

Even a cursory look at the hybrids developed by the Japanese cross-pollinations indicates clearly the influence of *Dendrobium regium*. It was abandonment of British hybridising in the early part of the century, probably to concentrate more on cymbidiums, which led to a gap in dendrobium production for almost forty years. The Japanese breeders simply moved on from where the British left off, particularly concentrating on the clones with cream monotone labellums and better shape.

Although *Dendrobium regium* flowers at a different time of the year from *Dendrobium nobile* despite the marked similarity in their morphology, this influence is not noticeable to any degree in hybrids. However, *Dendrobium* York (*D. nobile* x *D. regium*) does tend to flower a little later in the year than other *Dendrobium nobile* hybrids.

Dendrobium heterocarpum (Wallich) (syn. *D. aureum*, Lindley) is widespread in occurrence, changing morphologically from area to area. It is found in Nepal, Sikkim, Khasia, Assam, Upper Burma and as far away as the

Sir Jeremiah Colman

Celebes Islands and the Philippines. It prefers slightly warmer conditions than *Dendrobium nobile* as it occurs mostly below 1000 metres (over 3000 feet). The Indian species have rather short pseudo-bulbs, the flowers golden-yellow to pale yellow with a brown labellum and having a most delightful perfume, if anything reminiscent of freesias. It was first brought to England about 1837 from the Khasia Hills area and named by John Lindley, over whom the precedence of Wallich became accepted.

The form of this orchid which grows in Sri Lanka (Ceylon) is slightly taller than that of the Indian type, while the Philippines' type has even taller pseudo-bulbs and paler, scentless flowers.

The hybrid *Dendrobium* Ainsworthii (D. *nobile* x D. *heterocarpum*) is similar in importance to the first laeliocattleya — it is the background material from which most of the modern soft-cane dendrobiums are bred. Unfortunately, while *Dendrobium* Ainsworthii retained some of the perfume of *Dendrobium heterocarpum*, all or nearly all of this lovely attribute had disappeared by the third generation. Some hybrids, such as *Dendrobium* Euryalus, the back-cross of *Dendrobium* Ainsworthii to *Dendrobium nobile*, have a most disagreeable odor.

Possibly the grower with most influence on the production of hybrids was Sir Jeremiah Colman, from whose estate, Gatton Park, many of the dendrobiums in cultivation in the 1980 period originated. The combinations of dendrobiums *nobile, heterocarpum, findlayanum, signatum* and *hildebrandii* were paramount in the primaries, but a peculiarity of the hybrid register comes to light as these cross-pollinations are considered. Where three of these species have been used, at times two hybrids emerge where basic reasoning dictates that they are in reality one and the same thing. The combination of numbers 1 and 2 used to breed into number 3 has one name, while the combination of numbers 1 and 3 bred into number 2 has another. It occurs in genera other than dendrobiums.

For example, *Dendrobium nobile* x *Dendrobium findlayanum* x *Dendrobium aureum* produces *Dendrobium* Melanodiscus, but *Dendrobium findlayanum* x *Dendrobium aureum* x *Dendrobium nobile* produces *Dendrobium* Acis, and so on.

Dendrobium findlayanum was brought to England and cultivation about 1877 after its discovery by Parish in Burma. It is also native to Thailand and Malaya. Cool-growing, from a high altitude, it requires almost the same conditions as *Dendrobium nobile*. The pseudo-bulbs are remarkable, with a definite waist at each leaf axil and almost a circular section between each, something after the fashion of a string of flattened marbles. The plant grows to about 30 centimetres (about 12 inches) with the pseudo-bulbs semi-pendulous to totally so, giving the plant a somewhat straggling appearance.

This dendrobium needs a definite break in the temperature cycle in autumn to promote flowering, much the same as the general run of soft-cane dendrobiums. It assumed a major role in the hybrid list through association with the main group in producing *Dendrobium* Cybele from *Dendrobium nobile*. It is probably the most important of the primary hybrids.

The manner in which these dendrobiums impress their characteristics on hybrids is amply demonstrated in *Dendrobium findlayanum*, the labellum of which is prominent in the Japanese hybrids of the late years of this century. It is as unmistakable as that of *Dendrobium regium*. In a modified fashion, the waisted pseudo-bulbs of *Dendrobium findlayanum* are also passed on to many of the secondary and subsequent hybrids.

Dendrobium signatum is one of the least known of the species. As it is listed n *Sander's List of Orchid Hybrids* some speculation should be entered into. One of the poorest documented, it is impossible to find a consensus of opinion even as to its color. Described by some as bright canary yellow, one of the specimens preserved at the Kew Herbarium, England, is linked with Australia through a one-time English grower, Mr Cooper, and his specimen is described as having white tepals, a yellow lip and a chrome-orange centre. Such variety is not unusual, but the species used in conjunction with dendrobiums *nobile, heterocarpum, hildebrandii* and *findlayanum* as the background to many hybrids in *Sander's List of Orchid Hybrids,* was described as bright canary yellow with a golden labellum featuring a central area of brown-red radiating lines from two red-brown or purple-brown 'eyes'. With *Dendrobium nobile* it was one of the antecedents of *Dendrobium* Thwaitesiae and, as the illustrations show, this description was probably correct.

It has been linked with dendrobiums *friedricksianum, bensoniae, hildebrandii* and *heterocarpum*, flowering only from the upper parts of the pseudo-bulbs and then not too freely. It was supposed to have been collected originally in Indo-China (Siam, now Thailand) close to the Burmese border and was named by Rolfe. Although the opinion from the Kew herbarium discounts its origin as a natural hybrid, it does indeed concede that all these species are no doubt inter-related. *Dendrobium signatum* was grown at Gatton Park and used by Sir Jeremiah Colman's hybridisers, but Bartle Grant, who knew a considerable amount about the orchids of the Upper Burmese area, did not even mention it in his book.

Dendrobium signatum was far too important an orchid to leave unresearched because of its hybrid generation. R. A. Rolfe, as far back as 1910, was intrigued; so much so that in one of his contributions to *The Orchid Review* he commenced with the question: 'What is *Dendrobium signatum*?' Some seventy years later I asked the same question of the relevant department of the Royal Botanic Gardens at Kew, England. Unlike Rolfe, I did get a fairly definite answer, but before quoting it I would prefer to take you through the wonderland and the maze which engulfed Rolfe and perhaps others before and after him.

John Day delineated this orchid in color in his usual beautiful fashion and described it thus: 'Drawn at Mr Wm. Bull's, being a new species from Siam of his own importation and flowering now for the first time. The flowers were wanted for the Prof. [possibly Reichenbach - J. R.] so I could not make a sketch of column, &c. Although the flowers recall *D. bensoniae,* the growths are more like *D. tortile*, for which Mr Bull took it on arrival, and sold the entire box at Stevens' for a mere trifle.'

It was described in *The Gardeners' Chronicle* about three weeks later, Reichenbach noting that it looked a good deal like *Dendrobium bensoniae* and remarking: 'It is sulphur colored with a light longitudinal line at the base, on the situation where on some species velvet is to be seen. The disc is adorned by a broad transverse radiating brown blotch and on each side of the basal part there are four similar brown lines going out at nearly right angles and running of course nearly parallel... The circumference of the lip may best be compared to that of *Dendrobium nobile*.'

In 1889 Messrs Veitch sent to Kew a flower which had been received as *Dendrobium signatum*. It had clear, deep shining canary yellow flowers and the disc of the lip was puberulous, with a pair of small purple-brown blotches (the color being carefully recorded at the time). In February of the following year a named flower also came from Messrs Seeger & Tropp. Other flowers also came in for identification, from plants consigned ostensibly from the Philippines and Siam, which Rolfe understood to be the habitat. The collector

Roebelen also sent flowers from Siam, which he named as *Dendrobium friedricksianum*.

Possibly, the real clue to the habitat of *Dendrobium signatum* came to Sanders' as early as 1882, the origin given as Burma. Clear thinking on the whole subject would indicate natural hybridism from two and possibly more parents or grandparents, with all the evidence again pointing at *Dendrobium bensoniae*. It is unfortunate that the mystery has never been completely solved, because Sir Jeremiah Colman used what was known as *Dendrobium signatum* to produce some of the best hybrid dendrobiums which have ever been seen. The early cross-pollination of *Dendrobium nobile* with *Dendrobium signatum* in the Colman glass-houses produced *Dendrobium* Wiganiae and this was the starting point, for many of the 1970-80 hybrids including the Japanese contributions to the genus.

Dendrobium Gatton Diamond, which included the true *Dendrobium signatum* blended with *Dendrobium nobile* var. *nobilius* and *Dendrobium findlayanum*, measured just over 11 centimetres across (4½ inches) and it was only one of many flowers of the 1900 to 1920 period which have almost disappeared from cultivation. According to the illustrations they perhaps lacked a little of the rounded shape of the 1980 hybrids, which were generated more to conform to a set of artificial standards than for other reasons; but that in no way can be held against these rather wonderful flowers.

Gatton Park was always unsure of the credentials of *Dendrobium signatum*, tending to rely more on *Dendrobium aureum* (syn. *Dendrobium heterocarpum*) for color; but the various combinations of species and primary hybrids sometimes left Sir Jeremiah Colman and his orchid cultivators puzzled with the results they achieved. For instance, why should a rather dull colored *Dendrobium aureum* give a far brighter color to its seedlings than that given by the brighter *Dendrobium signatum*?

In closing off the rather confused history of *Dendrobium signatum* a tribute should be paid to both the Royal Botanic Gardens and their staff. This quote from Jeffrey Wood, of that establishment, is possibly the best explanation:

'*Dendrobum signatum* (Reichenbach f.) is treated in synonymy under the Burmese *D. bensoniae* (Reichenbach f.) by Kranzlin. It does indeed seem very close to this species, only differing by its slightly smaller flowers with narrower petals and less conspicuous purple-brown markings... I have examined two flowers of *D. signatum* in alcohol and they seem to differ little from *D. bensoniae* apart from the narrower petals. We have no living material of either *D. signatum* or *D. bensoniae* in cultivation at Kew. There does not appear to be any color illustration of *D. signatum* in any of the contemporary publications... I cannot find any reference to it possibly being a natural hybrid in the literature. I do not think that it is a form of *D. heterocarpum*, although all of these species are related to one another and hybridisation cannot be ruled out.

'Although originally thought to come from Thailand [Siam], I cannot find any mention of *D. signatum* by Seidenfaden and Smitinand in their authoritative *Orchids of Thailand* or in the more recent enumeration published by Seidenfaden. It seems more likely that the plants came from neighboring Burma. *D. bensoniae,* also recorded from Thailand in the early literature, is not regarded as occurring there by Seidenfaden.'

In the end we get back to the possibility of falsification of points of origin to confuse and delay the opposition until the market was satisfied.

Dendrobium hildebrandii (Rolfe) has several close affiliates which lead to speculation about the origin of some five or six Indo-Burmese species. It is freely acknowledged that most had a common origin in the remote past and although they have a similar habit to that of *Dendrobium nobile* most exhibit the yellow to gold tints of dendrobiums *bensoniae* and *tortile*. *Dendrobium hildebrandii* was discovered by Arthur Hildebrand, a civil servant in the Shan States, which was a conglomerate of provinces jointly under British and Burmese jurisdiction in the late years of the nineteenth century. He sent this dendrobium to Hugh Low & Co. who had a description of the flower as being light yellow colored with two maroon blotches in the labellum. It had considerable influence on the soft-cane hybrids in the primary hybridising stages. Arthur Hildebrand returned to England after some thirty years service in the area and died at the age of sixty-five. He was responsible for several other orchids being brought into cultivation.

Dendrobium hildebrandii is similar in habit to many other dendrobiums which are native to the Indo-Burmese area, the pseudo-bulbs partly pendant and finer at the base than the rest of the pseudo-bulb. It is rather shy flowering, which may account in part for similar characteristics in the yellow to gold hybrids.

Dendrobium wardianum is one of the most beautiful species in the genus. It was brought to England in 1856 by Simons and flowered quite soon after in Jackson's nursery at Kingston. At first it was mistaken for *Dendrobium falconeri*, but when Dr Ward of Southampton flowered it, recognition of its new status was apparent and it was named by Warner.

In common with many of the soft-caned dendrobiums, *wardianum* has the peculiarity of shedding all its leaves in transit from collectors to growers and the bare canes, when potted and grown in good conditions, produce the most amazing show of flowers, never to be repeated in either size or numbers. *Dendrobium wardianum* is deciduous to a marked degree, usually shedding all the leaves from the mature growths in the autumn as a prelude to flowering.

It is, like its close relative *Dendrobium crassinode,* pendulous by nature and flowering problems with either of these two can sometimes be debited to the tidy habits of growers who tie the pseudo-bulbs erect.

Dendrobium crassinode flowers are remarkably similar to those of *Dendrobium wardianum*, but the pseudo-bulbs are much swollen at the nodes — to quote a painful parallel, like arthritic fingers.

A stronger, hardier type of *Dendrobium wardianum* was later imported from Burma by Messrs Hugh Low & Co. and about 1930 this source was considered almost inexhaustible. Plants of *Dendrobium wardianum* or *Dendrobium crassinode* were available from Australian nurserymen at about 3 shillings and 6 pence (about 35 cents) and the buyers nearly all had the enchanting sight of the bare pseudo-bulbs flowering as they never did again. It is not an easy dendrobium to continue in cultivation for long.

Dendrobium wardianum, judged from the color and beauty of its flowers, should have been prominent as a progenitor, but it proved very difficult as a seed parent. It was much better as a pollen parent, but in most instances unsuccessful as a dendrobium from which to get hybrid improvement. It excelled as a species.

Nigro-Hirsute Dendrobiums

This section is named from the short, dark, hair-like coating which covers parts of the pseudo-bulbs, the leaves in some instances and particularly the flower sheaths and bracts. Once the plants have been seen the name is self-explanatory.

It may be thought that this group is numerically small, but nothing could be

155

further from the truth. Many species are seldom seen in cultivation, only two or three members being popular because of the size of their flowers. *Dendrobium formosum* is the warmest growing of the species, but even this comes from widespread localities and is subject to growing conditions different from what may be expected. Discovered in north-eastern India by Gibson, it was sent to the Duke of Devonshire's glass-houses at Chatsworth about 1837. His growers had their problems, but subsequently it was found to grow quite well when attached to blocks of wood such as sections of oak with the bark still attached. A warmer-growing variety, *Dendrobium formosum* var. *giganteum,* was sent to Low & Co. about 1856 from the vicinity of Rangoon, Burma, where it proliferated as a tropical lowland orchid.

Roxburgh predated Gibson's finding of the species somewhere about 1832 and had the privilege of naming it. His find was in much the same area as Gibson's and many other habitats were subsequently found spread over the various countries of Asia. Some of the environments could be classed as sub-tropical to temperate, but it is best to treat *Dendrobium formosum* as a tropical lowland orchid. In the Andaman Islands it was found growing in coastal mangrove swamps, a climate difficult to describe and much harder to duplicate. The temperature in such localities seldom varies from about 40 degrees Celsius (over 100 degrees Fahrenheit) over the whole year.

Cultivation of *Dendrobium formosum* in England was predated by Calcutta Botanic Gardens which had plants growing as early as 1812. It is one of those surprising things in horticulture that Smith, who brought it to the gardens so early in the century, did not register his find with any one of the many herbariums in existence at the time. He found it in the same area of Sylhet province, the home of *Paphiopedilum insigne,* as Roxburgh did in a lower and warmer area than where that orchid lives. Even so, it would be considerably cooler than the Andaman Islands habitat.

In cultivation this dendrobium tends to flower more than once from the same pseudo-bulbs. This is a cultivation problem where the latent 'eyes' which should all flower in the one year do not reach maturity as they should. Few growers reach the potential of *Dendrobium formosum's* flower production, but it is nevertheless a wonderful ornament to a collection grown in cattleya conditions. Its beautiful white flowers present a challenge which is better met in warmer climates than in glass-house culture in cooler climates, no matter how good the system.

Dendrobiums *infundibulum* and *jamesianum* have been considered by some authorities as one and the same thing and by others as separate species. It is probably best to regard them as related rather than synonymous, because they come from different regions and climates. Some of the later authorities list *Dendrobium jamesianum* as a variety of *Dendrobium infundibulum.* The flowers are almost inseparable from a labellum color point of view, because in both it may vary from pale to deep orange.

One of the earlier men to study them in their habitat was Major-General Berkeley who spent a considerable time in Burma during the later years of the nineteenth century, probably one of the most wonderful periods in orchid history. Modern warfare, subversion of natural resources and pollution, each of which is part of life in the world a century later, had not then occurred.

A short quote from his extensive survey of the orchids of Burma: 'In Veitchs' manual *D. jamesianum* is considered a variety of *D. infundibulum,* but I never found them growing together on the same hills. Each variety is confined to its own range of mountains... On the top of the range of mountains which can be seen from Moulmein grows in abundance a short, robust, form of *D. jamesianum.* It is found growing abundantly on the rocks

nd also on the trees. The flowers of this variety are very rich in color, but the
lants are dwarf and robust in habit, quite different from the variety found on
he southern range of the Arracan Hills, where the plants are found extremely
bundant and in habit quite four times the size of the Moulmein hill plants.

'*D. infundibulum* is found in the ranges of hills further away from
Moulmein and also in the north of Arracan far up the River Kuladan in the
ills which are probably the source of this river. There is no doubt that both *D.*
jamesianum and *D. infundibulum* require quite different treatment from the
ther forms. They are essentially mountain varieties and they continue to grow
hroughout the winter, flowering abundantly in the spring. I have seen in the
Arracan Hills five hundred plants of the variety *jamesianum* in flower at one
me, forming a grand sight. So profusely do these plants flower in their native
abitat that the plants become much shrivelled and should the heavy rains be
elayed many of the plants die.

'I should say of these two varieties, judging from the conditions under
which they grow abroad, that they should be grown warm in winter and cool in
ummer in our houses at home and I have experienced no difficulty in keeping
hem in good condition when treated in this way. They are two of the most
seful of the formosae section as they last such a long time in flower.'

The size of flowers on *Dendrobium infundibulum* varies considerably, but
ne noted particularly in 1895 was presented to the Royal Horticultural
Society by a grower named Woodhall. It measured 13½ centimetres (5¼
nches) across the petals and each petal was 5½ centimetres broad (2¼ inches).
The pseudo-bulbs on the plant were literally covered with these flowers.
But on reading this note it is impossible to put rather sombre thoughts out of
ne's mind. Where is the plant now?

It must have been a pleasant relaxation for such an army man as Berkeley to
get into the jungle looking for plants which he obviously liked so well.

Most of the nigro-hirsute dendrobiums should be treated in the way outlined
for *Dendrobium formosum* except in the matter of the varying degrees of
warmth needed to bridge them over cold and sometimes dark winters. They are
a sun or light loving group, a fact which should not be forgotten when
positioning them in the glass-house. Berkeley's little note about the delay of
rain causing the death of numbers of plants should also be heeded in designing
a living system for *Dendrobium infundibulum*.

Reverting to Mr Woodhall's plant, it should be remembered that it was
probably a newly acquired clone imported direct from Burma and on its first
attempt reproduced the galaxy of flower commonly thrown out by such plants,
never again to be repeated.

Most orchid growers who fancy these dendrobiums find them much more
difficult than other sections and a common failing is for the plants to slowly
deteriorate over about four or five years. Cultivation factors are obviously
responsible but the deficiencies are hard to pinpoint because of the relative
differences in growing systems from country to country and even from glass-
house to glass-house. Two areas to be sure of are potting and watering.

Newly purchased or imported plants of the whole group are mostly robust
but frequently leafless. Initial treatment should be aimed at holding the plants
stable until the correct growing season commences, which is usually in the
warmer part of the year. Instead of watering the plants once new growth is
evident, keep them in moist conditions until such time as new roots emerge
from the new growths. It is frequently impossible to revive root action on the
older part of the plants, therefore the new system must be kept in good
condition. Once the root system is well on the way and the growths are
extending, the plants should be watered a little more freely until, in the

157

warmest part of the year, it is almost impossible to overwater them in reasonable sense. It is here that the second successful programming comes into operation, which is in giving the roots something to grow on or in.

Potting material for all of the nigro-hirsute section should be coarse. Some such as the beautiful diminutive *Dendrobium bellatulum*, prefer a cork, tree fern or wood block to conventional potting. The group matures its growth well before the flowering period, which is usually in the spring following maturing. In their habitat the stems flower almost from top to bottom, but in artificial cultivation it is seldom more than the tip which has flowered. Wintering the plants correctly will result in survival, but if they are watered during this period it is possible that the root system will be irreparably damaged. Humidity and natural moistness of the surroundings should provide all the moisture they need, and in the spring and summer very little water should be given to the plants until again the new roots commence from new shoots. Even at this stage water should be applied sparingly so that the older roots may also develop new tips and branches.

Notwithstanding the restrictions on watering, at no time throughout the year should the root system dehydrate or the potting material become dry. This imposes a damp gravel bed system of wintering, a type of cultivation which suits many genera.

The Hard-Cane Group

Each of the hard-cane dendrobiums described is representative of a different section and most have different flowering periods. It is obvious that if they are to be grown in one collection a certain amount of movement of plants may be necessary to approximate their natural cycles. These flowering periods may not coincide seasonally with their habitats and could vary by as much as months — a spring-flowering species may become a summer-flowering type and so on. At worst, most cultivators will need to work out a program to suit individual plants. At best, they will find that the plants combine very well into spring flowering or some other season. It may be possible that a certain group or type may fit in very well with the conditions. It could be composed of such different dendrobiums as *Dendrobium chrysotoxum, Dendrobium aggregatum, Dendrobium farmeri* and *Dendrobium bigibbum,* which are as diverse a combination as can possibly be imagined.

Although they may all be in different stages of action throughout the year, in general they would all be growing vigorously in the summer in correct conditions. All need the same or similar potting materials, rather small pots relative to plant size and night-time minimum temperatures which should be carefully monitored, either automatically or manually. This does not envisage opening or closing ventilators to correct temperature fluctuations, as all would need copious air flow. The air flow should be the subject of temperature change, a process which is easy to arrange electrically.

Two dendrobiums should be given pride of place in this section, so they will be mentioned first. Both are Australian and spectacular in their flowering. *Dendrobium speciosum* is common to most of the Australian eastern coastline and up to 180 kilometres inland (110-120 miles) from there on the slopes of the Great Dividing Range. It is one of the ornamental flowers noted early in the settlement of Australia by the colonists and perhaps the convicts in the Sydney Cove area. It was taken to England by Sir Joseph Banks about 1800 as part of the botanical collection assembled for the Kew Gardens and has been known and admired world-wide ever since. It was named by Sir James Edward Smith, ut the origin of its colloquial name of Rock Lily, and why it is sometimes mistakenly called the King Orchid, are not known for certain.

One of the unforgettable sights of an orchid-growing lifetime is to see large numbers of naturally growing plants of *Dendrobium speciosum* in flower. It is still possible to see this in some parts of its extensive habitat; it is outdone in sheer numbers by no other Australian epiphyte or lithophyte except perhaps *Dendrobium kingianum*. *Dendrobium speciosum* is easily cultivated in a number of ways; as rockery plants in suitable climates, potted in rough mixes, as glass-house plants or even adorning the top of fence posts out in the bush — a most surprising sight. To a degree frost resistant, it has the habit of alternating growing years with flowering years and when growing as a rock plant in its habitat is extensively grazed by wallabies and other animals.

There are three main forms, but the flowering habits, if not the color, are constant in all its forms. The first and perhaps best known form is of short, stout pseudo-bulbs up to 45 centimetres long (about 18 inches); very stout at the base and tapering to the apex with its three to five large leathery leaves. The pseudo-bulbs of this form are thickly clustered.

The second form is much taller, rather more slender at the base and up to 60 or 70 centimetres high (24 to 27 inches), topped by the same number of leaves. The flowers are sometimes a little smaller, whiter, but just as numerous.

The third form is that of northern Australia, with short, bulbous pseudo-bulbs tapering off to at most three leaves, the new growths sometimes quite purple and retaining pigmentation over the first year and then gradually losing it. Where the flower spikes of the first two forms are usually held horizontally, those of this short northern form are erect and carry fewer flowers of a different shape, with rather blunt petals and sepals.

The root system of the larger forms has a peculiar habit of growing vertically so that a clump is formed, similar to the habit of some of the grammatophyllums and catasetums. This vertical root growth forms a food trap which fills up with leaves and detritus until quite a large root ball is formed.

In cultivation *Dendrobium speciosum* is one of the hardiest of all orchids, withstanding even direct summer sun for a large part of the day. It is not happy in a glass-house and over the summer should be grown outdoors whenever possible to promote flowering. While the pseudo-bulbs may shoot new growths as early as October-November (early summer), occasionally this orchid will produce them as late as March and then mature them. The flowering season is from September to November. Because of the immense size of the plants it is difficult to find pots which will contain them for more than a few years and breaking up a plant of *Dendrobium speciosum* is a formidable task, with inevitable losses in separating the rhizome.

In some literature *Dendrobium speciosum* is separated into more than three principal varieties and several sub-varieties, but for the ordinary everyday grower the three forms given are sufficient and simple. As a species it grows from sea level to about 1000 metres (just over 3000 feet) and is one of the most accommodating orchids to cultivate at all levels, with the North Queensland stubby colored form even coming down to southern Australia and growing well, although shy flowering so far from its habitat.

Dendrobium falcorostrum is more localised than *Dendrobium speciosum,* growing as far south as Dungog, New South Wales, on latitude 32 degrees south, to just beyond the border of that State and Queensland. It is found principally on the beech tree *Nothofagus moorei,* one of the anachronisms of the Australian flora because of its Antarctic origin.

'This beautiful Dendrobium I found growing upon the brush-trees and fern-trees in a mountain scrub on Mount Banda-banda, near the Macleay River.

The flowers are very large and numerous for the size of the plant, which is c compact habit. They vary from 10 to 20, are produced by every pseudo-bul and exhale a sweet perfume, very distinct from that of our othe Dendrobiums. From the height (about 3000 feet) [1000 metres] at which it wa found, it may possibly be suited for cold glass-houses and is certainly a ver fine addition to our Dendrobs. It flowers in October.'

That description is from the outstanding orchid publication of Australia, R D. Fitzgerald's *Australian Orchids*. He named this orchid and it was formall notified by publication of a description in *The Sydney Morning Herald* of 1 November 1876.

There is no variation in color of *Dendrobium falcorostrum*, although a variety named *pinkie* definitely has tinges of color in the buds, and the flower are slightly creamy instead of pure white. The growth habit of this form also i shorter and stubbier, the flower spike carrying fewer flowers. There are grounds for suspicion that it may be a natural hybrid from *Dendrobiun delicatum* or another of the variants from *Dendrobium kingianum*.

Growing techniques for both these dendrobiums are similar; *Dendrobium falcorostrum* thrives and flowers in much cooler conditions than *Dendrobium speciosum,* the spikes appearing in July on leafless as well as leafed bulbs which have matured for a season before flowering. The pseudo-bulbs will flower four or five times, perhaps more, before they are exhausted. From this it will be noted that provided the plant is maintained it would be second to none as a flower producer.

Dendrobium falcorostrum soon loses interest when grown in warm climates and does not thrive in lowland areas even as far south as Sydney, growing to perfection either at its natural altitude of about 1000 metres or in southern lowland climates. It dislikes hot, dry conditions and in such climates will need to be well shaded and given special treatment.

Most countries have their orchid 'puzzles' and, with *Dendrobium kingianum*, Australia is no exception. It has so many forms that it is almost in-describable, so many shapes and colors in its flowers that it is almost impossible to give them varietal names and, after all that, one saving grace: it is one of the easiest of orchids to grow.

Generally the pseudo-bulbs are club-shaped, thick at the base on an almost non-existent rhizome, tapering to about one-quarter of their basal thickness at the tips and carrying from two to five leaves. Most forms are colored, but some of the pseudo-bulbs are pale green. In addition to its vagaries in shape and color, some varieties apparently never flower at all, proliferating solely by growths from the flower nodes at the tip of the pseudo-bulbs. It is only by growing many different types that the peculiarities become apparent. After cultivating some thirty or forty different varieties in my garden for many years, I have produced flowers on most, but two have never flowered and show no tendency to do so in spite of fertilisers, different positions relative to light and northern orientation and other inducements like starvation or deprivation of water for long periods.

In studying *Dendrobium kingianum* in its habitats, it is apparent that it is invariably lithophytic but grows best in masses of decaying vegetation on rock faces, nearly always facing a south-eastern to north-eastern direction in the best aggregations, but also in fewer numbers in other directions. It will grow epiphytically, particularly on casuarina (sheoak or bulloak) trees, but is generally pot-grown as a glass-house plant. Like its associates in Australian dendrobiums, it prefers outdoor summer growing at least. In growing forty to fifty plants epiphytically on casuarina trees in southern Victoria, I found that birds and insects pollinate the flowers, seed pods set prolifically and natural seedlings germinate and grow in this latitude some 1200 kilometres south of the habitat. The numbers of seedlings, naturally, are an infinitesimal proportion of the seed scatter.

Dendrobium kingianum has cross-pollinated naturally with the other Australian dendrobiums and there is considerable weight of evidence that no-one can really distinguish, in the present evolution of these dendrobiums, between *Dendrobium kingianum* and a series of back-crosses into perhaps family three and four status. Its closest relatives are dendrobiums *delicatum* and *suffusum* and the work of Australian hybridisers during the 1960-80 period has revealed that it is particularly hard to break the chain of size and color. *Dendrobium kingianum* seems to dominate the larger species such as *Dendrobium falcorostrum* and *Dendrobium speciosum*.

Morphologically, *Dendrobium kingianum*, with its variation of pseudo-bulb length from 5 to 30 centimetres (about 2 to 12 inches), does not dominate the length of some of its hybrids, as forms of *Dendrobium* Bardo Rose (*D. kingianum* x *D. falcorostrum*) have been raised with pseudo-bulbs 45 centimetres long (about 18 inches). Some of these hybrids have flowers slightly larger than the best of the *Dendrobium kingianums*, with color varying as it does in *Dendrobium kingianum* from white to deep rose-purple. Possibly the outstanding primary hybrid using it as one parent is *Dendrobium* Ella Victoria Leaney (*D. kingianum* x *D. ruppianum*). Some clones are deep rose-purple.

Further information on these Australian orchids is obtainable from a number of publications, most of them out of print but available in libraries, possibly including those of the orchid societies.

Dendrobiums *phalaenopsis* and *bigibbum* are so alike that possibly they should never have been separated. At one time they were known as *Dendrobium phalaenopsis* and *Dendrobium phalaenopsis* var. *schroderianum*. Alex Hawkes, not always reliable, listed them as *Dendrobium bigibbum* and the variety *phalaenopsis*, while other pretenders to authority have variously distinguished them. So far as this book is concerned they are referred to as dendrobiums *bigibbum* and *phalaenopsis*, the first named usually shorter and less stout than the other. In general this is their main distinction.

Dendrobium bigibbum was first flowered in England about 1824, but there is good reason to suppose that it was *Dendrobium phalaenopsis* from somewhere north of the Australian mainland. *Dendrobium bigibbum* was named by Lindley in 1853 following the flowering of a plant in one of the larger collections of the period. It was mentioned in *Paxton's Flower Garden* of the same period, Paxton noting the region from which it came and setting out several sensible cultural recommendations, as he did for many of the novelties of that time. Many of the 'gardeners' were killing off plants of all types almost as fast as they could be imported.

The origin of Lindley's material was northern Australia, to which the original type must have migrated by island-hopping over many thousands of the preceding years. It is an 'interloper' and not a native like dendrobiums *speciosum* and *falcorostrum*, and its real source is the subject of speculation in another section of the book. For a good resumé on *Dendrobium bigibbum The Australian Orchid Review* of 1976 should be consulted and for the relative taxonomy, Alex Dockrill's *Australian Indigenous Orchids* is possibly the most authoritative text.

Dendrobium phalaenopsis and, more particularly, *Dendrobium bigibbum* thrive on extremes. In one period of the year it is all wetness and heat and in the following one it is dryness and milder warmth. *Dendrobium bigibbum* was most commonly found growing on scrubby trees in strong light and is a most hardy orchid. It was once common in the Cooktown area of northern

Queensland and in consequence bore the colloquial name 'Cookies' more frequently than its botanical title. Both dendrobiums commence growing at the start of the rainy season, October onward, produce their pseudo-bulbs quickly and by almost the end of the growing period are commencing to flower from older pseudo-bulbs as well as the new growths, which persist in flowering even when old and leafless.

By the end of March to April the dry season commences and the plants go into a dormant phase until the following growing season, with very little rain in the intervening period. The pseudo-bulbs have few leaves below the apex of the growths, which are sometimes striated with rather attractive purple lines down their length in the juvenile and pre-maturity stages. By the end of the dry season they are sometimes considerably ribbed and starved looking. Air flow in a warm glass-house is necessary for artificial conditions, but as natural garden plants *Dendrobium bigibbum* will grow as tree-mounted specimens as far south as Brisbane and even further south in suitable climates. The larger variety, *Dendrobium phalaenopsis*, is less at home so far south and even in the Brisbane latitude may need glass-house culture for the months from April to October.

Dendrobium bigibbum var. *compactum* is a totally different orchid because it is almost solely a lithophyte, growing in bright to quite open sunlight and said to be more free flowering once it is established. It grows in the northern parts of Cape York and spills over into the islands to the north of the continent. Generally the flowers of this variety are darker than the long-stemmed type and considering the height of the pseudo-bulbs at some 10 to 15 centimetres (about 4 to 6 inches) the spikes are longer but pendant. In cultivation there is little difference between the two types, both needing a warm atmosphere throughout the year.

The two varieties of *Dendrobium bigibbum* and also the variety or separate species *Dendrobium phalaenopsis* are becoming scarce in their habitats for various reasons, not least of which are greedy and foolish over-collecting by people anxious to make a 'quick dollar' and by growers from southern states who have the mistaken idea that as it grows as a pretty bush orchid in Queensland it should do the same thing in their colder climate. This dendrobium is the state emblem of Queensland and a better choice could not have been made. Its use has been extended in hybridising from the original production of the beautiful hybrids such as those illustrated to incorporation with other sections of the Australian dendrobiums in later years of the 1970-80 decade with most pleasing and promising results.

There is a slight difference between the environments in which dendrobiums *bigibbum* and *phalaenopsis* grow, with the island climates of *Dendrobium phalaenopsis* more humid throughout the year. Micholitz, one of Sanders' collectors, was among the first to send plants to England. His first collection of *Dendrobium phalaenopsis* was lost as a result of a shipboard fire and he sent a cable to Sanders asking for advice. Their answer was simple and to the point: 'Go back and get some more.' He did so, although most unwillingly because of the bad time he had in getting the first lot. The second collection, however, turned out to be easier, probably as a result of experience, and he included in the consignment plants of dendrobiums *atroviolaceum, dearei, johnsoniae, schutzei* and *superbiens*.

On reviewing some of the literature of the last century and the years of its first appearance as a glass-house plant early in the nineteenth century, it is obvious that the name *Dendrobium phalaenopsis* was all-embracing. Plants were grown in the Royal Exotic Nurseries at Cheltenham, England, in the 1880-90 period and the grower, James Cypher, had a considerable collection.

Each year he flowered hundreds of them, varying from the pure white form common to both types to the deepest of rose-purple. A pure white form gained First Class Certificate from the Royal Horticultural Society in 1895.

Dendrobium superbiens is one of the natural affiliates of *Dendrobium bigibbum*, the natural cross-pollination of this orchid with *Dendrobium discolor*. The first plants of it to arrive in England were sent by a member of the Macarthur family from Sydney, arriving in good condition at the Veitch nursery. This autumn-flowering dendrobium was named by Reichenbach and the intuition of several experienced cultivators was proved correct when hand-made cross-pollinations of the two species were flowered. *Dendrobium superbiens* also occurs in the islands to the north of Australia.

Dendrobium johannis (Reichenbach) was discovered in northern Queensland about 1865 by John Gould Veitch. It also appears to have some relationship with *Dendrobium discolor* (Lindley), which is common to great areas of Australasia and as far to the east as the Solomon Islands. For a considerable time it was known more by its synonym *Dendrobium undulatum* and reference to the illustrations supports the name as being appropriate.

It is not possible to conclude the section without reference to *Dendrobium dicuphum* (F. Mueller), which could be referred to as the 'poor relative' of the *Dendrobium bigibbum* family. It occurs in the northern part of the Northern Territory and across into Western Australia and some of the islands in the Gulf of Carpentaria. Smaller morphologically and florally than its relatives, it is a very attractive species, its color varying from almost white with some labellum color to paler pinks. This orchid grows mostly on melaleucas or paper-barks as they are known, which grow in proximity to marshy areas or streams and rivers. It is seldom seen in cultivation and appears unhappy when so grown. Its annual cycle if anything is more marked in the dry period than the wet, consistent with the type of country in which it occurs.

Dendrobium dicuphum is an 'outsider'. Like many of the north Australian dendrobiums, it comes from a separate group unrelated to *Dendrobium speciosum* and its affiliates. But again it is separate from the Indo-Asian series, which are products of an evolutionary system on the other side of the Wallace Line. This imaginary line runs between Borneo and the Celebes islands, separating the marsupials from other animals into two distinct and ancient groups. Wallace was as controversial a figure as Darwin, but his status as a naturalist, botanist and natural history authority is undoubted. An extension of his theory may be mistaken in its application to orchids, but it is attractive in this regard as an explanation of obvious differences in the dendrobium tribe, if not other orchids. The dendrobiums to which *discolor, bigibbum, dicuphum* and others belong are a group which could be termed 'migrants' to Australia from the southern islands of the Arafura, Coral and Timor seas areas.

Wallace, a contemporary of Darwin and by a strange coincidence the promoter of similar thoughts at the same time, although separately developed, had this to say of orchids: 'Their usually minute and abundant seeds would be as easily carried as the spores of ferns, and their frequent epiphytic habit affords them an endless variety of stations on which to vegetate, and at the same time removes them in a great measure from the competition of other plants. When, therefore, the climate is sufficiently moist and equable and there is a luxuriant tropical vegetation we may expect to find orchids plentiful on such tropical islands as possess an abundance of insects adapted to fertilise them and which are not too far removed from other lands or continents from which their seeds might be conveyed.'

What neither Dr Alfred Russell Wallace nor Charles Darwin realised was

163

that no matter how far a seed was wafted on the wind or otherwise transported, unless a spore of a fungus was awaiting its arrival in a suitable spot for germination and growth, the odds against its survival were considerably lengthened. Symbiosis did not enter their considerations at all in the period in which they lived and worked.

Dr Wallace died in 1914 at the age of ninety-one. He travelled extensively throughout the tropical countries of the world and the quote from his book *Island Life* in the above paragraph was a reflection of his knowledge of the Malaysian region. In the years he spent in that part of the world he built up an extensive collection of specimens and herbarium material which was totally destroyed in a shipboard fire. He was scornful and critical of the misapplication of the theories of Mendel and of other facets of plant development and evolution. For the approximate position of the supposed demarcation termed the Wallace Line the colored map on page 52 should be consulted.

Square Orchids

Nature produces some peculiar plants, all of which are in some way the product of an environment and ecology which influenced their metamorphosis. One cannot help wondering what induced the square cross-section of *Dendrobium tetragonum*, an Australian variant from the usual type with which it is included, the dendrocorynes, of which dendrobiums *speciosum* and *falcorostrum* are also members. It has nothing in common with other members on the score of growth habit — it is pendant and the flowers are spidery. Nature usually works in curves and rounds rather than squares. However, it is not the only dendrobium with this peculiar square cross-section, but the attribute is less marked in the others.

Dendrobiums *thyrsiflorum* and the variety *densiflorum* and *Dendrobium farmeri* are others with this characteristic, the last more pronounced. *Dendrobium thyrsiflorum* was originally found in Lower Burma by the Rev. C. Parish, and Low & Co. were possibly the first of the nurserymen to import it in quantity somewhere about 1860. It was named by Reichenbach, its title deriving from the shape of the spike just before the blooms open, as it resembles an inverted cone. The absolute derivation of the name may be traced out in encyclopaedias.

The flowers of *Dendrobium thyrsiflorum* are pale creamy petalled, the labellum a rich orange-yellow, with the buds just before and at opening having a pale flush of pink tinting them. The flowers of *Dendrobium thyrsiflorum* var. *densiflorum* are more richly colored.

Originally, under the order established by Sir Joseph Hooker, *Dendrobium densiflorum* was considered the main species, *Dendrobium thyrsiflorum* a sub-variety. *Dendrobium densiflorum* comes from the tropical Himalayan foothills and other areas of north-eastern India, now known in part as Bangladesh.

Newly imported jungle plants usually flower prolifically in their first season following acclimatising and after that a build-up must follow before they again produce such a show. This is common to most Indo-Asian dendrobiums. In cultivation *Dendrobium thyrisflorum* seems to do best in a moderately warm and humid climate through winter to induce free flowering, although it also has a dormant phase related to its pre-flowering period. Once the small acorn-like nodes are obvious the plants should be encouraged out of this false dormancy and the spike given sufficient moisture to bring development. The flower nodes at the tip of the pseudo-bulbs may endure and continue to produce blooms for some years. The leaves, usually some five or six at the apex of the growths, should be a dark, glossy green. The plants appreciate a good air flow about them in the growing period, ensuring, however, that the foliage does not burn. There is no limit, within reason, to the size that mature and well-grown plants may reach, but good drainage and perfect culture are needed to retain foliage and good health in them. Retention of leaves is advisable, but even in leafless condition the pseudo-bulbs may flower again.

Dendrobium farmeri, a similar type of orchid, is native to the eastern Himalayan foothills country, particularly semi-tropical zones at altitudes of 300 to 1000 metres (about 1000 to 3500 feet). This orchid also occurs in Lower Burma which is a tropical region, the Khasia Hills and as a minor species in other zones. The pseudo-bulbs of *Dendrobum farmeri* are more squarish than those of *Dendrobium thyrsiflorum*, which are slender and spindle-shaped.

Dendrobium farmeri was introduced to English growers by McClelland of Calcutta Botanic Gardens when he sent plants to the orchid grower W. G. Farmer, in whose honor it was named by Paxton. In the type form the flowers are a soft pink, but white varieties are known. The flowers lose their pink coloring as they age, in the same way as *Dendrobium thyrsiflorum*, and overall they live for about ten to fourteen days.

There is considerable variation within all these dendrobiums and this was noted early in their cultivated history by interested people in the army, civil administration and even the church in what were perhaps the golden days of the British Empire.

The Rev. Parish, who must have spent a considerable amount of his time between sermons pursuing his pastime of collecting and growing orchids, had this to say of *Dendrobium farmeri*: 'What if I were to say that *D. farmeri* and *D. chrysotoxum* were one and the same? I know both of them extremely well, having had them growing for years. There is no mistaking the two without flowers. Two days ago, on going down into my garden, I was astonished and could hardly believe my eyes at seeing a panicle of golden flowers of *D. chrysotoxum* proceeding from the bulbs of *D. farmeri*! The only difference being that the labellum is here rather pointed and not so round as in *D. chrysotoxum*.'

Parish was probably looking at the variety *aureoflava*, as it was then known, and had apparently not known of it. He knew the variety *albiflora*, but it is surprising that he should compare it with *Dendrobium chrysotoxum*, because the two are so different but grow in the same general areas. It is not beyond possibility that the plant on which he remarked was a natural hybrid between the two. The frequency with which this occurred in the tremendous orchid populations of Asia was well known and it is incredible from the standpoint of species paucity of the late years of the twentieth century.

It will be noted on referring to the illustrations how different the two species are. *Dendrobium chrysotoxum* is warm-growing like *Dendrobium farmeri* and to promote best flowering results must be given quite bright light in the maturing phase of the pseudo-bulbs, without running the risk of burning the leaves in direct sunlight. The pseudo-bulbs of *Dendrobium chrysotoxum* are shorter, stouter and more spindle-shaped than those of *Dendrobium farmeri*. Indeed, *Dendrobium ruppianum* is so markedly similar morphologically that it could almost be mistaken for it at times.

Dendrobium ruppianum is a stranger in the Australian dendrocoryne section and could be mistaken for an 'interloper' like dendrobiums *bigibbum* or *discolor*. There is no doubt that its fusiforme pseudo-bulbs are inherent characteristics of a species which possibly has since disappeared from the

Australian catalogue, although on looking at the pseudo-bulbs of the hybrid *Dendrobium* Hilda Poxon (*D. speciosum* x *D. tetragonum*) and some of the other *Dendrobium tetragonum* derivatives it is logical to look for the progenitor in that direction.

Dendrobium ruppianum, although coming from the north Queensland Cape York region, succeeds only as a cool-growing species and is usually difficult to flower under glass-house culture. It is a most beautiful specimen when free flowering in southern Australia. It is not a square orchid and should not be included in this section. Its resemblance to *Dendrobium chrysotoxum* brought it in.

Fully Leafed Hard-Cane Dendrobiums

There are many members of this group, some related but most with no affiliation with one another except their growth habits. Almost solely epiphytic, they are usually from the upper strata of the forest, with in some instances the yellow or cream flowers indicating that fact. They have different habits in casting their leaves, with some such as dendrobiums *sanderae, fimbriatum* or *pulchellum* retaining most of their leaves until adverse seasons or conditions force their discard.

Dendrobium fimbriatum (Hooker) was originally collected by Gibson in the Khasia Hills, a region saturated with orchids of many species. He found it growing at about 1000 metres (about 3500 feet) in almost full sunlight and sent it to the Duke of Devonshire's collection where it flowered in the following spring in 1824. Joseph Paxton, the man in charge of this collection, produced some wonderful results compared with the standard of the time. *Dendrobium fimbriatum* produces racemes of flower from the tip and nearby lower nodes for some years in good conditions. It also grows in northern India at about the same altitude and needs warm cultural conditions, quick growth where possible and a pause before flowering in the spring of the same year.

Dendrobium discolor (Lindley), also known as *Dendrobium undulatum*, which was Robert Brown's name for it, may grow up to a metre and a half high normally and has been known to exceed this in naturally growing plants. It casts some of the lower leaves as the pseudo-bulbs elongate but retains them on at least half of the new growths. The flower nodes appear at the tip of older, mature pseudo-bulbs at varying times in artificial conditions.

Dendrobium pulchellum (Roxburgh) is one of the most beautiful of the tall-growing hard-stem dendrobiums. A native of north-east India and adjacent regions, its habitat extended to the border of Burma and Thailand. The description of Parish needs no qualification: 'A noble species. Stems often 5 to 6 feet long when found in damp, shady forests which it affects; drooping flowers in loose racemes, near the end of the stems, of 6 to 7 flowers 5 inches across, cream-gold, lip large, saccate, but hardly slipper-shaped, with large, deep blood-red blotches on the inside, the middle and front part projecting forwards and covered with a soft velvety pile. Abundant in the Tenasserim forests. The stems, however long, are but of one season's growth, at the close of which they flower for the first time, while the leaves remain on; but the same stems will flower also the second and third year after the leaves have fallen off, new racemes proceeding from the leaf axils next below those of the preceding year. The lip is bagged or boat-shaped, villous, with the central margin turned outwards; column and anther dark purple, stems marked with red-purple lines.' It is illustrated in the color photo section.

The description, so far as the morphology or habit is concerned, is applicable to most of this section. *Dendrobium sanderae* (Rolfe), also illustrated, shows the type of growth to be expected and the note in the Parish description relative to the length and speed of growth in getting to maturity indicates in some measure the type of natural or artificial climate in which the plants should be grown.

Dendrobium moschatum (Willdenow) is a similar species, the flowers having more than passing similarity to those of *Dendrobium pulchellum*. *Dendrobium agrostophyllum* (F. Mueller) is an Australian member with morphological similarity to the well-leafed Indo-Asian group. It grows in the tropical section of northern Queensland on the higher peaks like the beautiful Bartle Frere at about 1000 metres (over 3000 feet) and, as Dockrill remarks, in lower cool gorges. The leaves persist on the pseudo-bulbs for some years in suitable conditions, the flower racemes issuing from about the upper four to six pairs of leaves and even on bare pseudo-bulbs. The flowers, although small, are bright golden yellow. This dendrobium transfers easily to cooler climates at lower altitudes and a photograph in the color section shows it growing as an epiphyte on a casuarina tree in the author's garden in southern Victoria some 3000 kilometres (about 1800 miles) south of its habitat. Like many of the Australian dendrobiums, it is not suited by glass-house culture and gradually deteriorates if so grown.

As the largest or near enough to the largest genus of orchids, dendrobiums could be elaborated into a separate volume in order to do them justice. However, from this review of some of the types and possibly those most grown in artificial cultivation enough information can probably be gleaned to estabish a cultural program for most of the family which are not mentioned separately. Only in the instances of Niugini species and some of the lesser known species of other island orchid communities, would difficulty be found in formulating a system for them as company for other orchids in a general collection. Unfortunately, in such cases the treatment would need to be so insular that the rest of the collection would be adversely affected. These 'strangers' usually give up the fight against what to them are totally unsuitable conditions. With artificial heating and copious air flow so incompatible as components for their climate it is usually difficult to strike a balance in their favor.

Cultivation

Overpotting dendrobiums should be avoided with pot size appearing at times to be quite out of proportion. For the *Dendrobium nobile* type hybrids the correct size is approximately 3 centimetres of pot for each mature and leafed pseudo-bulb. This is a rough figure, but in practice such a pot and plant will look well suited to each other. Mostly these orchids have comparable root systems, regardless of how tall their pseudo-bulbs may grow. It is possible that some of the taller plants may be top-heavy and in such instances a smaller pot should be half-buried in a much larger pot which will stand upright. The filling between the two pots should be crushed rock of about 1½ centimetres (¾ inch) aggregate.

A well-planned cultural program should be thought out for these soft-stemmed dendrobiums, starting with the repotting or moving on of plants which obviously need a little more room. This should be taken in hand as new roots are noticed in early to late spring and early summer, handling the plants progressively as it occurs, and leaving the slow ones until last. Most of these orchids will tolerate fairly bright light in this period and watering should not be too free until the plants have had time to get over the post-operative shock. Give them four to five weeks, by which time the roots will have become accustomed to new material. Throughout these weeks the pots should be stood in the most humid, fresh part of the glass-house or growing area and the surroundings should be frequently damped down.

Locality will have marked effects and although soft-stemmed dendrobiums are grown in sub-tropical, temperate and even cool zones and thrive in all of them, a fairly fast summer or warm period growth pattern should be encouraged, with stand-by heating available right through summer in those areas where it may be needed to keep internal growing temperatures up about the 12 to 14 degree Celsius mark. In mixed collections, naturally, this pattern cannot be followed, as the general collection usually dictates what will be going on in the glass-house. Those growers who are fortunate enough to be able to grow these orchids under shade-cloth right through the year have little need to worry, even on cold nights, as the compensatory features of their climate make up for most deficiencies.

It is better to get this continuous type of growth and people growing soft-caned dendrobiums in cool climates should be prepared to note failures, which are beyond their control in some seasons. By late autumn in the best of possibilities the growths should be completed and fattened out, changing from the mid-green of the growth stage to a green-yellow. This is the ripening period but not necessarily the budding stage. Under shade-cloth there is no need to change anything to get the plants into this ripening period, but in glass-house culture the shade should be reduced by as much as half in order to get the same results. Sun values may be quite different for various parts of a country like Australia and this will also be a factor in other countries. Some recognition should be given to this, so that regardless of the home territory of various growers they all get the same results.

The formation of flower buds is a most perplexing thing. It defies all rules and recommendations and is based principally on the relative dominance of one or another of the species in particular cross-pollinations, even when long removed from the primary hybrid stages. Some clones flower easily, others are difficult and it is these which may at times form buds on the lower part of the pseudo-bulb and not on the upper portion, which may form buds in the following season. Others may flower on the upper portion of the pseudo-bulbs and not on the lower portion and these very seldom complete flowering from the lower part of the growths in following years. Mostly the characteristics of a particular clone will be constant year after year and no amount of fiddling with chemicals will change them.

Very few clones of the soft-stemmed dendrobium hybrids flower regularly or on the total length of the pseudo-bulbs. Where they are noted they should be sought out and bought if this type of flowering pattern is the aim. It is unwise to take note of photographs which purport to show this type of flowering, as it may not be a constant characteristic or it could be a 'faked' photograph.

Once the tiny swellings are noted at the joints in the pseudo-bulbs the plants should be taken along in a steady pattern without overwatering or any additional fertilising. At this stage too much water or a cold spell of weather may cause the buds to lose vitality and turn dormant. It is some weeks before the swellings mature enough to see the tiny buds beginning to form at the head of the nodes. Even temperature is a factor at this stage which, unfortunately, occurs in late winter and early spring. Do not try to force the plants ahead of their set pace, although if a 'hot-box' is available it will certainly advance the opening of the flowers by a week or two.

The most common sequence with soft-stemmed dendrobiums is for pot-life of some three or four years for mature plants, over which period they gradually build up to a maximum flowering stage, with preferably some six or even pseudo-bulbs all flowering together. This depends, naturally, on planning and attention to cultivation. Following this it is usually best to dismember the plant, starting off again with at least three mature pseudo-bulbs, one of which should be unflowered, and begin the process all over again. Occasionally it is possible to have a clone which proliferates and pots-on well into a specimen plant. This is mostly a five year plan, again followed by dismembering. It is fairly accurate to say that plants of these dendrobiums have only one maximum flowering in their pot-life. Once the flowers open the plants should be allowed to dry off slightly and there should be enough vitality in them to hold the flowers for some weeks.

Various theories have been promoted to account for the initial swelling on the pseudo-bulbs turning into growths instead of flowering. In the first place it is a natural habit of the soft-cane dendrobiums and occurs for two reasons in artificial cultivation. The first and most disastrous of these is that if they are overwatered the plants are provoked into this reaction by root loss and seek to propagate by adventitious growth instead of floral pollination. The second has to do with the general cultivation conditions and indicates that a change should be made in the direction of increasing light aiding winter dormancy instead of stagnation and perhaps night-time temperatures in glass-houses where other genera are grown. Although these dendrobiums like the same sort of conditions as cattleyas, they do not like a warm humid atmosphere at any stage of the plant cycle, particularly in the bud formation stage.

Many of the soft-stemmed dendrobiums such as *pierardii* and *chrysanthum* are naturally pendulous and the various habits of such species as well as the hybrids should be noted and encouraged. To tie them erect usually induces poor flowering more than growth and this stage in their life to which we all look forward is frequently spoiled by inattention to such details. With any of them a little shrivelling from late autumn to summer is not a bad thing and it will be frequently noted that such 'ribbing' of the pseudo-bulbs may not fill out until the next season's pseudo-bulbs are maturing.

The dendrobiums with rigid, tough pseudo-bulbs, usually referred to as hard-canes, are so diverse in origin that no general cultural program can be recommended. If anything, they complete their growths and then flower, with some waiting up to six months before producing spikes. As far as light is concerned, most of the hard-cane dendrobiums withstand much stronger light than their lush, green-leafed soft-cane relatives and to promote flowering the light intensity should be increased.

The general rule regarding pots applies at times more rigorously to the hard-cane group; with a plant of, say, *Dendrobium bigibbum* with four or five pseudo-bulbs growing quite happily in a 10-centimetre pot containing almost nothing. It is wrong to imagine that root systems of dendrobiums should be enclosed in pots if cultivated, as they are naturally partly or completely aerial in nature although clinging closely to some host. There will always be exceptions and these will need quite an amount of understanding to get much out of them.

Some dendrobiums are far more at home tied to slabs of tree-fern, wood and at times cork. This last material is suited more to warm climates than cold and in glass-house culture may be completely useless as a dendrobium mount.

Wooden slat baskets also have a place in cultivating some of the hard-cane series such as *Dendrobium chrysotoxum* and similar plants. The advantage of this type of container is appreciated when dendrobiums requiring a shift into brighter light are planted in them. It is much easier to arrange a new hanging spot than if they are planted in pots.

169

The fully leafed dendrobiums like *Dendrobium fimbriatum* and, for that matter, some of the 'squares' may be thought too tall for small pots or slat and basket culture. This may be an instance where a natural wood pot such as illustrated would not only suit the plant but provide a natural container much more attractive to orchid roots than our mass-produced substitutes. Common sense usually dictates the 'home' each type of dendrobium needs, but always be ready to copy an innovator who seems to have something suitable. One of the things uppermost in mind should be the wintering-over of root systems and the suitability of containers to allow an easy dormancy. Overpotting at any time is a dangerous habit when growing dendrobiums, reaching its worst proportions when quick drying out is needed and water is not shed from pots too large or 'heavy' mixes.

The most important feature in the lives of nearly all dendrobiums is the radical change in climate and moisture deposition they experience naturally. It must be duplicated as nearly as possible in artificial conditions. At times cultivators manage to do much better than nature and may exceed the natural flowering of these orchids.

Dendrobium Mixes and Fertilisers

Root systems of dendrobiums are what might be termed fine to medium thickness and somewhat different from those of other cultivated orchids. Naturally growing plants develop a considerable pattern of surface roots designed to attach the plant to its anchorage and to feed from available moisture and natural fertilisers. Roots of pot-grown plants are exposed to a totally different set of conditions, with the root system almost totally enclosed. Because of this, consideration should be given to the type of material used as well as its drainage.

Regularly accepted potting mediums comprise bark of various trees, which is a natural medium for epiphytes, and various additives. The plants may be grown in a wide choice of containers, such as pots, slat-type 'baskets', scooped out sections of tree-fern trunk, 'blisters' cut from the trunks of fallen eucalypts such as illustrated, and a number of others which at times are either novel or unusual. These containers should be selected with an eye to their suitability both as to size and materials. Of the pots themselves, little may be said in favor of one type over another, plasic or clay. But a large volume of opinion still favors clay pots, which are my preference, for epiphytes; perhaps this is a hangover from the time when plastic pots were new and occasionally even toxic.

Whatever the style of container, drainage should be a primary thought, even if it is a portion of similar material like bark used for the potting medium, but with the stipulation that it be coarser than the potting material. The overall size of the mix should be related to the size of the container rather than the type of plant. Some hard-cane dendrobiums such as *Dendrobium bigibbum* and its hybrids and the smaller hirsute types should be grown in the smallest pot which will accommodate the plant, as outlined in the previous section. It is not an economy measure, but rather a reflection of experience.

Some growers, perhaps a little lazily, use ordinary cymbidium mixes for dendrobiums. This is inadvisable, although if properly handled there is no reason why it may not be successful. As the root systems of these two genera are totally different there is too much scope for error in misguided or careless watering programs. Nearly all the dendrobiums have a period in their annual cycle when they are completely dormant and when they need only enough moisture to keep the mixes from drying out, the plants subsisting entirely on he humidity in the air either at night or in the daytime. In open-air conditions drying out may seem more intense, but occasionally even these open conditions provide moisture at night. If this does not occur it may be necessary to water the plants occasionally in their dormant stage. But something better than cymbidium mix should be used.

If charcoal is used as a part-blend it should be proved; it may be from an unsuitable timber and so lack the necessary characteristics to attract dendrobium roots. If suitable it may be used as a half-and-half mix with bark, each component being made up of different sized pieces. If a large plant is to be potted in a 12 centimetre pot the bark used should be from 5 to 10 millimetres and the charcoal from 5 millimetres down.

Natural additives may be included such as dry leaf of oaks and composted grass clippings. The clippings should have completely decayed into hard peat, a rather unpleasant semi-solid like black grease, which must be dried out. This is one of the best natural additives, however unattractive it may appear in processing. Chopped bracken and tree-fern fronds also have something to contribute.

The term of pot occupancy varies, but to grow a representative plant of any species or hybrid it should be not less than three years. The mix should therefore be designed to stand up to that period and be capable of retaining vitality even after being dried out in a dormancy.

All this may seem rather complicated, but dendrobiums must be treated with a little more care than cymbidiums. Plants which look unhealthy mostly suffer from root loss caused by overwatering at some period of the year or a potting mix which is unsuitable because it is too acid or charcoal retains adverse mineral salts. Instead of charcoal some growers use red scoria and this should also be proved suitable by the 'bird-seed test' which has been outlined elsewhere. Scoria could even be a major part of the mix in warm climates where the plants never seem to go through the cold dormancy stages of cooler climates.

Choice of fertilisers should be influenced by certain factors such as the need of dendrobiums for stimulants in some seasons and not in others. Hundreds of propositions could be detailed and it is in growers' interest that they work out programs which suit cultural styles. If good-looking plants are produced the worst part of a sort-out has been mastered; if unsatisfactory flowering follows then something remains to be modified in the program without necessity for scrapping it as a whole. In dormancy, which is common to nearly all the genus, the plants are incapable of absorbing much nutriment at all as the root system has tapered off its activity and 'gone to sleep'. One of the reasons for discarding slow-release fertilisers for most dendrobiums is the possibility that residual pellets may be left behind and their effect of still releasing nutrients which are not needed affects the root system and the potting mix.

One of the best systems is to make up a very weak solution in a bucket, which should be about one-quarter the strength recommended on any container, and to use this as the plants need it after they have been thoroughly watered with good quality water. As each genus seems to need a slightly different formula a little experimental work may be needed over a year or two. Even with this, the seasons and general environment have as much to do with success as the fertilisers.

A weak solution to be used in this way would be about a level teaspoonful of any of the usual soluble fertilisers to a bucket of water (about 14 litres or 3 gallons). A small amount of Maxicrop or seaweed fertiliser, sufficient only to barely color the water, and about a teaspoonful of fish emulsion may be added to this. If these are added the quantity of water should be increased by half.

With such a fertiliser the plants may be watered frequently without any i effects and the only thing to beware of is the temptation to increase the amoun of fertilisers in the hope that even better results may be obtained. Once plant indicate that their growing season is at an end all fertilisers should be withhel and only clean water used to irrigate them when necessary.

Many types of refined and borderline techniques are sometime recommended, some with almost lethal amounts of fertiliser, but these ar principally designed for the conditions under which they are used and are quit useless to anyone in a type of environment which may be totally different They cannot be quoted for general use.

Blood and bone meal is a stimulating fertiliser if used correctly. It should b stored after purchase to allow it to partially break down and this may take up to twelve months. Old ice-cream containers are ideal storage bins. At the enc of the storage period the material may have broken down to a light fluff powder which releases its growth energy quite rapidly. As it is a concentratec form of fertiliser containing most trace elements as well as the basics, blooo and bone should not be used as heavy applications. As some form of guide, as much as will cover a 10 cent piece is sufficient, and this application should be repeated three times over the growing cycle of dendrobiums.

When used in conjunction with liquid fertilising, the nutrient liquid should not be used for about two or three weeks after the blood and bone has been applied. As there is little or no residue from the blood and bone there is no need to worry about removing unwanted fertiliser at the changeover of the plants. The only part left will be bone granules which are inert and harmless.

Use of lime is frequently advocated, particularly to correct alterations to potting mixes caused by liquid nutrients. It is best used as a dip if possible and the method is to put about a cupful of slaked lime into a bucket of water and allow it to stand for about two or three days, stirring it occasionally with a stick. Pots should be individually immersed in the solution for three or four minutes, held to drain some of the surplus away and then returned to the bench or hanger. Lime residue which may be floating free in the dip will not harm the plant or the roots. An alternative to this is to put free slaked lime into a salt-shaker or something similar, lightly dust the surface of the potting mix, then water it through the mix with a fine spray from a hose, taking into account the usual watering program and using this as a replacement for it.

Top-dressings or incorporation of dolomite, shell-grit or limestone are almost completely ineffective as the breakdown time for these materials to be effective is far too long for the ordinary pot-life of dendrobiums.

The effect on flowering dendrobiums may be summarised in a fairly short last paragraph: All the efforts of the plants may be reduced to nothing by over-anxious and over-helpful use of the hose and fertilisers. The build-up to flowering is a long process and the price of failure is ultimate poor quality flowers and wasted years of effort.

Propagating Dendrobiums

Some species lend themselves to orthodox propagating methods better than others because they may be persuaded to produce what are commonly called aerial growths. These take the place of what would normally be flower spikes and *Dendrobium kingianum* is probably the best example of this natural method. Some species never produce aerial growths, but others like dendrobiums *loddigesii* or *falconeri*, to mention only two of the soft-cane species, habitually grow from the pseudo-bulbs at points higher than the basal nodes which develop new growths on most of the genus.

The normal rules of division apply to dendrobiums and it is unwise to sever lants into single or dual pseudo-bulb propagations; three is an ideal propagating division and preferably one of the pseudo-bulbs should have most r all of its leaves. Plants may be divided by severing the rhizome between elected pseudo-bulbs and if the divisions are left intact in a plant clump until he following growing season it is possible to obtain better propagations than if he plant is stripped of its potting material and severed into pieces which are otted in new mix.

The aerial growths which develop instead of flowers should be left on the ged or leafed pseudo-bulbs until the second growth springs away from them n the next season. These must also be left until the new growths develop new oot tips and then the growths should be carefully parted from the old seudo-bulbs and potted. None of the roots on the older aerial growths, which ave been growing in the air since they developed, will live if they are put into he potting material. They should be spread on the surface of the new potting nix, while the younger roots from the second growth will make their way lown into the mix if it is suitable. In this way a strong plantlet of a worthwhile ariety is quickly produced. If the first growth is taken away, despite the fact hat the roots may enter the mix, there always seems to be a blank period when t finds itself severed and it may take quite a lot longer to develop into a new olant than one which is treated in the correct way.

Occasionally these aerial growths seem reluctant to produce a new shoot from the base. If, after a year, there seems to be no progress, the old pseudo-bulb on which it has grown should be cut off at the base. Counting one joint on each side, above and below the point of development, sever the old pseudo-bulb so that it has a full segment above and below the growth. This piece of pseudo-bulb is then fastened flat on to the surface of a pot containing new material or sphagnum moss and benched with the rest of the collection. No special treatment, other than spreading the existing roots on the surface, is necessary. To hold this propagation firmly on the surface it may be necessary to pin it down with wire loops.

If a plant fails to produce aerial growths and they are wanted, a flowered or unflowered pseudo-bulb may be severed and stood in a wide-necked bottle like a milk bottle in about 5 centimetres (2 inches) of water. It is not necessary to change the water very often and nutrients or formulations for rooting the plants should not be added. It is necessary, however, to have only 5 centimetres of water in the bottle, as it is the humidity in the main part of the bottle which is most likely to produce a growth or growths from the old pseudo-bulb. Sometimes it works, but sometimes it fails.

If a seedling which is promising is propagated in any of the above ways it may seem a slow process and it is possible to have the plant mericloned by any of the propagators who handle this method. While it produces small plantlets which are said to be patterns of the original, in dendrobiums strange things may happen because, like cymbidiums, they are the product of several generations of hybridising from a number of species and this alone destabilises most orchids.

A number of the hard-cane dendrobiums do not produce aerial growths at any time. One example is *Dendrobium thyrsiflorum*. It is necessary to wait until these plants have grown sufficiently to divide. Premature division is a very wasteful process because pieces are frequently lost to fungus infections in the rhizome or leaf loss and subsequently the whole of the premature division.

Severed portions, as well as the rhizomes or pseudo-bulbs from which they are taken, should be treated with an anti-fungus powder or spray and if this is not available a little free lime rubbed on to the cut surfaces is usually quite enough to stop entry of spores or diseases.

173

Masdevallias

This genus was discovered and named by Ruiz and Pavon in Peru in the decade 1780-90 and dedicated to Dr Jose Masdevall, a Spanish botanist and physician. It belongs to the pleurothallideae, a very large family of plants, occurring over a widespread area of Central and South America.

Masdevallias were popular as a genus in only one period of their cultivated history and during that time growers in England and Europe specialised in them and bought at times hundreds of plants to build up collections of a particular species. Their greatest popularity was enjoyed between 1880 and 1900.

Masdevallia uniflora, discovered by Ruiz and Pavon, is the species on which the genus was founded and named, as outlined in the first paragraph. It is similar morphologically to the bulk of the genus, caespitose, that is, growing in a clump, and the leaves of most species are club-shaped to a greater or lesser degree. On the larger species these leaves are 30 centimetres and more long, about 1 to 3 centimetres broad and rather fleshy and brittle. There are no pseudo-bulbs, the leaves acting in this capacity and capable of retaining and sustaining moisture for fairly long dry periods. The single leaves grow direct from an ascending rhizome in most species and last for upward of two years in good cultivation.

Masdevallias are epiphytic and terrestrial, as the following quote from Veitch's *Manual of Orchidaceous Plants* indicates:

'*Masdevallia coccinea* ... was discovered by Chesterton in 1871 near Sogamosa (Colombia) and was introduced by us in the same year... Its principal locality is on the eastern Cordillera between Sogamosa and Concepcion, where its vertical range is 7000 to 10,000 feet [2000 to 3000 metres]; it is particularly abundant on that part of the Cordillera called the Sierra Nevada de Chita, where it spreads for miles in uninterrupted masses covering acres upon acres of the upland slopes, growing in the partial shade afforded by the low shrubs that abound in the place.'

Chesterton was not the only collector finding them thus, as another collector almost complained that all he could find in one whole day's travelling were masses of masdevallias all in flower, mostly *Masdevallia coccinea*, growing both on the trees and the ground. He was looking for other things like odontoglossums. The variety found by Chesterton was *Masdevallia coccinea* var. *harryana*, possibly the best of the species. It is cultivated in many Australian glass-houses, mostly disseminated from the original plants brought into Australia by members of the first orchid club, the Victorian Orchid Club, in the 1920 decade.

The first cultivated masdevallia appeared to be *Masdevilla infracta,* found in Brazil by Descourtilz about 1809 and flowering in cultivation about 1828. There are about 100 species in the genus, most of which are known only as herbarium specimens.

Masdevallias were not grown as much as the numbers collected and despatched to the European and British markets might suggest and there is the

ather desolate fact that they die off so easily in cultivation. There has not been
a great number of hybrids raised, but one which has lasted very well is Bocking
Hybrid, the result of cross-pollinating *Masdevallia veitchiana* and *Masdevallia
ucculata,* a Colombian species.

The Veitch nursery raised several hybrids and one or two other fanciers also
did some hybridising, but generally in the 1980 period the genus has fallen into
disfavor. It is surprising how a well-flowered plant soon rekindles interest.

One of the first botanists to stimulate interest in the genus was Jean Linden,
who was born in Luxembourg in 1817. He was educated at Brussels University
and on graduating went to South America for some years. He became most
interested in orchids and gave John Lindley a beautiful collection of dried
specimens which included *Masdevallia coccinea.* He also made very careful
notes on the habitats and the climate and it was this information which
prompted John Lindley to persuade changes in the cultivation habits of the
British growers.

Sir Harry Veitch

Linden had this to say of *Masdevallia coccinea*: 'This magnificent orchid
grows on the ground on the southern slopes of the high mountains near
Pamplona at the height of 9500 feet [about 3000 metres] ... its brilliant
flowers resemble at a distance those of begarias, vaccinums and other plants of
those lofty regions.'

Jean Linden was accompanied by his half-brother, who discovered another
masdevallia later in the 1830-40 period and Linden named it *Masdevallia
schlimii* in his honor. Schlim was a noted collector and recorder in the South
American region for many years.

Linden began a nursery business in Brussels about 1845 and was later
appointed director of the zoological gardens in that city. Schlim and Wallis
were two of his collectors, and both worked for other nurseries, including
Sanders'; Linden was also responsible for some beautiful printing in *Lindenia,*
highly prized by owners in the twentieth century for the beautiful drawings and
lithographs. Unfortunately many of these books were cut up for the
lithographs and so destroyed.

One of the most outstanding species is *Masdevallia veitchiana*, discovered
originally by the collector Pearce in the Peruvian Andes at an altitude of about
3500 metres (more than 10 000 feet). Although growing at this altitude, in
cultivation it is apparently not suited at all by cold climates or winter
conditions and much better results are obtained with an all-round minimum of
about 12 degrees Celsius (54 degrees Fahrenheit).

Veitch's collector Davis followed Pearce in harvesting it again about 1870
and added to the stock they obtained and flowered in 1867. Davis, whose
career is given briefly in a previous book, also described the altitude as correct
and noted that he found the plants growing in crevices and hollows in the rocks
above the timber line and with almost nothing in which to take root, the best
plants growing in the part shade of the stunted shrubbery covering the
mountains. Davis also noted that the daytime heat from the sun directly
overhead was most intense, with the nights very cold and damp, the humidity
constantly high and the rainfall frequent even in what was known as the 'dry'
season.

Masdevallia veitchiana is illustrated. Its foliage is similar to that of
Masdevallia coccinea and other members of the genus, but not all members are
large. *Masdevallia rolfeae*, one of the diminutives, has leaves about 5 or 6
centimetres long (a little over 2 inches) growing from a tufty rhizome and with
its small flowers clustered down in the leaves.

Masdevallia schlimii was not introduced into cultivation until the Veitch
collector Burke sent a consignment from Colombia. He found it growing at

175

about 3000 metres (over 9000 feet) on the eastern Cordilleras, completel[y] epiphytic, growing only on old trees which had decayed to the point wher[e] their wood, with other decaying vegetation, proved a most suitable medium.

There are some twenty-four other masdevallias native to Venezuela including *Masdevallia tovarensis*. This beautiful little masdevallia, occupyin[g] a niche for size midway between the largest and smallest, with its pure whit[e] flowers and happy habit of flowering from the same stems for two or thre[e] years, was the subject of exploitation to the same extent as the other over[-] collected species. It was discovered by Wagener in 1849 at a considerabl[e] altitude in Caracas. He sent plants to Germany and the English growe[r] Sigismund Rucker obtained one and flowered it in 1864. It was rare i[n] collections until about 1880 when Low & Co. obtained a consignment. *Masdevallia tovarensis* will grow in cold conditions, but grows and flower[s] better in a moderately warmed glass-house if kept cool and shady in summer.

Some idea of the depredations committed by collectors may be gained from the fact that Sanders' collector Arnold in 1880 consigned 10 000 plants o[f] *Masdevallia tovarensis* to them from Venezuela, followed in 1881 by a further 7000; also 2000 *Masdevallia maculata,* 500 *Masdevallia triangularis* and all the plants he could find of *Masdevallia picturata*, a completely new species.

It is interesting to note the diminished number of plants of *Masdevallia tovarensis* in the second consignment, which probably cleaned out the entire area. It is even more interesting to note that as he described the plants they were of forty to fifty leaves in each. Much of that foliage would have been lost, as masdevallias were notoriously poor travellers and at times whole consignments were lost if collected and packed at the wrong time or in the wrong way. Arnold's consignments for Sanders usually comprised seventy or more large packing cases containing thousands of plants of various genera.

F. C. Lehmann, a collector for Hugh Low & Co., England, was probably the most knowledgeable man of all time about masdevallias. He originally went to Colombia, Peru and Ecuador for this firm about 1876 and consigned a fair amount of material to them. Lehmann later went into business for himself as a collector and exporter and masdevallias became his favorite flower. He also had the extraordinary experience of seeing acres and acres of *Masdevallia coccinea* in flower, in all colors from white to deep fluorescent reds. He collected commercially for some years in Guatemala, Costa Rica and other Central American habitats as well as Colombia.

Lehmann married into a wealthy Colombian family and became German Consul for that State. He devoted a great deal of time to management of a portion of the family business interests, but also much time to his chosen occupation. *Masdevallia rosea* was a centre of intense interest to growers in Europe and Britain, and Lehmann set out to find it. Originally discovered by Hartweg in 1842 in Ecuador, it had been found most difficult to prepare and ship and all attempts had been unsuccessful. As it grew at a high altitude, when it was brought to the intensely hot lowlands it quickly decayed. Its habitat was some 4000 metres up in the Andes.

Lehmann handled his collection most carefully, sailing with it on the ship for Europe. Unfortunately the ship was wrecked on the Azores islands and he managed to save only his masdevallias, risking his life in the process, finally landing them in England.

Lehmann knew where to find some forty to fifty masdevallia species, and prepared and sent quite a lot of dried material to the various herbariums in England and Europe. He spent most of the years between 1876 and 1904 journeying through the South and Central American countries and was unfortunately drowned in a boating accident on the Tibique River in Colombia n December 1903. There is very little on record in English publications about either his career as a collector or as the original finder of many species orchids. He supplied a great deal of material to various authors, particularly on masdevallias. His apparent favorite, *Masdevallia rosea,* is not grown in collections as much as its beauty warrants.

Most reports of the number of plants consigned by collectors are credible. Although those given for Arnold are no different from those of other collectors, he is said to have consigned 40 000 plants of *Masdevallia tovarensis* to Sanders from Tovar. Perhaps it was correct, but 40 000 plants of any orchid species, particularly of such a size as described by Arnold, is a vast number and must be doubted. It enters the class of stories told by the would-be adventurous orchid hunters when the romance of such an occupation had an attraction for a somewhat unsophisticated reading public. For anyone reading the following account of his brief life, however, there is little doubt that reality sometimes may eclipse fantasy.

Frederick Arnold was born in 1860, but very little of his background is known until he became one of Sanders' collectors about twenty years later. In 1881 they despatched him to Merida, Mexico, on the Yucatan peninsula, to collect orchids for them. In the same year he also went to Venezuela for *Cattleya percivaliana,* one of the *Cattleya labiata* affiliates. He collected, prepared and despatched forty packing cases of plants of this species and others including a single plant of a pure white form which apparently was cultivated and owned by a native woman from whom he had great difficulty in obtaining it. On this trip Arnold saw one specimen cattleya plant well over 2 metres in diameter (some 8 feet) and carrying, as nearly as he could estimate the number, some 400 flowers. It was growing on the steep rocky banks of a river at about 1750 metres (6000 feet). During 1881 he also went to Colombia and at and near Santanda, a mining district, he collected and packed 1100 plants of *Odontoglossum triumphans,* 4500 masdevallias, 700 plants of *Cattleya mendelii* and 600 other mixed odontoglossums. Although he was only young, he must have had a busy time. He returned to Europe with this collection.

In 1882 he returned to Venezuela and Colombia to pack and despatch some 100 cases of various orchids. These included thirty-eight cases of *Masdevallia schlimii, Epidendrum atropurpureum (Encyclia cordigera)* and a mixed lot of cattleyas. Arnold knew intuitively when he should collect and despatch the plants and perhaps he was also instructed by either Sander himself or other collectors. He rarely went out collecting until midway through the year and his latest consignment was always packed and gone by October. Unfortunately, other than from meagre verbal reports and still more meagre notes, little is known about the method of operation of the collectors such as Arnold. He did keep a good record of his collections, however.

In 1883 he had an order for odontoglossums from New York, possibly from the American branch of Sanders', and he consigned 118 cases to fill this order. Again we do not know the dimensions of the case, but it would involve a considerable number of plants — and they did not despatch small plants. He also sent eighty-three cases to England. He covered enormous distances during the year and the number and variety of his collection seem incredible when viewed from this end of the next century. He found and despatched to Sanders', plants of cattleyas, zygopetalums, odontoglossums, masdevallias, anguloas, ornithidiums, epidendrums, peristerias, stanhopeas, sobralias and phragmipediums.

Arnold rarely stopped for long and early in 1884 he was still at work collecting odontoglossums and masdevallias. Among the latter he found a new species which measured about 20 centimetres (8 inches) from tip to tip of the dorsal and petals. By March he had packed and despatched no fewer than eighty cases of plants from some of which he carefully removed the new growths which were too soft to stand the journey. By the middle of the year he had packed and sent off about fifty more packing cases. In this period he apparently turned to woven baskets, if they were not used before, and sent a large number of plants packed into sixty of these containers.

During 1884 Arnold suffered bouts of sickness, was beset by thieves and was involved in a revolution, although not taking an active part in it. He nevertheless found time to collect some 400 anguloas, 450 *Phragmipedium schlimii*, 150 *Rodriguezia secunda*, 30 *Stanhopea eburnea*, 100 *Odontoglossum naevium*, 5000 *Odonto. triumphans*, 5000 *Odonto. pescatorei*, 50 *Maxillaria venusta*, 500 *Epidendrum atropurpureum*, 400 *Xylobium hyacinthinum*, 1500 *Miltonia phalaenopsis*, 25 *Acineta humboldtii*, 85 burlingtonias, 150 various epidendrums, 300 physurus, 360 *Sobralia virginalis*, 600 warscewicziellas, as well as a mixed lot of catasetums, mormodes, oncidiums and other orchids. By the end of the year he had sent Sanders' an additional large collection, the last of which was 4000 plants of *Ada aurantiaca*.

In 1885 while still in Venezuela, Arnold started collecting again, particularly *Cattleya gaskelliana*, the whereabouts of which he kept secret, as it was then still a recent discovery. He had to wait until May to collect the plants, as they were still soft and flowering until then. He also visited Trinidad to collect *Diacrium (Caularthron) bicornutum*. It grew so freely there that it could be collected right on the coast, at times without getting out of the boat. It was obvious from his records of that year that he made considerable use of the natives to build up his collections because he records the expenditure of 100 pounds on trade goods. He also recorded his experiences during 1885 in the headwaters of the Orinoco River when collecting *Cattleya superba* (syn. *Cattleya violacea*). Strangely enough, this cattleya flowers in the rainy season in its habitat.

By January 1886, Arnold had travelled far up the Orinoco River to again collect *Cattleya superba*. In June Sanders' received news of his death in San Fernando, Venezuela. It appeared that he was shadowing a rival collector G. T. White to find the origin of a particular species quite unknown to him and stimulating him to get further into some unworked country. His rival did not know he was being followed and it was only by chance that he was forced back along his route and found Arnold lying in a coma and dying of fever. White stayed with Arnold until he died and buried him in the remote place, so far from the coast that it was impossible to take the body back with him. And so ended the remarkable career of a young man of only twenty-five; a term into which he had probably crammed more living than most people would experience in a lifetime.

The number of plants collected by Frederick Arnold must have been verging on 300 000 and possibly more if the number of specimens of *Masdevallia tovarensis* is any guide. There is no real reason to doubt the figure quoted, but at least it does strain the credulity of most orchid growers of the 1980 period.

Cultivation

Although classed as epiphytes, masdevallias have a root system which is moderately coarse and prolific and grows well in the mix usually made up for cymbidiums. As this system becomes quite extensive in good cultivation, plants should not be grown in too small a pot. It is common to find small pieces of *Masdevallia coccinea* on offer, mostly with three or four leaves. In general this is too small a propagation and the genus as a whole should be left in clumps of no fewer than six leaves if possible. Pot drainage should be perfect, as masdevallias prefer to grow undisturbed for some years.

Potting should be such that the bases of the leaves, which are enclosed in pale, thin bracts are just below the rim of the pot. These growths are succulent and attract pests such as slugs and snails. The flowers usually come from the inside of the leaf base on completed growth, new or old. The stems are brittle and succulent in juvenile form but harden up to bear the flowers. Height of the stems varies from species to species, with some of the larger ones like *Masdevallia coccinea* reaching 50 to 60 centimetres (about 2 feet). The flowers of this species are among the largest and may measure up to 6 or 7 centimetres (2 or 3 inches) across the lower sepals. The petals are minute, decadent flower parts, but overall the flower may measure up to 10 or 12 centimetres (4 or 5 inches) from top to bottom.

Most of the cultivated species conform to a pattern or set of conditions which is rather easy to design. They should not become dry at any stage of their annual cycle, but neither should they be grown wet. Paphiopedilums are usually grown in a set of conditions which suit the genus ideally and both these orchids may be cultivated together in moderately shaded conditions. The upper range of temperatures, however, should be watched fairly carefully, as the leaves and flowers scald easily if exposed to the range between the upper 20s and 30 degrees Celsius (about 80 to 90 degrees Fahrenheit).

Masdevallias do not need fertilising as much as more vigorous orchids like Slippers, and the best time to apply weak solutions or moderate amounts of blood and bone with a little hoof and horn is when the leaves are about half grown and new roots or older root activity are noted. Do not use slow-release fertilisers or slow-release pellets.

Black tops on the leaves or black patches usually indicate insufficient fresh air, overwatering, root loss or over-fertilising. Exposure of the plants to winter or cool temperatures in the 6 to 10 degrees Celsius range (40 to 50 degrees Fahrenheit) may also cause foliage disfigurement and even plant loss.

Masdevallias flower at various times during the year, the majority in spring and summer, but they are liable to vary from grower to grower. They are generally unsuitable for semi-tropical or tropical climates and would not stand hot or humid conditions. After the flowers open the plants should be kept cool and shaded and slightly less water should be given, in which conditions the flowers last for some weeks, possibly losing a little of the fluorescent color present when they are fresh. The actual colors of masdevallias *coccinea* and *veitchiana* change with the changing light of bright and dull days, glowing most brilliantly in bright conditions.

Following flowering most masdevallias commence growth, with a dormant period at the end of that phase. Sometimes they may be non-conformist and remain dormant until the next growing season, producing flowers and growth simultaneously. Having no pseudo-bulb system to fall back on, the plants should never be dehydrated, but kept barely damp only in their dormant stages.

The type of pot is immaterial, but a preference would indicate clay pots; preferably again the tubby fern pots rather than deeper types. Repotting should be carried out only in the growing period and just before the plants show new roots, with a break-up of a clone second preference and potting-on the ideal until the plants obviously need handling.

Some idea of the plants cultivated in the days of their popularity may be gauged from an exhibit by Mrs T. B. Hyward in 1907 of eighteen large plants of *Masdevallia tovarensis* which gained the Lindley Medal from the Royal

Horticultural Society. Each of the plants bore about 100 spikes of flower and it is easy to imagine the delightful perfume shed on the surroundings by such a profusion. *Masdevallia tovarensis* is not the only scented masdevallia, but it is the most pronounced.

The principal pests to be watched for are scale insects which may infest the undersides of the leaves and mealy bug which will attack the soft young shoots, flower stems and buds. Slugs and snails will also damage both immature young growths and eat out the 'eyes' at the bases of the leaves as well as quickly destroying the flower buds and stems.

Catasetums
and Cycnoches

Catasetums: This genus was named by L. C. Richard ex Kunth, the origin being two Greek words — *kata* (down) and *seta* (bristle). The reference is to the two spikes which are attached to the column and turn downward in the male flowers. Not all the catasetums have them, however. The genus was named in 1822.

Cycnoches: This genus was named· by Lindley in 1832, again using a combination of two Greek words — *kyknos* (swan) and *auchen* (neck). In this instance the reference is to the slender, curved column of the male flowers, which is visible in the photographs of the genus in the illustrated section.

These two genera belong to the section which also contains mormodes, and there are differences of opinion among the various authorities as to which section the group belongs to. Schlechter's inclusion in the pleuranthae sub-tribe cataseteae is probably the most modern, classifying them as sympodial orchids — that is, growth by lateral shoots from previous growth bases.

The flower spikes come from the base of the various segments of the pseudo-bulbs in both genera.

It was indeed a wise man who put pen to paper about catasetums, cycnoches and the allied genus mormodes for many years following their discovery and absorption into the collections of Britain, Europe and America. How can one analyse them? Most of them are mysterious because of their flowers — one year male, another year female, sometimes both on the one plant in the same year, even (rarely) on the one spike or raceme. Apparently there were also some combinations of both male and female flowers in some years in cultivation, which is normal for most orchid genera but not for catasetums or cycnoches. Orchid cultivation history is full of records of gross abnormalities and insufficient is known about the occurrence of such in nature.

Following that summary of the possibilities, it is worthwhile taking a look at catasetums and cycnoches in the period following their discovery, when their quaint and unpredictable ways of reproduction were not even to be guessed at. Prominent botanists of the period were totally confused and made their judgments on incomplete examinations of the flowers, which was a fault quite readily understood when gauged by the standards of present-day knowledge.

The involved story of clarification of cycnoches was published in the Orchid Society of New South Wales bulletins in 1980. Although the vagaries of catasetums have been understood for many years, why they switch over from one gender to another in flowering is still poorly understood. Some people closely associated with them in their natural surroundings are fairly certain that the stamina of the plants is a determining factor, but the not too remote idea of the plants' predetermination of the prospective seasons relative to seed germination should not be completely disregarded. Birds have some sense of this which has possibly been obliterated in humanity in the process of civilisation, and too frequently we are apt to judge all processes in the light of our own experiences. With plants one cannot explain their reactions in human terms and there are some of us who hold that they 'think'.

The catasetums occur in most of tropical Central and South America. Their leaves are somewhat impermanent and are cast either at the commencement of the dormant period or even through it and the flower spikes appear on the new growths at maturity or slightly before that phase.

Catasetum cristatum became known in Britain about 1824 when a plant from Bahia, Brazil, consigned by G. Don, produced dimorphic flowers, the term used to denote flowers of different gender. Lindley, usually so observant and intuitive, missed the implications spread before his eyes and spoke of 'a curious monster of this plant which we observed on an individual in the Horticultural Society's garden. Among flowers of the ordinary structure, two or three others were observed in which the labellum was precisely of the same nature as that of *Catasetum tridentatum*, that is to say destitute of the crested appendages and perfectly galeate and naked'. As Rolfe remarked, Lindley not only failed to see the significance of the phenomenon but many years afterwards could not credit his own words.

On a later occasion in cultivation of these orchids in Britain an unusual happening was again observed when a plant flowered in the glass-houses of the Duke of Devonshire in 1836, producing flowers such as described by Schomburgk in a following paragraph. Dr Lindley, who had been mistaken in his earlier observations of the 'strange genera', corrected himself and remarked in explanation: 'Nor do I think that as a botanist I could be blamed for these errors, the genera being founded upon characters which no one could *a priori* have suspected could pass into each other in the manner that has now been seen.'

The prehistory of confusion began some time before this. The genus was established by the Frenchman Achille Richard, referred to, perhaps scathingly, by Paxton as a 'traveller', which was something less than a botanist or naturalist. From an unstated source, a plant of the catasetum family flowered in Britain in 1817 at the Kew Gardens and inconsistencies in the flowers were noted. Some were male, some female and others what are now termed hermaphroditic. Little of the comment caused by this unusual instance survives and certainly the real implications were entirely missed.

The fertilisation of flowers of *Catasetum tridentatum* is typical for the genus and is worth noting in an extract from *The Orchid Review* of 1913. Darwin had published a paper entitled 'On the Three Remarkable Sexual Forms of *Catasetum tridentatum*'. It was later shown that the females of three different catasetums passed under the name of *Monachanthus viridis* and that *Myanthus barbatus* was the male of one of them and distinct from *Catasetum tridentatum* with which it had been confused.

Schomburgk originally supplied the key to the puzzle and if his analysis of observations had been heeded a great deal of supposition and mistaken identification could have been avoided. He had noted that the three genera were one and the same thing and based this on the fact that only the plants titled monachanthus bore seed pods and the other supposed two genera none. It took some time and careful analysis to reach these conclusions and Rolfe was apparently the man who first clarified the points. A portion of his analysis follows. Writing at that time (1913) he remarked that only some thirty odd female flowers of the genus had been identified, so that even his previous figures had been revised only a little from a 1902 estimate. However, reverting to the quote on fertilisation, the following Rolfe extract conveys some idea of their peculiarities:

'The economy of fertilisation in the genus is remarkable. The propulsion of the polinia by means of the sensitive antennae was fully explained by Darwin and the method of fertilisation in *Catasetum tridentatum* was afterwards described and illustrated by Cruger, who was able to observe the species in Trinidad where it is common. The visiting insect is described as a large bumble bee, noisy and quarrelsome, which visits the flowers of both sexes for the purpose of gnawing some cellular tissue in the interior of the sac. On visiting the male flowers the pollen masses are thrown on the back of the insect, and Cruger had often seen them flying about with this peculiar looking ornament on them. On subsequently visiting the female flower the pollinia were caught by the upper margin of the stigmatic cavity and were left behind on the retreat of the insect. The function of the sensitive antennae in the sections Eucatasetum and Myanthus is thus apparent, but these organs are not developed in the more primitive Ecirrhosae and Pseudocatasetum, so that other mechanism must be available, which it would be interesting to work out.

'The scarcity of female as compared with male flowers is well known, in connection with which the following note by James Rodway is suggestive: "In some species of catasetum there are male and female flowers, quite distinct in appearance the one from the other, and what is more curious, borne on the same plant at different times. It appears as if the orchid is able to choose whichever of these it is able to bring to perfection. The male necessarily requires a less continuous strain, as it is saved from the labour of ripening the capsules, which takes several months. When, therefore, the plant is comparatively weak, only male flowers are produced, but when the pseudo-bulbs are plump and strong, females." '

Catasetums are uncommon in cultivation in countries outside their natural occurrence because they are ill suited by the conditions applicable to growing mainstream orchids. *Catasetum longifolium* (Lindley) is perhaps a good example of this. It was discovered by Sir Richard Schomburgk in British Guiana, growing almost exclusively on palm trees in swampy areas where the climate for the major part of the year was extremely hot and rainy, at the end of which the weather changed, the plant flowered and then experienced a fairly long, dry hot season during which a great amount of foliage was discarded by the plant. As soon as the rainy season commenced it came into growth and again followed out the cycle. The leaves of this catasetum grow to a metre or more long, but the inflorescence is shorter.

An equally vivid description is given by James Rodway in his book *In The Guiana Forest*: 'In the savannah rises a great eta palm, perhaps sixty feet high, its masses of roots standing above the water as a mound, from whence proceeds the rough but bare stem to a height of fifty feet, where a great dome of fan-shaped leaves crowns its apex... Below the crown stand the remains of a hundred clasping leaf stalks of different ages, their axils filled with decaying vegetable matter in which revel the roots of that unique orchid *Catasetum longifolium*. With ribbon-like flexible leaves streaming downwards and great flower spikes bent outward to greet the sunlight, the plant appears to have no rivals.'

How do we hope to duplicate such a habitat or modify our facilities to have even a glimmer of hope of ever growing such a plant? While this may not be a general set of conditions applicable to the genus as a whole, it is a good example of the type of climate and environment to which most catasetums have adapted.

Catasetum gnomus (Lindley and Reichenbach f.) illustrates quite well the extraordinary shape of flowers of the genus as a whole. It is most variable in color, with plants from different areas being totally dissimilar. It is never a good idea to stipulate the color of the flowers when ordering anything like these catasetums. James Veitch & Sons gained an Award of Merit for *Catasetum gnomus* at a Royal Horticultural Society show in England in 1893, but it would be difficult to win an award for a species such as this in the 1980s. Apparently theirs was an outstanding specimen, possibly just acclimatised and not subjected to the winters for which England was then known or the tremendous smogs caused by burning coal polluting and staining the atmosphere for months on end.

Time and experience serve to drive home to perceptive growers the necessity to recognise variations within species for what they are and to teach them not to be too dogmatic about identification or to perhaps wrongly identify and describe orchids, or to hammer the table on the basis of recognition from printed descriptions, photographs or paintings without actual experience of the genus concerned.

If beauty becomes a consideration then it is most difficult to find one to outdo *Catasetum pileatum* (Nathaniel E. Brown), the synonym for which is *Catasetum bungerothi*. The illustration is sufficient evidence. This catasetum was first recognised about 1882 in a dried specimen from Venezuela. It was confused with other species, as so often occurred in orchid botany and taxonomy derived from such specimens. The collector, Bungeroth, who worked for the Belgian botanist and nurseryman Linden sent the material, which was submitted to Reichenbach. Based on a drawing from the collector, an illustration appeared in the book *Lindenia* in 1886, accompanied by a description. In the same year plants were sold at Stevens' auction rooms on consignment from Linden. One of them bore seven flowers and it was purchased on behalf of Baron Schroder. The best plant of the day brought fifty guineas, the relative value of which may be worked out as being the annual income for a large number of employees in various occupations at that time.

This orchid qualified for an award, an attainment still possible for it at any time. The flowers in that instance were described as ivory white, but as the illustration in this book shows, it also has in the male flower the beautiful form known as the variety *aurea*.

The bracketing of the names Lindley and Reichenbach and the listing of the synonym resulted from the closure of Reichenbach's herbarium material for twenty-five years following his death and a little more information on this is available in *The Orchid Review*, volume 23, page 295.

A collector named Spruce sent dried specimens of the flowers of *Catasetum pileatum* to the Kew herbarium about 1860, but in the confusion following receipt of so many thousands of specimens from all over the world it remained unidentified until it emerged from the pile of material many years later.

An interesting snippet also appears in *The Orchid Review*, in which a resident of Para, north-eastern Brazil, had this to say: 'Did I ever tell you that I had *Catasetum bungerothi* long before Bungeroth discovered it? My plant did not bloom for a long while; when it did, I found it was new and sent half of it to Linden. It was the yellow variety figured last year... Meanwhile Bungeroth had sent the white variety to Linden and it became the type. The plant is Amazonian. The white is from Venezuela and has been long known in Trinidad.' At that time the female flower, which is depicted in the color illustrations, was unknown.

Catasetum fimbriatum (Lindley) began its cultivated life in England under a cloud. *Paxton's Flower Garden* Volume One, a beautiful and instructive book, describes it as follows: '*Catasetum fimbriatum*, alias *Myanthus fimbriatus* ... (is) a terrestrial orchid of unknown origin, with dirty-white and pink flowers. Introduced by the Belgians... It appears to be a species of no great beauty with the habit of *Catasetum cernuum*.' One wonders whether the description may not have been more flattering and effusive had the species been a British nnovation. The description of it was also wrong in noting it as a terrestrial orchid. Few, if any, of the genus could be so classified.

Mormodes, which are bracketed in this section with the cycnoches instead of appearing separately, have bisexual flowers and are non-divergent. A new genus has been formed to take in the catasetums which also have bisexual flowers and they are designated clowesias. This title is included as a sub-genus in *Orchidaceae Brasilienses* by Pabst and Dungs who also include a beautiful set of water-colour illustrations of these strange genera in Volume One of that publication. Two transferees are named in this book, clowesias *rosea* and *warscewiczii*.

In Britain, as far on from the original appreciation of the true characteristics of catasetums as the year 1902 less than half of the known catasetums, numbering some seventy-odd, were recognised in both sexes, according to R. A. Rolfe, at that time Editor of *The Orchid Review*. At the end of that year only twenty-three had been positively identified in both gender, and since that time some thirty species have been added to the genus from subsequent discoveries and naming. It is not to be wondered that even so eminent a naturalist as Sir Charles Darwin was puzzled.

The generic title clowesia was originally attached to the catasetums by John Lindley following the flowering of *Clowesia rosea* by the Rev. John Clowes in Britain about 1840. While the catasetums have flowers of separate sexual character and only occasionally produce imperfect flowers combining both gender, the clowesias never vary. That is not to state emphatically that they never did nor could do so, which again might be dogmatic and perhaps untenable.

Morphologically the plants are similar and their cultivation identical. However, as with so many other genera which have been renamed, the involvement of *Sander's List of Orchid Hybrids* means that the clowesias will continue to be known as catasetums for some time to come.

All told there are more than 100 members of the family and some additions have been made in comparatively recent times. There are also several natural hybrids and the indirect inference is that there may be a number of others included in the total but so far unidentified.

The Rev. John Clowes was born in 1777 and apparently from an early age was charmed by orchids. A graduate of Trinity College, Cambridge, he was attached to Manchester Cathedral. In 1833, on inheriting the family estates, he retired from the ministry and became a more ardent orchidophile. Several species were named in his honor before he died in 1846.

The green-and-white form was first flowered by an Antwerp (Belgium) grower named de Hamis, exhibited at an exhibition in Brussels and awarded a gold medal. This probably prompted the tone of the extract from *Paxton's Flower Garden* as it was commented: 'In this country people would have hardly remarked it'.

The female flower of *Catasetum fimbriatum* appeared in 1891 in England, when a spike bearing two male and two female flowers was shown at a Royal Horticultural Society meeting. This spike was subsequently preserved in the Kew Herbarium. The plant came from a collection owned by W. Wright, the origin being Montevideo. The habitat of the plant is widespread and the labellum more variable than the color of the flowers.

A brief description of one of its habitats is given by a writer in 1908: 'I was on my way to the great and little heard of waterfall of the Iguazu ... in the month of May, the cold, wet mist a little thick ... and there was the plant I now have growing on a dead tree.' Although it is a little unclear whether the plant was growing on the dead tree at the waterfall or in the writer's collection, it is commonly found on that type of host and even on weathered fence post in suitable climates, like so many others of the genus. It is accustomed to very high daytime temperatures and is known to the natives in this South Brazilian area as 'casaea romana' — the Roman coat orchid.

The male flowers of *Catasetum fimbriatum* were known some seven years before the female flowers were identified.

Cycnoches and Mormodes

Cycnoches loddigesii was the plant on which Lindley established the genus; it was sent to Loddiges' nursery in England by J. H. Lance, an English legal personality who for reasons unknown lived for some years prior to 1834 in Surinam (Dutch Guiana), on the north coast of South America, with a border common to Guyana. *Cycnoches loddigesii* was named by Lindley in 1832.

Another plant from the same source bloomed shortly after this with quite different flowers and Lindley named it *Cycnoches cucullata*. Botanists generally were at a loss to explain why two apparently similar plants should produce such different flowers. The solution to the problem came with the production of two spikes on a pseudo-bulb of a plant flowering in the glass-houses of the Horticultural Society. One spike had male flowers, the other female, one *Cycnoches loddigesii*, the other *Cycnoches cucullata*.

Lance also sent a plant to Bateman some time between 1832 and 1834. It flowered soon after with twelve flowers on the spike, which he dried and sent to Reichenbach in Europe. It also was *Cycnoches loddigesii*. Both Bateman and Lindley were impressed by the artistry of Lance, who apparently sent them either drawings or color paintings of the orchids abounding in the area where he lived. When he returned to England in 1834 he brought a large number of various orchids with him.

Cycnoches ventricosum was described from a plant sent to England from Guatemala by G. Ure Skinner. The flowers, dehydrated and long dead on the spike attached to the plant, were identified as male, but the plant bore a huge seed pod. This cycnoches caused more confusion than any other, although probably exaggerated and intensified by the advent of *Cycnoches egertonianum*. But first a little space to *Cycnoches ventricosum*. It is variable in color and the accepted variety *chlorochilon* has sometimes been accorded the rank of separate species without any real right to the privilege. It is a little larger than the type form and lighter in color, the largest and brightest of the varieties. But the variety *warscewiczii* sometimes is passed off as it. Both are lemon-yellow colored.

Where other cycnoches have notable differences in the flowers of the two gender, *Cycnoches ventricosum* has male and female flowers which are remarkably similar, the greatest difference being in the column. In the male flowers the column is long, curved and slender like the neck of a swan artistically portrayed; in the female flower it is short and stubby. Unlike the male flower which carries the pollinia at the tip, the column has only the receptive cavity. One of the remarkable attributes of the genus as a whole, however, is that no matter how different the male flowers are from species to species, the female flowers of many are all remarkably similar and like the flowers of *Cycnoches ventricosum*.

Turning to *Cycnoches egertonianum*, it is perhaps best to refer to the explanation of James Bateman himself. He published in his beautiful book *The Orchidaceae of Mexico and Guatemala* a lithograph of this orchid and for a long time a curious error remained unnoticed. It portrayed flowers of both male and female gender, but as subsequently shown the two female flowers at ie top of the picture, on a separate spike, were identical to the male flowers of *ycnoches ventricosum*, also illustrated in this book, so far as the column at ast was concerned. But let us look at Bateman's frustrating experiences with iis orchid as detailed in *The Orchid Review,* Volume 15, of 1907:

'Among Mr Skinner's earliest Guatemala collections attention was articularly directed to the specimens of a plant which to the habit of a ycnoches joined the long pendulous spikes of a gongora and for the ossession of which, in a living state, no small anxiety was entertained. Some lants were speedily transmitted by Mr Skinner, but these, on flowering, roved to be merely the old *Cycnoches ventricosum*. A mistake was of course uspected, and Mr Skinner being again applied to, sent over a fresh supply of lants, for the authenticity of which he vouched, but these were scarcely ettled in the stove when flowers of *Cycnoches ventricosum* were again roduced. Mr Skinner being importuned for the third time, and being then n the point of returning to this country, determined to take one of the plants inder his special protection during the voyage, which, flowering on the assage, seemed to preclude the possibility of further confusion or lisappointment. The specimens produced at sea were exhibited and the plant tself placed in the stove at Knypersley, where it commenced growing with the utmost vigor. The season of flowering soon arrived, but brought with it a recurrence of the former scene of astonishment and vexation, for the blossoms, instead of those of the coveted novelty, were not distinguishable from the old *Cycnoches ventricosum*. They were still hanging to the stem when the inexplicable plant sent forth a spike of a totally different character and which was, in fact, precisely similar to the specimens gathered in Guatemala, and to those produced on the voyage. It is at present impossible to attempt any explanation of so strange a phenomenon, especially on the supposition that the two forms of flower are analogous to the male and female blossoms of other tribes, for *Cycnoches ventricosum* alone not infrequently perfects seeds. The species (if such it may be regarded) was named in honor of Sir Philip Egerton, before any of its eccentricities had been discovered, otherwise the compliment might have been deemed a dubious one.'

Bateman died in 1898 and it was not until shortly before his death that Rolfe helped to solve the riddle of the lithograph in Lindley's book. In this account of the misunderstanding of the genus some confusing aspects still remain. It helped neither Lindley nor Bateman to receive from another grower a spike of five flowers, of which one was green, two were purple and two mottled green and purple. No explanation of this phenomenon is possible other than that the spike bore flowers of two separate gender and at least two composite flowers, occasionally termed 'hermaphrodite', which bear both pollen and ovaries, although possibly they would be sterile.

This spike was apparently from *Cycnoches egertonianum*, but it was not preserved and the plant was subsequently lost, to join all the other strange mysteries attached to the genus. The male inflorescence of this cycnoches grows up to a metre and a half long, but the female inflorescence is usually shorter and consists of only a few flowers on a short stem. It was named in 1849 by Bateman after the man in whose collection it originally flowered. This strange orchid is native to extensive areas of Central and South America and, like most of the genus, with the type of weather pattern in all those localities of lowland tropical heat suiting its proliferation.

Cycnoches pentadactylon, among the more colorful of the species, might almost be imagined, considering its name, to have an association with the dinosaurs. The shape of the flowers may also add to that impression. It was first described by John Lindley, who had only a passing knowledge of the species he was handling and was tentative about making firm pronouncement about its identity. His difficulty is expressed in his addendum, when he alludes to the whole group, catasetums, cycnoches and mormodes, as an extraordinar collection 'among which we find the most astonishing deviations from ordinary structure and the most startling variations from what appears to b the rule in other parts of the organic world... If we were informed that the camelopard in the Zoological Gardens had shortened the vertebrae of its neck till it was no longer than a cow's, or that the kangaroo had exchanged its tai for the switch of a Shetland pony, a more surprising thing would not b announced than those changes with which we are now familiar in this group o orchidaceae'.

The female flower of the species was unknown until appearing about 1889 on a plant which had until then always produced only male flowers.

The technique of growing and flowering *Cycnoches pentadactylon* was mastered by many early cultivators and one instance is worth noting. James Simmon, the orchid grower and gardener for W. Mann, produced a plant carrying six spikes of flower, three on one pseudo-bulb, two on another and a single on the third, in all carrying 247 flowers. The photograph accompanying the report shows it fully leafed at the time it was presented for consideration of the Royal Horticultural Society, who gave it an Award of Merit at their meeting in January 1893, which was just past midwinter.

This specimen, however, must have been far surpassed in the habitat according to the description of Edward Rand, who lived in Para, Brazil. He was most interested in the genus, as well as catasetums and mormodes, of which he had a large collection. He considered it the most beautiful and fragrant of all the Amazonian orchids and had seen plants with pseudo-bulbs a metre tall (about 3 feet) and about 5 centimetres in diameter (2 inches), carrying both gender of flowers on the same pseudo-bulbs. The male flowers, numbering some fifty to seventy flowers, were carried on the upper parts of the pseudo-bulbs, the females on the lower parts and borne only in threes or fours. As Rand remarked, a single flower will perfume the air for metres around the plant, filling it with a delicious vanilla-like fragrance.

Mormodes

These orchids, although morphologically similar to the previous two genera, do not possess the same eccentric flowering pattern. However, they too are most curious in their proliferation techniques.

Lindley remarked of mormodes: 'We find among them the most astonishing deviations from ordinary structure and the most startling variations from what appears to be the rule in other parts of the organic world.' Some explain these strange characteristics as floral evolution over great periods of time to ensure that the species continue. But it could be argued against these views that continuous development through hybridism and survival of conforming types to climatic, evolutionary and pollinating agents could just as easily be the determinants, brought about over the migratory paths the plants have followed in various countries over periods quite unimaginable.

For instance, how and why did mormodes develop pollinatory systems which contort the column and place it in the position where it flicks the pollen out at the slightest touch on its tip? By just what stretch of imagination can we visualise the development of the flower to conform to the habits of an insect? Why does the insect approach the flower by this path if not directed to do so by the conformation of the flower? Who did it all? Strange, too, is the way the human mind gives up so easily when faced with this type of questioning.

One of the first of the species brought into cultivation was *Mormodes xatum*, sent from Mexico to England by a collector named Ross somewhere about 1842. The genus was named by Lindley in 1836 and the name refers to the strange appearance of the flowers. It is derived from the Greek word *ormo*, meaning a phantom or frightful object, 'which represent the most astonishing deviations from ordinary structure and the most startling variations from what appears to be the rule in other parts of the organic world'.

It is not strange that these orchids were confused with the catasetums and even as late after their discovery as 1885 there was a lot of mistaken identification and *Mormodes luxatum* was thought to belong to the monocanthus' which Lindley originally confused with the catasetums and cycnoches.

The cultivation of mormodes parallels that of these two orchids; they have the same periodic dormancy and growth, casting their leaves and renewing the root system annually.

Observant growers noted one feature common to all mormodes in the way the root system tends to vertical habit, away from the potting material surface. They are not alone in this habit, which one may also find in the species *Cymbidium tracyanum*, *Dendrobium speciosum* and many other orchids. I prefer to regard this habit as the formation of a food trap rather than a plant eccentricity, as previously noted. (See illustration on page 109.)

H. A. Burberry, a noted grower of some 100 years ago, had this to say of these three genera: 'Those quaint orchids cycnoches, catasetum and mormodes have now finished flowering and must be given a long dry rest throughout the winter months. They object to a cold temperature at any time, even when they are perfectly dry and resting. They will pass the winter very well at the warmest and dryest end of the cattleya house, or it will be quite safe to keep them in the East Indian department altogether. Too much cold and wet is the ruination of this class of orchid; even when in full growth during summer, and when the compost sparkles with bristling live roots it is necessary to water very carefully, otherwise the new growths may damp off. The roots of all the above species invariably perish when the plants are resting, but this fact does not seem to much matter so long as new compost, small receptacles and plenty of warmth is given when they again start to grow in the spring.'

Like most of his contemporaries, he understood the genera very well. Little need be added to that short paragraph to summarise what they need for their welfare.

In cultivation catasetums, cycnoches and mormodes are better grown in wooden slat baskets. They grow on dead wood more frequently than on other hosts, although some grow on live trees and palms. If pot-grown the plant habit of casting off the root system as well as the leaves could cause problems unless the plants are repotted each year. The new roots would hardly enter a potting material contaminated by rotting root systems. If grown in slat baskets the plants may be hung away from the reach of the hose during their dormant stage.

The annual cycle is rather sharply divided into two, with growth in conditions of high humidity and warmth, the dormant stage one of aridity in the container but fairly humid air conditions. The amount of light the plants will tolerate is also related to the two seasons, with light shade provided in the growth phase and the plants able to withstand fairly bright light when defoliated. Even if one or two leaves remain over the dormant period they will be cast almost as soon as the plants recommence activity and produce new shoots and roots.

Watering should be controlled at all times, but in the early growth stage when these orchids are beginning to awaken, the amount of water should b enough to only dampen the potting material. As the root activity increases th water should be increased until in the full flush of growth and maturing th plants may be flooded each time they get to the just damp stage. The whorl c leaves in juvenile growths should be kept free of excess water or sprayed wit an anti-fungus pesticide to prevent mould and disease spores from getting hold and rotting out the growths. As the new leaves are soft and prone t attack by red spider and other pests they should be sprayed with Capthion o something similar, and although the leaves become patchy with the residue thi may be sponged off when the danger period is passed or it is intended t exhibit the plants.

Temperatures throughout the year should be fairly high, that is withi cattleya range and above, with an absolute minimum of 15 degrees Celsiu (about 60 degrees Fahrenheit) being the aim. It is much easier to cultivate thes orchids in subtropical or suitable tropical areas than in glass-house condition in cooler regions, as a better division of the seasons is natural in such climates In either season, the wet or the dry, air flow about the plants is a great aid a catasetums, cycnoches and mormodes are certainly fresh-air plants. Stagnatior can lead to loss of new growth, old growths and even pseudo-bulbs ir dormancy.

Root systems of catasetums and cycnoches are medium type, in some profuse and a times aerial, as illustrated in the photographs, in others not sc dense and at times even sparse. In general it is almost completely lost and regenerated each year, which may create problems with growing mediums. The best of these is probably a pine-bark combination, but others may be thought up and partial replacement of material each growing season considered. While the mix should be free draining, it should also contain some moisture conservation property if the plants are grown suspended in free air rather than benched, a proposition they enjoy. Moisture retention should be achieved by using rotting wood, leaf content (although in general these plants avoid it in natural habitats), peanut shells or even peat-moss. Addition of fresh sphagnum moss to the surface of growing materials at regeneration will help to build a healthy root system.

Overwatering in the flush of growth is scarcely possible with good temperature maintenance. For this it may be necessary to consider a booster system like a fan-heater for cooler climates to keep the temperature above about 15 degrees Celsius (about 60 degrees Fahrenheit). Continuity of leaf and root growth, once started, is essential for plant development and flowering. The spikes appear almost as the growth matures, but wide variations from this are possible. Once visible they should be kept free of excess water and pests and the flowers, once they commence to open, kept dry and clean.

With slat basket culture watering is best and more thoroughly carried out by soaking the container in a shallow dish of water to which very weak nutrients may be added, the container left to soak for up to five minutes or more. Normal hose watering of these containers is often sketchy and incomplete despite a careful approach to it. Pot-grown plants are more difficult to handle, but this does not mean the system is impossible; it simply takes a little more time and care than an open system where almost total plant activity can be monitored.

There is an understandable urge, once flower spikes appear on any orchids, to apply fertilisers to boost the number of flowers or their size. However, the length of the spike, the number of flowers and their size have been predetermined long before this by the awakening of the plant into growth, the eather patterns and so many other small factors that fertilisers are simply an afterthought. Whatever fertiliser is used should be in weak solution at all times, tapering off once the flowers begin to open and ending as the spike develops. The general growing conditions will determine how long the flowers last while taking into account the plant habit anyway.

Following flowering the three genera and even other similar orchids round out their pseudo-bulbs and add a little to height before slipping into their dormant stage. This is usually indicated by a slight yellowing of the foliage on the lower parts of the pseudo-bulbs, a condition slowly progressing toward the tip of the growths and finally a leafless condition. Although root loss occurs at the same time, the pseudo-bulbs should not shrivel. This pattern may not be consistent year after year, but it is a good general average performance. Leaves should not be cast in the growing phase and if this happens the cause should be sought out and not repeated if it is a cultural failure.

Propagation of the genera may be slow because the plants do not proliferate as well in cultivation as they do naturally. While it is uncommon for two growth 'eyes' to break from the base of the pseudo-bulbs, it will happen if the growing conditions are right. It is not good culture to sever the pseudo-bulbs into units of less than two and even this is unwise if there is a possibility of getting a better 'cut' the following year.

In repotting some care should be taken to keep the bases of the pseudo-bulbs above the potting mix, as the growth 'eyes' tend to rot out if buried. The addition of growing sphagnum moss to the top of the mix seldom causes this loss and it does hasten production of new roots from the bases of very immature shoots. If the basal 'eyes' should all be lost the pseudo-bulbs may produce new shoots from higher up the growths. Although these shoots seem to be progressively weaker as they distance from the dead basal 'eyes', at least plants may be saved from them. It does involve, however, peculiar potting methods such as laying the pseudo-bulbs on their sides on the surface of the mix so that roots may enter the moss or mix without needing to travel too far.

Red spider is one of the worst pests which attack these genera and they will be found on the undersides of the leaves. Aphids will also proliferate on the flower stems and buds and should be killed off with a fine misting of 50 per cent water and 50 per cent methylated spirits, a suitable treatment also for red spider.

Maxillarias

This genus was named by Ruiz and Pavon in 1794, with the root of the title in the Latin word *maxilla*, loosely translated as 'jawbone'. In the type form the column and labellum appeared similar to the jaws of an insect, but in many of the flowers, such as *Maxillaria picta,* even the petals bear this resemblance. Ruiz and Pavon, Spanish botanists, collected in Peru in the years 1777 to 1788 but it was Dr John Lindley, the English botanist, who finally revised the inclusions in the genus and reallocated some of them.

Maxillarias grow in most Central and South American States and the Caribbean islands, also at all altitudes, some withstanding almost extreme low temperatures in the 6 degrees Celsius range (about 42 degrees Fahrenheit). Among the warmer growing species is *Maxillaria sanderana*, which prefers a minimum of about 15 degrees Celsius (about 59 degrees Fahrenheit). *Maxillaria porphyrostele* is almost a garden plant in moderate climates and down to the already mentioned minimum.

In earlier times Lindley grouped lycastes and many other orchids in a general species level under the name of maxillarias and a great amount of separation has gone on ever since. The maxillarias comprise a large genus, mostly epiphytic, some rupicolous or lithophytic. In Peru alone, the original collecting area for Ruiz and Pavon, there are more than ninety known and named species, of which a number are still known by synonyms, mostly a result of different nationals collecting and sending their plants to various herbariums in England, Europe and America. There is also a persistence of binominals which cause confusion and sometimes even arguments.

The habit of the general run of the genus could be described as a system of clustered pseudo-bulbs on a close-set rhizome and with corresponding short root systems. Variations naturally occur, with some, such as the species *Maxillaria tenuifolia*, having the ascending type of rhizome common to a number of oncidiums.

Maxillaria flowers are mostly borne as singles from the bases of pseudo-bulbs almost as they mature. Most cannot be mistaken for new growths, which are flattened and pointed. The buds appear from the sheathing bracts at the bases of the bulbs in the same manner as the growths, but will seldom come from older pseudo-bulbs.

There are usually only one or two growth 'eyes' at the base of the pseudo-bulbs and if the plants are buried in potting mixes they will possibly rot out and the expected proliferation common to most of the genus will not occur. They reach their ultimate in large aggregations of pseudo-bulbs all bearing flowers.

In a manner common to most epiphytes, maxillaria species have their own particular host trees and some will be found only on that type of tree and no other. Lithophytes should not be regarded as any different and may grow on only one type of rock surface, whether it is limestone, sandstone, granite or any other type. It is little wonder when taken into common cultivation that some of the species will thrive where others languish. Although we need to

·educe them to a common cultivation program there is still scope for
experiment where members of the genus appear to be unsuited, with the root
system always telling the story for the rest of the plant.

Maxillarias had the same phases of popularity at their introduction and
subsequent discard which occurred with other genera, each having its turn to a
greater or lesser degree. Novelty caused their popularity in Britain about the
middle of the nineteenth century, although the original introduction occurred
much earlier. The collector Henchmann sent *Maxillaria variabilis* to Europe
from Mexico about 1837. It also grows in countries further south. It differs
from the general run of the genus in adopting a scandent habit like some of the
oncidiums and other climbers. Some, indeed, have quite a long rhizome
between the pseudo-bulbs. Single flowers from the base of the newly formed
pseudo-bulbs are not a general rule, as some species have trailing spikes with
terminal flowers numbering ten or more.

Maxillaria variabilis was brought into England in quantity by Low & Co.
about the same time as it appeared in Europe, the flowers varying from pale
colors through to deep purple.

Mrs Harrison of Liverpool, England, who introduced so many beautiful
Brazilian orchids, flowered *Maxillaria picta* in 1831. It was sent to her by a
relative living there from the source of so many lovely orchids, the Sierra dos
Orgaos, north-east of Rio de Janeiro. The nurseryman Loddiges imported
Maxillaria picta in quantity in the following years. It is easily recognised by its
canary yellow flowers, the color prominent on the outside of the sepals and
petals in purple-red bars instead of the inside. *Maxillaria prophyrostele* is
frequently mistaken for it. The flowers of both are fragrant. The flowering
season for both is variable, but usually the last named species flowers in early
winter or late autumn following the maturing of the pseudo-bulbs.

Long after the genus had passed its zenith of cultivation new species were
continually introduced, including the beautiful *Maxillaria longissima,*
collected and despatched from Colombia just before 1900. Sir Trevor
Lawrence flowered it well enough to receive a First Class Certificate for his
efforts. The flowers are densely spotted with red-purple on the 10 centimetre
long petals and sepals, with even darker shades in the central parts of the
flowers. Some varieties have an almost clear, creamy colored area midway
from tip to base of the petals. It is among the larger flowers of the genus and
scented like *Maxillaria picta..*

Maxillaria sanderana would probably be considered the most prominent
member of the genus. It was discovered by collector Edward Klaboch in
Ecuador about 1880 at some 1000 metres (over 3000 feet) and introduced to
cultivation by Sanders' in 1883. Baron Schroder, an ardent bidder for
novelties at sales rooms and nurseries, flowered and exhibited it at an orchid
conference at South Kensington, London, in 1885. The Royal Horticultural
Society sponsored this conference and a record was created with the prize
money of £184. That was rather small change considering the amount
expended on plants by the connoisseurs.

However, let us again digress into history to consider just what this
conference was. At the time it was the greatest event which had occurred in
cultivated orchid history. The gentlemen exhibitors, naturally, were mentioned
first, the trade exhibitors last. But all contributed, with Sir Trevor Lawrence
heading the list with 64 plants, followed by W. Lee with 72, the Duke of
Devonshire with 40, Baron Schroder a lesser number but having most of the
best plants in the show. The total number of genera exhibited was 56, with 347
different species. Perhaps readers will note those numbers and reflect on the
small number of genera and species exhibited in shows in the late years of the

twentieth century. The prize money would scarcely buy any of the best plant exhibited in the show, but many suitable silver trophies were also given — and in that period silver was taken to mean silver and not plate. It is refreshing to get carried away by history, but away to the maxillarias again.

Some flowers in the genus are not spectacular, but *Maxilaria sanderana* is one of the exceptions. The plant produces its flowers from the base of the pseudo-bulbs and frequently downward, therefore it should be grown in a fashion to give it scope to do so, much the same as for stanhopeas. The heavy texture of the flowers, their coloring and the perfume make it an outstanding species, but it is useless except in moderate climates, whether glass-house grown or as an outdoor subject.

Maxillaria porphyrostele is probably the most commonly grown of the genus because of its durability and ease of culture. As remarked previously, it is morphologically similar to *Maxillaria picta,* but the latter usually has longer foliage. The column of *Maxillaria porphyrostele* may be deep purple and this contrast to the pale yellow of the flowers makes it most attractive in well-flowered plants. It was introduced from Brazil into English glass-houses by nurseryman William Bull about 1873.

These are only a few members of a large genus which inhabits mostly light forest country, growing in half shade, but with the type of foliage which will withstand strong light and cold winds without showing the ravages of poor conditions. Morphologically they vary in plant size, with *Maxillaria sanderana* probably the largest-growing of them all and standing leaves up to 40 or more centimetres (about 16 inches).

In cultivation they should be treated as epiphytes, some pot-grown, some in wire baskets and slat baskets, particularly the species *Maxillaria sanderana*, as illustrated in the color photographs. Most of the genus prefer to grow into large undisturbed plants and small propagations are always slow to get away and make up into flowering specimens.

Potting or growing materials may vary according to cultivation, but generally should be based on bark mixes which will withstand drying out and allow for reabsorption of moisture. The rest phase of some maxillarias may be as long as six months, but others may be in continual growth and flowering phases through the year, depending on the species cultivated. It is only by watching what the plants are doing that this can be noted. A topping of growing sphagnum moss may suit very well in the restarting stages after dormancy, as it will prevent the potting material from drying out too quickly and promote new roots.

The root systems of most maxillarias are a little more permanent than some of the epiphytes and surface growth rather than immersion in potting mixes seems to suit them. This leads to cork slab, tree-fern or sections of suitable tree limbs rather than pots as growing positions. Again, reference to the pictures on growing systems may give some new or unorthodox ideas in their cultivation.

Temperatures recommended for maxillarias vary considerably, at times colored by local knowledge and forgetting how much climates may vary from country to country and State to State or even getting down to the street-to-street level in one suburb. Some background information is always valuable when it refers to altitude. In this respect, it would be inadvisable to grow *Maxillaria sanderana* in lower temperature minimums than 12 degrees Celsius (about 52 degrees Fahrenheit) summer or winter, as its habitat is at altitude 1000 metres (over 3000 feet) and slightly lower in a region almost on the equator.

The climate associated with these factors would be tropical, yet not with the humidity associated with a sea-level habitat in an equatorial region. Similarly, those species from higher altitudes, such as *Maxillaria porphyrostele*, although in a cooler climate, would be in areas where wind currents would vary from fresh to strong almost throughout the year.

Watering maxillarias should be governed by the various stages through which the species grow. First stage is appearance of small green shoots at the base of the pseudo-bulbs, which on some at starting could frequently be mistaken for flower stems. Without knowing what they are, water should be applied sparingly if at all and once they are perceptibly grown the amount of water given should be increased slightly at each application, particularly if root action can be established or is apparent. In full growth the plants may be thoroughly watered every second or third day as necessary, with an occasional lapse of four or five days to allow the plants to almost dry out. In the dormant phase the plants should go without water almost completely, disregarding what shrivelling occurs, but atmospheric moisture should be consistent with normal glass-house conditions.

In cultivating the species outdoors, which is possible and advisable in areas where there is no frost, the plants may be left to nature during the dormant phases and watered only in times of poor rainfall or hot, drying conditions. In the growing stages it is almost impossible to overwater outdoor-grown plants. In borderline conditions, such as those in which the illustrated plants are grown, it is surprising how some of the species accommodate to adverse and opposite weather cycles to which they are normally accustomed. They are apt to miss flowering one year in every three and the growth phase may extend beyond that normally expected. This produces an out-of-phase system and a pick-up of normal phase for flowering at the right season every three years. It is all very complicated to describe and analyse, but watching the plants go through their cycles makes it quite clear.

If plants are potted in bark mediums and are dried out at the onset of the dormant period a top-dressing of sphagnum moss helps to recondition the bark on resumption of the growth cycle. Roots may adhere to it, but the moss should later be removed.

With *Maxillaria sanderana* sphagnum moss should be used to line the wire basket usually holding the plant. It should, however, be only a thin layer against the wire. If the moss lining is too bulky the roots will probably suffer in the long run and the viability of the plant be seriously affected. A far better lining is either the husk or fibre from elk or stag ferns, again only a thin layer through which the flower spikes can penetrate easily. *Maxillaria sanderana* is a very poor plant to try adapting to normal potting systems.

Flowering habits vary considerably, from those which produce blooms on new growths before maturity to those which almost mature before the flowers open. Some flower in winter, but most in spring to early summer. In either northern or southern hemispheres the summer is almost exclusively the growing time for maxillarias, during which they display their hardiness in the bright light most will tolerate.

Fertilisers for this genus may be a little different from those applied to other epiphytes. If liquids are used they should be very weak applications in the later growth stages and stopped as soon as the pseudo-bulbs approach maturity.

Solid fertilisers such as hoof and horn or blood and bone should be applied sparingly to glass-house grown plants, but a bit more liberally to outdoor-grown plants. The usual rate would be as much as would cover and heap on a 10 cent piece for a 10 or 12 centimetre pot, applied as soon as root growth is noticed, as it takes some time to break down. This would also apply to any of the slow-release fertilisers, which should be completely dissipated, preferably by the time the pseudo-bulbs are maturing. Any fertiliser carry-over is adverse and may sour the potting medium.

Plants mounted on cork slabs or any other type of mount should be immersed in a bucket of water containing one small teaspoon of Aquasol or similar fertiliser, plus one large teaspoon of Maxicrop or other organic derivative for a couple of minutes once a week or less frequently.

All sorts of variations may be thought up, but the plants will suffer from overfertilising just as much as from too little. If the roots are destroyed for any reason the rehabilitation of maxillarias may take from two to three years and result in loss of most of the leaves. Any potting mix should be capable of retaining a little moisture, but all excess water should be able to run freely from the pot almost as soon as applied. It is much harder to overwater slab-grown or outdoor-grown plants.

Phalaenopsis

The genus was named by Karl Ludwig Blume in 1825, but the history of these plants commenced about seventy-five years earlier. The name is derived from the Greek words *phalaina* — a moth, and *opsis* — appearance, and the flowers are aptly named, as the illustrations show. Some philosophical thought could also be given to the amazing resemblance of these orchids to *Dendrobium phalaenopsis.*

The history of the genus commenced about 1750 when a traveller named Osbeck, on his way back to Europe from China, called at Western Java and came into possession of a spike of beautiful white flowers. These he dried and pressed and sent to Linnaeus, who could probably be called the father of systematic taxonomy. Linnaeus called it *Epidendrum amabilis* and this flower spike became the type specimen for the flowers of the species. His original flowers of *Phalaenopsis amabilis* were still held in fairly good condition some 150 years later and possibly are still carefully treasured. It was also known to George Eberhard Rumph (also known as Rumphius), author of *Herbarium Amboinense,* who named it *Angraecum album.* It was also known over the years following its discovery as a cymbidium in a résumé by Swartz and later renamed a phalaenopsis by Blume, still with the species name of *amabilis.*

Phalaenopsis amabilis appeared in John Lindley's *Genera and Species of Orchidaceous Plants,* although still not in cultivation in Europe or England. A collector or interested person named Cuming, who lived in the Philippine Islands, later sent plants to Lindley which he thought were *Phalaenopsis amabilis.* Finally Lindley obtained plants from the original area in West Java which, he thought, were not the same as *Phalaenopsis amabilis* and he named this species *Phalaenopsis grandiflora.* This was corrected by the German botanist Reichenbach. Meanwhile another consignment of plants was imported from West Java and they also were thought to be another species and were named *Phalaenopsis rimestadiana.*.

Australia also proved to have a species from the northern areas of Cape York peninsula and it was named *Phalaenopsis rosenstromii.*

With minor differences, no doubt evolutionary in separate environments, these species were later consolidated under the name of *Phalaenopsis amabilis. Phalaenopsis amabilis* var. *rosenstromii* may be said to be a species which has broken the Wallace Line, as it is unlikely to have migrated northward to the separate development of the variety *Phalaenopsis amabilis* var. *rimestadiana* of Java, or, indeed, any of the other species.

The Australian phalaenopsis, in its separate development, is now becoming rare through over-collection and forest destruction, which is a form of vandalism however it is done. It was found originally by Rosenstrom, growing high on large trees in the Daintree River area about 1907. Usually it has fewer flowers than its counterparts in Java and elsewhere.

Some of the notes on collection of various phalaenopsis are very interesting and condensed into a book such as this they do not reveal all the history of a beautiful genus. It should not be thought that the better known and more used species for producing the hybrids of the 1980 period are the sole representatives of a small genus. The habitat of the genus as a whole is widespread, most of the countries of the south-west Pacific region having representatives on even the smallest islands at times. Phalaenopsis are lowland tropical orchids thriving in conditions which are almost intolerable for humanity.

Paxton noted in his *Magazine of Botany* in 1847: 'It [referring to *Phalaenopsis amabilis*] has the merit of continuing a long time in blossom, one single plant in the Royal Gardens, Kew, having been in bloom during the whole of the present winter.' The English winters being what they are, it must have been an achievement to keep the flowers clear and unspotted during that time.

The Royal Horticultural Society sent a collector to China about 1840 to gather various genera for the members and after carrying out his assignment he visited the Philippines about 1845. He packed a consignment of *Phalaenopsis aphrodite* (another variant name for *Phalaenopsis amabilis*) and sent it off to England. Included were some very large specimen plants and the whole consignment cost him only a matter of a few pounds. The specimen plants were natural and the records show that the branching rhizomes of some of the plants had up to eight and more heads. *Phalaenopsis amabilis* is still known as *Phalaenopsis aphrodite* to some people, a name originally conferred on the species by Reichenbach.

Early commercial exploitation of the genus was disastrous, as nearly all the plants in large consignments rotted during the journey to England and Europe from Java and the Philippines. Never defeated for long, either the collectors or the agents, or possibly the nurserymen such as Veitch, devised the method of cutting the roots back to about 10 centimetres (about 3 or 4 inches). The plants were then tied to small slabs of wood or fern or even sticks about 15 centimetres long (about 6 inches). They then waited for the roots to grow on to them before packing and shipping the plants. The correct season for gathering and the proper way to partially dehydrate the plants also made the proposition lucrative and successful. In the packing sheds many thousands of plants were treated each year and consigned to the various markets, as illustrated in the photograph, page 199.

Phalaenopsis schillerana is one of the most colorful of the Philippines species. In addition to its shell-pink to rose-pink flowers it has most attractive dark green foliage barred and marked with greyish white. It has long, branching spikes of flower and it is not uncommon for a plant to produce three or four of these spikes at once, carrying anything up to 200 or 300 flowers. Warner, an English grower, sent a plant to the St Petersburg Exhibition in Russia in 1869 with 120 flowers open at the time it was despatched. There is meagre information about that feat, but no doubt it was an interesting exercise in transport for those times. Another authentic report recorded in *The Gardeners' Chronicle* for 1875 tells of Lady Ashburton, whose gardener produced a plant carrying three spikes with 378 fully opened flowers. Modern equivalents are rare indeed, but they do occur.

Phalaenopsis leucorrhoda and *Phalaenopsis intermedia* are synonymous but were once thought to be distinct because of different sources of the plants. *Phalaenopsis intermedia* was sent to Veitchs' nursery by Thomas Lobb, whose brief biography is given in *Growing Orchids* — Book Two. He sent it to them about 1852 from the Philippines and it was noted by Lindley in *Paxton's Flower Garden* as a probable natural cross-pollination of the two species *Phalaenopsis aphrodite* and *Phalaenopsis rosea,* the first occurrence of a tropical natural hybrid to be noted in England. Veitch's nursery subsequently

Part of a consignment of *Phalaenopsis schillerana* taken from the Philippine Islands about 1900. This may convey some idea of the depredations of plant gatherers as was possibly equalled by many others operating in the area for the commercial distributors.

proved the speculation correct some thirty-three years later when they flowered a Seden cross-pollination between the two species.

R. A. Rolfe described the original plant and flower in *The Gardeners' Chronicle* of 1886 and in a tribute to the perceptiveness and skill of Lindley he remarked: '. . . the shrewdness of Lindley's observation will be inferred when it is remembered that *Calanthe* x Dominyi, the first artificial hybrid among orchids, did not flower until 1856'.

Phalaenopsis rosea is one of the smaller Philippines species, the flowers about half the size of *Phalaenopsis schillerana*. At the time Thomas Lobb collected plants in that region he remarked that *Phalaenopsis rosea* was particularly common around the Manila area, growing thickly along the borders of the streams and in a climate of high temperature and extreme humidity. He found it there first about 1848 and sent samples to Veitch's nursery, sending larger consignments about 1852, as noted in a previous paragraph.

The largest foliage of the genus is borne by *Phalaenopsis violacea* (Teijsman), found by him in Sumatra in 1859. The flowers are sparse, growing on a short stem almost in the axil of the leaves, pale creamy yellow and purple colored and quite small considering the size of the plant. Singapore Botanic Gardens were instrumental in sending plants to a grower in Cornwall and to the Chelsea Gardens, where they flowered in the 1860 period. The collector Curtis later sent more plants to England when he was in the region. *Phalaenopsis violacea* has a delightful perfume.

Phalaenopsis rosea has been renamed *Phalaenopsis equestris,* the name originally given by Reichenbach. Most authorities now recognise the transfer, but growers seem to prefer its synonym, which may also be said to a degree of *Phalaenopsis amabilis*. Reichenbach also named *Phalaenopsis schillerana* after the Hamburg grower Schiller. There was never any of the confusion surrounding other members of the genus and it has always been so known.

199

Taken generally, the whole of the family, although related to such orchids as the Australian sarcochilus, is very similar morphologically.

It seemed to become necessary in the 1970-80 period to look for something different from what became the pink and white monotony of these orchids which were raised in so many hundreds of thousands. Breaking out into new colors was accomplished with at times quite small species and to look at the catalogues of the 1980 decade is something very different indeed, with considerable branching out into other genera, particularly the doritis. What was sought to be avoided in other genera, namely stripes, became one of the high marks of the phalaenopsis hybrids. It is common to have seedlings flowering within two years of removal from flasks and in the right climates the plants grow to their maximum production size in four years. In cool-climate glass-house culture, however, that would be asking a little too much from them.

The genus cannot be left without reference to some of the inter-generic hybrids containing phalaenopsis. Without doubt one of the most interesting of the 1960-1980 period were the sarcanopsis developed first by William and Jean Cannons, of Wayside Orchids, New South Wales. About 1963 they experimented with sarcochilus as an introduction to the phalaenopsis. After some difficulty they managed to get viable seed and produced three hybrid strains from *Sarcochilus hartmannii* with *Phalaenopsis schillerana*, *Phalaenopsis* Aristocrat and a large white unnamed flower. The resultant seedlings were named, in the order of the parent phalaenopsis, *Sarcanopsis* Jean Cannons, *Sarcanopsis* Macquarie Sunset and *Sarcanopsis* Macquarie Lilac. Although few seedlings resulted, the best of them, *Sarcanopsis* Macquarie Sunset, was an outstanding primary hybrid but a recalcitrant propagator. Two of these sarcanopsis are illustrated and it is a tribute to the hardiness of *Sarcanopsis* Macquarie Lilac that I grew and flowered a propagation of this orchid completely outdoors in southern Victoria under the same conditions as I grow sarcochilus, attached to casuarina trees. The best of these hybrids, Macquarie Sunset, is moderate size. The large white phalaenopsis used to produce *Phalaenopsis* Macquarie Lilac was later named *Phalaenopsis* Federal Monarch.

As a genus of tropical orchids which nearly all originate in humid lowland regions, phalaenopsis should be grown in conditions specially designed to give them this type of environment. As few other orchids will tolerate the year-round environment so provided, they should be grown almost as an isolated genus with the temperature adjusted automatically if it falls below about 18 degrees Celsius (about 65 degrees Fahrenheit), a rather expensive procedure in colder climates. The upper limits must be handled with discretion, but provided shade and humidity are adequate they will safely withstand temperatures in excess of 35 degrees Celsius (about 95 degrees Fahrenheit). The amount and quality of the flowers is affected by lower temperatures and while a little latitude may be allowed with the minimum, it will certainly be reflected in the growth, size and flowering capacity of the plants.

Shading is very important. The density is indicated by the positions of the plants growing naturally in forest areas. Usually they grow on vertical surfaces of the trunks of large trees, but are also found on the branches. The best plants, according to descriptions of the early collectors, grew on the shady side of the trees, the leaves pendant and the roots travelling up and down the trunks or branches for several metres. The density of shading in glass-house culture should be in the order of 70 to 80 per cent on bright, sunny days.

Recognising the nature of the root systems, with their flat profile, the underside a dense mass of tiny adhering papillae or hairs, it is obvious that hey will go into dark potting material only partially, with the bulk of the roots preferring light and open air. Their length in natural habitats also indicates that it would be most difficult to cram them into a pot. They seek flat surfaces and ideal containers for the very coarse potting material are flat fired-clay saucers of varying size and depth, such as were once sold as containers for pots. The general size of such pots used, even plastics, should be much larger than considered for most epiphytes. The depth of material should not be more than about 10 centimetres (about 4 inches) and coarse slabs and chunks of bark are best, with charcoal or smaller bark making up the gaps. Initially fastening the plants firmly into such containers is a little difficult and it is only by boring holes in the bottom and looping wire over the base or rhizome of the plant and twitching it tight that they may be secured in a tidy way. Preferably use copper or stainless steel wire of about 22 gauge. Finer copper wire may be used, but make sure that it does not cut into the leaves or rhizome.

If space allows for hanging plants they may be tied to sections of tree branches, cork slabs, or old weathered slabs of eucalypt. Any old pieces of flat weathered wood may be tried, but if the roots show aversion to attaching themselves the wood should be discarded and another sort tried.

Phalaenopsis live on decaying vegetation and a little of this in the form of oak leaf should be incorporated in the coarse bark mixes used in saucers or pots. Some commercial producers of the genus in seedling form raise hundreds of thousands of seedlings under controlled liquid nutrients, but this is scarcely possible in the usual collections of private growers. The state of the plants in growth, flowering and their brief dormancy, if any, should be the guide in the use of fertilisers. Everyone seems to recommend different solutions and the use of fish emulsion and seaweed derivatives. It is best to work out a program with a solution which is weak and innocuous enough to be fed continuously without ill effect on any of the plants.

Periodic root growth and sealing off usually indicates that the temperature or the light are at fault and fluctuations which occur between day and night temperatures will have the same effect if they are too drastic. Most of the species and the hybrids have rather soft leaves and they will burn easily if the shading is inadequate.

Occasionally water may affect the growth of the plants and alkaline or saline water will quickly stop all plant activity and stunt the leaves. If there is any suspicion that the water may be unsuitable it is best to have it tested and if proved faulty to then put in a tank and store rain-water. The difference when using it is incredible, and the plants should never be allowed to dry out.

Few of our common pests will live or multiply in the conditions provided or recommended for phalaenopsis. However, mealy bug will thrive if it gets a foothold and it should be kept out either by regular disinfecting or hanging several Shelltox pest strips in the air currents which should flow over the plants all through the year. They are silent workers. Aphids may also enter to get the advantage of the warmth in cooler months of the year, but they will also be dealt with in this way.

Some growers prefer to fasten their plants into wooden slat baskets and hang them on angled wire mesh frames so that the baskets are almost on their sides and the leaves hanging freely in the air. This is most successful, the only problem the destruction of the root systems when repotting every year or two.

Propagating phalaenopsis is far from easy, but occasionally if the old flower stems are left on the plants with a joint or more than one joint in the stem, small plantlets may develop at these joints. Once it is certain that it is not a branching flowering stem, a small pad of sphagnum moss may be tied to the stem immediately below the bud and it should develop roots. Once developed, the roots will sustain the plantlet and the stem section may be removed and put on a small bed of moss for a few weeks or until it is ready to be treated as the adult plants are treated.

Generally speaking, unless it happens to be a particularly fine variety, propagation is scarcely worthwhile. In addition to the above method, or if it fails, propagators of meristems advertise freely in orchid publications and may be contacted to obtain propagations in this way. Natural development of small plantlets from the existing 'eyes' on the monopodial stems of the plants is rare but should be a natural process. These should also be allowed to develop roots before they are removed.

Lycaste

The genus named by Lindley in 1843, the dedication to the daughter of Priam, King of Troy. The legend of the city of Troy and King Priam is to be found in Homer's *Iliad* and *Odyssey* and the flowers of this genus match the reputed beauty of Priam's daughter.

Few orchids have retained the devotion and continuity of culture in the fashion of *Lycaste virginalis*, once and possibly still known by most as *Lycaste skinneri*. It is the outstanding member of a genus of some thirty-eight species which grow in Central and South American states and was early in its history known as a maxillaria.

Its origin in cultivation came from the collector G. Ure Skinner, who found the plants in Guatemala somewhere about 1840. Following the flowering of the lycaste in the collection of the Rev. John Clowes, it was described in *The Botanical Register* of February, 1842, as follows: 'This, the facile princeps of all known maxillarias, has at length flowered in the collection of the Rev. John Clowes with a vigour and beauty that could not be exceeded in its native haunts...'.

During the preparation and publication of James Bateman's book *The Orchidaceae of Mexico and Guatemala* shortly after this publicity, John Lindley named the genus lycaste and portion of the credit for this reverted to James Bateman. The specific name *Lycaste skinneri* was also bestowed by Lindley and it was only in the late 1970-80 period that the name was changed to *Lycaste virginalis* (Scheidweiler), the precedence of which was established by his earlier descriptions.

Skinner did not disclose his points of origin, but it was probably first found in Honduras, which at that time was British territory. *Lycaste virginalis* also occurred in Mexico, and Salvador. The plants were both epiphytic and lithophytic, growing usually in partly shady conditions as indicated by the large leaves, thinly textured as they are, and mostly at about 2000 metres. The climate at this elevation is moderate to cool and the species *virginalis* accommodates to this type of environment.

There are many hundreds of varieties of *Lycaste virginalis* and in the early days of its cultivation the naming of such varieties was taken to the point of ridicule. In the most authoritative literature available J. A. Fowlie lists many types or varieties and they are sufficiently distinct to merit the listing. Several fine types were cultivated in the years 1880 to 1900, the best of which probably is *Lycaste virginalis* variety *Mrs Hamilton Smith*, which has large flowers with wide segments, a photo of which appears in *The Orchid Review* of March, 1981.

There is a misconception about *Lycaste virginalis* which should be corrected, however, that it is supposed to have petals or sepals which do not furl or reflex. Its natural habit has always been to suffer this fault (in the eyes of some non-growers), the only time at which they are concave and full being as the flowers open before maturity.

Paxton's Magazine of Botany in 1884 described how Skinner brought

thousands of plants of *Lycaste virginalis* into England. One grower, M
Wray, whose gardener was a competent orchid grower named Brewster, too
the trouble to ask Skinner about the habitat and Skinner described it t
Brewster. Subsequently he grew the orchid to perfection in an open basket-lik
container in a mixture of 50 per cent moss and 50 per cent leaf mould and at
temperature of about 10 to 22 degrees Celsius (about 50 to 70 degrees Fahren
heit). (The author's great-grandmother was a Brewster, her brother presiden
of the Bendigo Horticultural Society in 1880 and noted for the beautiful flowe
gardens he cultivated at Axe Creek, Victoria. But let us get back to th
lycastes.)

The first flowering of *Lycaste skinneri* was recorded as a plant in th
collection of Sir Charles Lemon in 1827, but the species never became we
known until many years later. The pure white form, *Lycaste virginalis* var
alba, first appeared about 1856 in the collection of T. Jackson & Sons, o
Kingston, England. It is still comparatively rare, although many thousands o
self-pollinations have been raised in the last 100 years.

The artist-grower John Day remarked in 1881 of *Lycaste skinneri,* an orchic
which he regarded most highly: 'It has now 19 splendid flowers, all ir
perfection... Mr Skinner used to send grand masses to Veitch and from 20 tc
50 flowers on a plant was not uncommon.' He also remarked on the grea
variation in the flowers of plants imported into England.

The best plant cultivated by the author came from a back-bulb propagation
developed over some four years which carried thirty-two flowers, a
photograph of which appears in the color section.

Some of the best varieties found in the early days of *Lycaste skinner*
importation seem to have vanished, like *Lycaste skinneri* var. *armeniaca,*
which was a white lycaste with apricot-pink petals and a slightly fainter tinted
labellum in the same color. There were many such specialties, passing from
grower to grower and finally vanishing almost as though they never existed,
appearing only in the records of exhibitions and presentations to the Royal
Horticultural Society committee for their approval.

There are several distinct types of lycastes and whereas *Lycaste virginalis*
flowers on the matured new growths and occasionally again on a two-year-old
pseudo-bulb, *Lycaste deppei* flowers on the very immature new growths and
most plentifully on well-grown plants. The new growths commence about
early summer and by the time the shoots are anything from 10 to 18
centimetres high (4 to 7 inches) the flowers are fully out.

As the new growths take off the root system also recommences, both from
the older parts and from new growths. The roots of all the lycastes are similar,
about the same diameter as dendrobium roots, but most profuse and
thickening in pot culture into a very tight ball. In clay pots they tend to cling
and proliferate against the inside of the pots, making the plants most difficult
to remove for division. As the roots grow, the yellow tip, usually about 1 or 2
centimetres long, is the only visible sign that the root is good, because the
remainder turns brown, becomes covered with a quite hairy overcoat and
branches freely.

Lycaste deppei is not the only member of the genus to flower from the new
growths. But as an easy orchid for beginners it has outstanding merit because
it flowers in the summer, matures the pseudo-bulbs in the autumn and,
provided the rules are obeyed, in the winter a continuity of growth and flower
results. The winter or colder months of the year, naturally, is a period of
complete dormancy, no matter if the plants shrivel a little.

The species was introduced to cultivation by Loddiges about 1828, so that it
is one of the oldest lycastes in cultivation. It was originally collected by an

gent named Deppe in Mexico and first flowered in England in a collection near Sheffield. Deppe found it growing in Guatemala and Nicaragua at about 000 to 2000 metres (3000 to 6000 feet) and remarked on the faint but delightful perfume. It was originally named *Maxillaria deppei* in his honor by Loddiges and later renamed *Lycaste deppei* by Lindley.

Lycaste aromatica was also named by Lindley and as the name implies it is quite strongly though not unpleasantly scented. It has the same cinnamon odor which some of the other yellow lycastes have, very sweet on a sunny day.

It was first sent to Britain by Lord Napier from Mexico about 1826 to the Edinburgh Botanic Gardens, but neither the habitat nor the elevation was recorded. Later notations gave the elevation as 1500 to 2000 metres (about 4000 to 600 feet), which would give it some scope in a moderately warm glass-house or in a climate where the winter minimum did not fall below about 10 degrees Celsius (about 50 degrees Fahrenheit).

As *Lycaste aromatica* is another summer flowering species it is quite a good acquisition for a beginner. It has the reputation for flowering on bare pseudo-bulbs, but also flowers on leafed bulbs and in profusion on both. It is the smallest of the lycaste flowers and as the color of the flowers indicates it should stand bright light just short of leaf burn. As the leaves are tender in immature growths they should be allowed to harden off before the plant is taken into bright light.

Disfigured leaves on lycastes are never quite so much a burden to the plant as on, say, vandas because they are replaced almost annually and do not carry over much beyond the second year of their advent. Disfigurement is mostly caused by overwatering, particularly of the foliage, which often displays brown tips to about 4 or 5 centimetres (1½ to 2 inches) from the leaf ends. It is common to all the genus and can be avoided with a little care. The most certain sign that the culture applied is first class is for the leaves to reach maturity with the tips still green and to remain in that condition until they are cast.

Lycaste cruenta was discovered in Guatemala by Skinner about 1841 and was named by Veitch. It is also reported to occur in Colombia, but frequently these sighting reports are of isolated plants and do not indicate that they are endemic. However, it is also native to Costa Rica and other parts of Central America and was first handled in England by James Bateman.

Lycaste cruenta is truly one of the lycastes which flower on bare pseudo-bulbs and it is common to see most beautifully cultivated and flowered plants without a single leaf remaining. *Lycaste cruenta* and some of its near relatives retain a very sharp spike at the point of leaf dehiscence and can inflict a rather painful stab to the fingers. The flowers do not need a description as they are illustrated in the color photographs and they appear on the plant almost as the new growths are appearing in the growing season. However, the flowering season is most variable and I have seen plants in flower in summer, autumn and even in spring.

In the habitat *Lycaste cruenta* grows at from 800 to 1500 metres (2500 to 5000 feet), so is more at home in a warm glass-house in winter with a minimum temperature of about 13 or 14 degrees Celsius (about 55 degrees Fahrenheit). It makes a rather good companion for a cattleya collection.

It is not easy to build up a collection of lycastes in the same way as a collection of paphiopedilums may be built up, partly because of poor availability and also because of incompatibility of so many of the species among the thirty-eight-odd known.

Most research associated with orchids is frustrating, but little of that aspect has been made in these books. However, the lycastes offer some of the most confusing information possible. *Lycaste ciliata,* an illustration of which, it is believed, appears in the color section among the photographs of the genus, is good example. This plant was sold as *Lycaste horichii,* which was discovere in Costa Rica by Horich. Investigations, however, disclosed that Reichenbac had described and filed a description of the plant and flower under the titl *Lycaste tricolor.* This species is quite different from the flower illustrated i this book.

Lycaste ciliata has had a varied history and if plants could speak they woul most likely indicate quite clearly that they were sure they could get on in lif much better without humanity in any of its phases. This lycaste was discovere by Spaniards Ruiz and Pavon in 1798 and they named it *Maxillaria ciliata* Apparently it was rediscovered and renamed in 1836 by Poeppig and Endliche as *Lycaste fimbriata.* Lindley first named it *Maxillaria costata* in 1838 anc later changed its generic title in 1843 to *Lycaste costata.* Alex Hawkes give separate species rank to *Lycaste costata* (Lindley) and *Lycaste ciliata* (Persoon) but in reality they are one with *Lycaste fimbriata* and several other synonymou terms. Reference to Schweinfurth's *Orchids of Peru* gives a clear run-down o the history of its naming and Fowlie's book on the genus is also interesting i somewhat confusing when compared with other literature.

Things have not changed much over the years since the publication of Veitch's *Manual of Orchidaceous Plants* in 1887 to 1894. They have this to say of *Lycaste ciliata:* 'Materials for description, under the name *Lycaste barringtoniae,* were sent to us from the Royal Botanic Garden at Glasnevin by Mr F. W. Moore, who called our attention to the confusion that has long existed respecting this species.'

As in other genera and even among other lycaste species, they were so widespread in occurrence and there is apparently so much cross-pollination between the species, probably into second-generation families, that the determinations are not only blurred by different authorities, each dealing with their own discoveries, but clear derivations and descriptions are almost impossible. That is, however, not to blame the botanists and taxonomists themselves, but rather the system which allows such things to occur.

As will be noted in the illustration, the flower stems are rather long, but those of *Lycaste ciliata* as illustrated in Fowlie's book are quite short; Schweinfurth does not give a length of flower stem; and Hawkes says of *Lycaste costata,* 'Scapes several at once, to 8 inches tall, rarely taller'.

Leaving the frustration for the orchid itself, *Lycaste ciliata* occurs in Peru at about 1000 to 1200 metres (3000 to 4000 feet), mostly on the banks of streams and in many instances on the inaccessible rock walls of the gorges confining the rivers. Ruiz and Pavon were among the earliest explorers and possibly exploiters of the orchids of Peru, where *Lycaste ciliata* occurs in several regions. Apparently it grew in a variety of environments from open rocks to terrestrially in light forest. Wherever it grew, however, it probably lived on aggregations of rotting vegetation in crevices or as decaying detritus on open country.

The flowering habit of *Lycaste ciliata* seems to vary. Some plants appear to flower on mature pseudo-bulbs, others on new growths as occurs with *Lycaste deppei.* It should appear on this orchid, however, in the spring, at the same time as new growths appear.

A small but important member of the genus is *Lycaste macrophylla,* which is most variable florally. It was named by Lindley in 1843 after having borne the usual generic title of maxillaria for some years. It is native to Costa Rica, growing in tropical forest at about 600 to 1500 metres (2000 to 5000 feet), but in cultivation is quite at home in moderate conditions in the glass-house. Very few people grow these orchids in natural surroundings in the open, although they lend themselves well to it in suitable environments. *Lycaste deppei,* for

nstance, is illustrated in the color plates growing in the author's garden in
outhern Victoria.

The amount of shading as well as the time of year in which the various types
of *Lycaste macrophylla* flower have marked effects on the color of the
blooms. As it seems to bloom intermittently in various seasons, it is possible to
have an olive green flower tinged with red-brown for one season and on the
same plant in a warmer period to have a coppery-brown colored flower. But in
most instances the labellum remains constant both in color and markings.

Lycaste macrophylla flowers from mature pseudo-bulbs in most hands,
although it is possible for the same pseudo-bulb to flower again either later in
the year or in the following season. It likes shady conditions and a periodic
year of growth and dormancy, encouraged by sun and warmth in the growing
period and less light and warmth and moisture after the plant has made up its
pseudo-bulbs.

There are a number of other beautiful lycastes which could be included in
compatible groups in the temperature ranges cool to moderate, the type of
climate from which many of them come. None of these is easy to obtain and
the cost of importing them is prohibitive when plant loss added to the cost of
quarantine in Australia is considered. In this regard, so far as the system in
Australia is concerned at the time this book was published, it is so far out of
date with the processes in other countries that a revision would do nothing but
good.

Of the species which from time to time appear in plant lists, *Lycaste locusta*,
green, from Peru, originating at about 3000 metres (9800 feet); *Lycaste crinita*,
yellow-green, from Mexico, growing at about 2000 metres (6500 feet); *Lycaste
lasioglossa*, light to chestnut brown, from Guatemala, about 2000 metres;
Lycaste schillerana, pale pearl colored to pale green, from Colombia, and
growing at about 3500 metres (11500 feet), are all species which add color and
variety to collections of species orchids.

Potting material for lycastes is common to all the species, with a little fining
out for smaller species, small propagations and seedlings, A cymbidium mix is
too bony and coarse and it is best to put together a separate blend using coarse
gravelly sand and some leaf content, preferably fresh autumn drop before they
have had a chance to get wet or begin to decay. Oak leaf is one of the best
inclusions, with other deciduous trees such as ash or old dry eucalypt leaves.
Pine needles and other leaves with aromatic oil content should be avoided.

A starting point should be made along the lines of three parts of bark to one
part gravelly sand and one part dry leaf which has been partly crumbled. The
bark should go through a 5 millimetre (3/16 inch) sieve after taking out the
finer part through flywire. A little coarser bark should be used in the instance
of pots over 10 millimetres (4 inches). Peanut shells and other things may be
added, but the bulk should still be only in the same proportions as outlined
above.

Pine bark should be weathered or boiled to remove harmful resins or oils
and preferably used in a damp to wet condition to make up potting mixes.
Occasionally pine bark can be bought only in sizes which are unsuitable for
finer rooted orchids such as lycastes and it should be reduced by pounding it
with the end of a length of 5 centimetre (2 inch) pipe.

The root system of lycastes should be understood as different from that of
dendrobiums, although of the same or similar diameter. In maturity it is
covered with a rough brown, hairy-looking coating and in this condition looks
quite dead. The only live-looking part of the root is the growing yellow to
greeny-yellow tip. Roots are produced prolifically from the rhizome and when
plants are repotted most of this root should be removed from the older parts of
the plants, treating carefully that which is issuing from the newer parts of the

rhizome. Sometimes it is most difficult to untangle the root ball of lycastes and when ready for repotting a large amount may have to be removed.

The drainage holes in pots for lycastes should preferably be in the bottom of the pot and a thorough drainage pattern of crocks or rough pieces of bark put into the bottom before potting plants. As with most orchids, the correct time to repot, divide or propagate lycastes is the growing season, which is summer in Australia and most other countries. In this period plants to be repotted should be pushed out of their pots and the root system on the outer surface of potting mix examined. Unless there are signs of growing roots the plants should be replaced until they appear.

Lycaste plants should be divided with a sharp knife and not pulled apart. Rough treatment destroys the growth 'eyes' on the base of the older pseudo-bulbs and potting to a depth lower than the base of the pseudo-bulbs will do the same. Propagations smaller than the usual two bulbs behind the lead bulb are unwise, although in this regard lycastes are not so touchy as some other genera. Leafless bulbs appear on some lycastes at the same time as the plant is flowering and these species should be left intact and not handled until new growths are up to the stage of producing roots before the plants are repotted or disturbed such as by potting-on.

It is frequently necessary to remove back-bulbs and they should be severed with a fine-bladed knife in pairs rather than singles. The strike rate with pairs is much higher than for singles and when the first growth has been made up and the new roots have fattened out the probable shrivelled condition of the pair, the new growth may be severed and a try made for a second strike. Rather than pot such back-bulb propagations in the standard mix for the genus, they should be put into as small a pot as will contain them with some sphagnum moss about the base, with the plantlet removed put into ordinary mix.

Sometimes it is necessary to make a decision which means sacrificing the flowers to get lycastes repotted in the flush of the growing season. In such instances it is best to approach it hard-heartedly and pull off even immature buds, taking care that they are not growth buds. It will mean a better flowering in the following season.

After repotting, the natural humidity of the surroundings should be kept high and not too much water poured into the pot. Plants may shrivel, but if they are stood on a bed of gravel, scoria, shell-grit or other materials and the bed kept wet they will soon send out roots and possibly not fatten out again until the next pseudo-bulbs mature. There is little cause to worry unless the propagations cast their leaves, in which case it is best to continue with the leafless plant but being careful not to overwater it. The potting material should be damp and that is all.

Lycastes like plenty of air flow and fairly bright conditions except when newly repotted, when shade should be more dense than for growing plants. They frequently go into a dormant stage where nothing at all seems to be happening and in this state they should be kept fairly dry, as this is the period when root damage occurs by watering plants which have no need for it. If the natural humidity is kept fairly high the pseudo-bulbs may shrivel a little, but this does not seem to be detrimental.

Fertilisers are always good talking points, as so many of them do similar jobs while growers insist on their preferences. Lycastes are a little different from single-genus orchids like cymbidiums that flower at one period of the year and grow in another. Some lycastes flower on almost fully matured pseudo-bulbs while others flower on very immature new growths. Taken all round, fertilisers are best applied to the genus as afterthoughts rather than incorporating them nto a mix. Although solid animal manure fertilisers may seem a little out of place, a few hard knobs of old sheep manure cannot do anything but good. Blood and bone is also an ideal solid fertiliser which breaks down quickly and releases nutrients as well as trace elements. Slow-release pellet fertilisers are best left to such coarse-growing genera as cymbidiums, where unwanted residues can do little damage. Lycastes need a fairly rapid boost in growth and then a fairly sterile pause until flowers need a little weak fertiliser to stiffen them up and strengthen the petals and sepals.

It could well be asked how it is that naturally growing plants do not suffer from residues in their environments? Anyone who has grown orchids in natural environments and not in pots could supply the answer very easily. Pot culture is about as alien a system as could be imagined for any plants and it is possibly more by good luck than good methods that peak results happen. There is no such possibility as overwatering in natural culture, as the residue quickly drains away, the plants may be saturated for days on end and suffer no ill effects when there are left-over fertilisers.

For those lycastes with a combined growing-flowering season regular or even irregular feeding with weak liquid nutrients should be continued, preferably after the plants have first been thoroughly watered. In addition, as much blood and bone as will cover a 2 cent piece should be sprinkled on the surface of the mix in a 10 millimetre pot (about 4 inches), repeating the application about every three weeks until the plants have finished flowering. During the maturing phase for the pseudo-bulbs the golden rule should be followed with both water and fertilisers so that the roots are induced by weak fertiliser to chase about after it and not killed off by too much concentrated in the small space of a flower pot.

For the lycastes which flower on mature pseudo-bulbs the system is a little different, more care being needed to bring the flowers along while protecting a semi-dormant root system. The preliminary culture leading to flowering is the one with most effect, particularly in the final stages of building maturity into the plants.

Few diseases or pests attack lycastes, but in over-humid and warm conditions leaves may develop black spotting. It may be caused by fungus and if the immature growths are early sprayed with a solution of Capthion, which is an all-purpose soluble powder formulation, the effect is long lasting and so far as grubs and fungus are concerned there is little chance for them to attack.

The flowers should remain spotless and if they mark with little brown to black spots the ventilation is usually at fault and more air flow should be given by a fan or more ventilation.

One of the pests which attacks the immature buds is mealy bug and it should also be dealt with by sprays in earlier stages than finding it on the flowers and buds. However, if it appears, it may be quickly checked and killed off with a spray of 50/50 methylated spirit and water forced through an atomiser. Most of these atomisers may be bought cheaply since plastics came into orchid cultivation and one should be always kept in the glass-house with this solution.

Watering should be such as normally given orchids in growth, but for lycastes the plants should be allowed to almost dry out between applications. The growing stage may be divided into three parts. First new leaf shoots appear and lengthen. In this period watering should be only sufficient to keep the potting mix damp. The second stage is the lengthening of the leaves into almost their full size and during this time the plants should be given a little more water plus fertilisers. The final stage is the complete broadening of the foliage and the growth of the pseudo-bulbs. This is the time when the older, perhaps shrivelled, pseudo-bulbs will fatten out and thus the plants need a little more water but only the same amount of fertiliser as applied previously. Both fertiliser and water may be cut out when the plants show fully developed pseudo-bulbs and from then on are kept only damp.

Some surprises come along with lycastes as with other orchids and it will be found that even when the pseudo-bulbs seem to have reached full maturity the plants will occasionally take another fertiliser application of the same weak strength and put on quite an appreciable increase in the size of the pseudo-bulbs. But again, remember the dangers of taking things a little too far.

Hybridising

The manual cross-pollination of lycastes began about 1890 with the production and naming of the hybrid *Lycaste* Imschootiana by Alfred van Imschoot, of Ghent, Belgium, one of the few people not identified as hybridists in *Sander's List of Orchid Hybrids*. The advent of this orchid was confused. Sander's list gives the parentage as *Lycaste skinneri* x *Lycaste cruenta*, both illustrated in the color section. It is best to go back to 1894 for clarification. In that year the raiser received a First Class Diploma of Honor for the hybrid at a meeting of the orchid society in Brussels and the parentage given at the time was *Lycaste skinneri* x *Maxillaria nigrescens*. A glance at the illustration of *Maxillaria nigrescens* in the color section must convince most people of the impossibility of this parentage. Perhaps it was a tongue-in-cheek hoax to put other hybridists off the scent, in the same way as the various collectors in the orchid habitats tried to throw others off the trail of genera over which they had a temporary monopoly.

Whatever the reason, *The Gardeners' Chronicle* then recorded it as a new lycaste from Peru, possibly a natural hybrid. In a following issue this magazine changed its derivation and said that it was raised by van Imschoot and that the suggested parentage was *Lycaste skinneri* x *Lycaste cruenta*. Rolfe, who knew his orchids very well, saw the flower and he came to the conclusion that the parents were indeed these two lycastes. He ruled the maxillaria out completely and described the flower as having light greenish-fawn sepals spotted with purple except near the tips; the petals similar but a little yellower, the labellum yellow spotted with orange-red at the base and on the callus. The combination, for anyone knowing the two parents, could have only one conclusion. It was midway between the two and on appearance alone the maxillaria could not have been one parent. A portrait appeared in the *Journal of Horticulture* for December, 1893, and a description of the flower at the time indicated it as having large flowers, the sepals soft greenish-brown dotted with purple, the petals clear yellow with red spots at the base and the labellum yellow with orange-red blotches at the base.

J. A. Fowlie in his book on lycastes perpetuates the story of this hybrid being the result of the cross-pollination of *Lycaste skinneri* and *Maxillaria nigrescens* and this is unfortunate, as the authority for his entry is none other than *Lindenia*. However, it was typical of the times that cross-pollinations were poorly recorded and orchid history is full of the 'wrongs' as well as the 'rights'.

Hybridising in the next half-century was spasmodic and to the year 1945 only thirty-one hybrids had been registered in Sanders' list. However, the hybrids like *Lycaste* Balliae (*L. macrophylla* x *L. skinneri*), raised by Sanders in 1896: *Lycaste* Sunrise (*L.* Imschootiana x *L. skinneri*), Cooke, 1941; and *Lycaste* Auburn (*L.* Balliae x *L.* Sunrise), Oddy, 1957, led to the cross-pollination of *Lycaste* Auburn again with *Lycaste skinneri* by Wondabah

Most lycastes are readily deciduous and do not hold their leaves for longer than a year or two. Although they may produce double shoots from the leading pseudo-bulbs where they are culturally suited, in general they produce only one and it is common for them to have leafless pseudo-bulbs behind the leaders, remaining dormant until prodded into growth. They are best severed in pairs and on this plant the two in the foreground should be severed to promote viable eyes into growth. Growers may become alarmed when they see pseudo-bulbs shrivel after the fashion of the leafed bulb, but this state is common to the genus and unless the leaves show that something is wrong there is little cause for worry. Unless lycaste plants are repotted and the back-bulbs are severed away they should be left intact in pots so that the main root system is undisturbed. By the time the plants are repotted the back-bulbs will have produced shoots and perhaps fattened them out into small propagations.

1

Many epiphytes with pseudo-bulbs like these, including zygopetalums, odontoglossums and some of the miltonias will produce adventitious growths like this lycaste. The two propagations here are obviously different, with one proceeding from a growth eye at the base of the pseudo-bulb, the other from the apex of the bulb. As will be noted, they were both taken away in pairs, but there were no viable growth eyes on the right-hand pair. Although there are roots on this propagation, it is best left 'on its perch' until such time as a second growth commences to make roots. Unless the old pseudo-bulbs rot away this should occur in the next growing season and the new plant may then be removed and potted in the normal way. The roots are typical for all lycastes — a growing yellow-green and white tip proceeding from a leathery, dead-looking root.

2

211

Orchids to produce *Lycaste* Koolena. These hybrids were of all colors from almost pale pinky-white through to deep velvety-red tones with a hint o indefinable color tempering the flowers, perhaps the last residual influence o the species *Lycaste cruenta* showing through. All this, of course, led to the complete inbreeding of the hybrid range and the Koolenas are still being worked on by Australian hybridisers Alcorn and Apperley as this book was published.

It will be noted that throughout this review of the hybrids the original name or synonym for *Lycaste virginalis* has been used. It was a little late in the development of the genus to try name-changing and probably it would have been better to retain the well-known specific name *skinneri* and have made the true name *virginalis* the synonym. There is no doubt of the superiority of *Lycaste virginalis* in dominating the hybrids and the development of the richer colors came from such other species as *Lycaste macrophylla*. Other hybridists in England and Europe worked on the genus, but in the 1970-80 decade much of the development was Australian and by minor growers rather than commercial nurseries. Their achievements speak for themselves in the flowers illustrated.

A branch into other genera occurred when *Lycaste* Queen Elizabeth (*L. locusta* x *L. skinneri* var. *alba*) was used with *Anguloa clowesii* to produce *Angulocaste* Tudor. With its half-brother *Angulocaste* Apollo, it proved a little difficult to flower in most hands. *Angulocaste* Apollo had *Lycaste* Imschootiana as the other parent.

Lycasteria Darius (*L. skinneri* x *Bifrenaria harrisoniae*) was another essay at intergeneric hybrids and this time it was a little easier to flower them. Reworked into *Lycaste* Auburn, this gave a most beautiful finely pink-spotted flower in *Lycasteria* Alkina, representing another first-class hybrid from W. G. and J. Cannons.

There seem to be few other genera with affiliations in the lycastes, but with the keenness for innovation in the 1980 period it is difficult to say what might not be brought out from them.

The genus was named by Frost, with some influence by Hooker, in 1829. They belong to the gongoreae and the name was in honor of Philip Henry, fourth Earl of Stanhope, president of the London Medico-Botanical Society from 1829 to 1837

Gongoras

Named by Ruiz and Pavon, dedicated to Antonio Caballero y Gongora, Bishop of Cordoba, Spain and at one time Viceroy of New Granada (Colombia). Natives of Central and South America, a genus seldom noted in cultivation but having remarkable floral characteristics like the stanhopeas. Named in 1794.

Coryanthes

Named by Hooker from the Greek words *korys* (a helmet) and *anthos* (a flower). The reference is to the helmet-like epichile of the labellum. The genus was named in 1831.

Stanhopeas, with the two associates in the preceding paragraphs, present some of the most fascinating and unusual flowers of the orchid world. In addition, they represent the most intricate and fully developed examples of evolution toward a continued existence of the genera. To some growers the voluptuous fleshiness of stanhopea flowers is repulsive, but apparently they give little thought to the reproductive systems of flowers of any kind, let alone stanhopeas.

The relationship between insects and flowers is part of this reproductive system, one depending upon the other — the insects for food, the flowers for their pollination and seed production. The most intriguing facet of this relationship is the timing. The insects hatch for the opening of the flowers and their maturity. Normal pollination by honey bees is understandable, as they maintain a community. But for what appears to be the calculated arrival of short-lived insects coinciding with opening of the flowers is apparently something which developed long before man arrived on the scene or at least assumed his present form. This is compounded again in complication by the way some orchids do not depend upon insects at all and are self-pollinating.

The pollinators of stanhopea flowers are mostly bees and the intricacies of the flower construction appear to be aimed at amusing or feeding or even at times intoxicating them as incidentals to the transfer of the pollen to another flower. The construction of the flower is such that the pollen is removed as the insect leaves the flower and not on entry, so preventing in most instances the self-pollination that makes for inbreeding. Why the flowers have developed in such a way, constructed something after the fashion of an amusement park for

213

children, with all sorts of things to stimulate them, has been subject to speculation from some of the most brilliant analysts to no good purpose. Most admit defeat and accept the fact that the flowers have evolved over many millions of years to a degree that ensures continuance of each species and, indeed, the generation of completely new species following cross-pollination.

Orchid Flowers, Their Pollination and Evolution, by Van der Pijl and Dodson, goes some way toward explaining all this, if at times expressed in terms beyond the scope of everyday orchid growers. Breathtaking is an overworked word, but the mind boggles at the implications of insect behaviour. Perhaps it is simplified if it is understood that total species and even genera disappear when pollinators are excluded and the whole of the orchid world has undergone many changes in its history from such causes.

Stanhopea flowers are aromatic and the scent or odor develops almost as the flowers open. In the warmth of the morning sun it is possible to watch them develop, the large buds opening and reaching maturity in a short period. It is certain that the bees or insects which fertilise their flowers are attracted by the scent, but they also attack part of the flowers with their mandibles and appear to eat portion of the soft tissue which is not related to the reproductive part of the flower except as being part of the whole. While the bee or insect may enter the flower from the side, the construction of the labellum is aimed at inducing or forcing it to leave through the main entrance. The labellum is intricate, with three main parts — the hypochile, which is the basal portion attached to the column; the mesochile, which consists of two horn-like projections which act like guide rails to channel the pollinator up the floor of the labellum toward the exit, so that as it forces its way past the tip of the column it detaches the pollen with the upper part of its body behind the head; the frontal part of the labellum is the epichile or apex of the labellum, which in orthodox orchids like cattleyas is termed the front or central lobe and the most decorative part of the flower.

The tip of the column is so designed that a backward facing projection may be passed by an insect entering between the epichile and column, but when leaving this projection would be forced away from the tip and the pollen firmly attached to the insect by the viscid adhering surface formed by the break. The bee or insect may dislodge the pollen at any stage of its activity with the flower and it may adhere to other parts of its anatomy, including the legs; but when attached to its back just behind the head it is implanted on the only spot which insects cannot reach if preening or cleaning — a situation akin to the spot between our shoulderblades. And this spot is the logical contact point with the next flower visited if the bee or insect forces its way between the column tip and the epichile or frontal lobe of the lip. If attached to any other part of the insect the chances of pollination for another flower are significantly reduced.

It would be most difficult to assess the proportion of flowers pollinated by this means to finally produce fruit. The number would be influenced by prevailing weather, the durability of flowers and the timing or arrival of the pollinators and numerous other features. But it is made understandable from pod counts of such an orchid as *Dendrobium speciosum* growing naturally in the bush, where in some years not one fruit may form from the thousands of flowers on one large plant. However, even with a small proportion of stanhopea flowers pollinated the seed scatter would be of incredible numbers, the germination and progress of seedlings to maturity an infinitesimally small number. Usually stanhopea flowers are short lived, with at most a few days of full life and even slow deterioration from about the second day on.

The genus has rather small pseudo-bulbs considering the size of the flowers. Most are rounded and markedly ribbed, about 5 to 8 centimetres tall (2 to 3 inches), occasionally larger, with a rather hard broad leaf of anything from 20 to 40 centimetres long and about one-third as wide, standing on a short, stiff stem attached to the apex of the pseudo-bulb. The flowers are produced on a pendant spike of from two to seven blooms which emerge in a downward direction from the plant. For this reason they must be grown in slat or wire containers and may never flower if pot or hard container grown.

John Lindley was intrigued by stanhopeas and listed some twenty odd in *Folia Orchidaceae* (1852), in which he remarked: 'The species of the genus are almost all known from garden specimens, the fleshiness of their flowers rendering their determination in herbaria extremely difficult. Hence their native countries have been often incorrectly stated. They vary greatly in the colors and a little in the form of their flowers. The botanist will find safe characters in the hypochile or lower cavity of the labellum or middle part from which the horns usually proceed, and the epichile or front lobe.' On examining a stanhopea flower there is no doubt that Lindley and his contemporaries must have had difficult moments trying to prepare specimens for inclusion in their herbariums, as they are among the most fleshy of all orchid flowers.

Lindley included stanhopeas *wardii* and *devoniensis* in his *Sertum Orchidaceum*. *Stanhopea devoniensis* was first flowered at Chatsworth, the Duke of Devonshire's home, in 1837. It is richly colored in golden-yellow, blotched and barred with red-brown. Lindley had the privilege of naming the species. He appeared to have the free run of Chatsworth. The plant apparently was sent to Chatsworth from an unnamed source, although some authorities give definite details of its advent in England. One of the curious inconsistencies of orchid history occurs in *Sertum Orchidaceum* in the second paragraph of Lindley's description of *Stanhopea devoniensis*, in which he states: 'I cannot doubt that this was the famous lynx flower of Hernandez, when his figure, rude as it is, and his description are considered.'

Stanhopea tigrina is usually considered to be the species which Hernandez mentioned in his book on the natural history of Mexico. Hernandez was a Jesuit priest whose original mission no doubt was to convert the native races to Christianity, but like other men of similar persuasions in the Indo-Asian area, he also took a keen interest in the country to which he had migrated or perhaps only visited. He is said to have called *Stanhopea tigrina* by its native name, 'coatzontecoxochitl', a name subsequently also applied to other orchids. Hugh Low introduced *Stanhopea tigrina* into England when it was consigned to them by their collector Henchman. Hartweg also discovered the orchid near Vera Cruz and it also was found in Guatemala and Colombia. It is one of the most strikingly colored stanhopeas, large and pendulous like all the genus, with an overpowering, sweet perfume, once likened by a naturalist to a cross between vanilla and melon. The perfume deteriorates to an unpleasant odor as the flowers age.

Stanhopea insignis was the species on which the genus was founded. It was discovered by Humboldt and Bonpland in Ecuador about 1800. It is pale yellow all over with some varieties densely spotted with purple to red-purple.

Stanhopea eburneum was sent to England from Trinidad by Sir Ralph Woodward, one time governor of that colony who collected and sent many orchids there, including *Brassavola* (now *Rhyncolaelia*) *digbyana*. His plants were sent to Loddiges about 1824. The same species was later found by Wagener in Venezuela and sent to Europe and it is common to other Central and South American regions. Like all the stanhopea species, it is perfumed, the flowers rather short-lived.

Stanhopea occulata was found by the collector Deppe in Mexico and sent to Loddiges in 1829 and it flowered for them in 1831. It was also found by

Skinner's collectors in Guatemala. The flowers are pale to orange yellow spotted with red-purple and this species carries more flowers than usual for the genus, plants with spikes of seven flowers having been recorded.

Stanhopea ecornuta, creamy white, was found by the Polish collector Warscewicz in Guatemala about 1845 and introduced to Europe by the nurseryman van Houtte. It is creamy white spotted with purple and the labellum is yellow and orange. Joseph Ritter von Rawicz Warscewicz was one of the early collectors in the American region. It is always hard to say which was the most important discovery of individual collectors, but possibly *Cattleya warscewiczii* would be his greatest tribute. He discovered it in Colombia in 1848. The greater part of this initial collection was lost in a boating mishap on the River Magdalena and only a few of the plants were salvaged. These also later died. J. C. Stevens, who operated an auction system in London for plants imported from America, notified a sale of imported plants in these terms: '... a collection of plants received from Mr Warscewicz, who had succeeded at great peril in penetrating into the territory of the Xivaros Indians near the source of the Maranon, one of the tributaries of the Amazon River, and whence no European ever before returned'. That was neither exaggeration nor overstatement. Warscewicz died at Cracow, Poland, in 1867, where he was Inspector (virtually director) of the Imperial Botanical Garden. According to Polish purists his name should be spelt Warszewicz and not as it generally appears. The penchant of the race for over-whelming groups of consonants defies pronunciation and perhaps we are fortunate for the initial error being perpetrated.

Mr Paxton, later Sir Joseph Paxton, the orchid grower, naturalist and botanist at Chatsworth, who also produced a comprehensive botanical dictionary in the years 1820 to 1860, is worth quoting in his method of cultivating stanhopeas. It is an insight into the methods of trying to duplicate the habitat in the initial stages of thoughful orchid growing. It is from Lindley's *Sertum Orchidaceum*:

'The following treatment is not only applicable to the growth of stanhopeas and others of like habit, but an advantage in the growth of any species of orchidaceae. (The terrestrial and those that grow in moss excepted.)

'Over the drainage hole of the pot to be used is inverted one of a smaller size generally covering about half the bottom of the pot, over this is carefully thrown a quantity of broken pots, sufficient to fill the former to within one-third of the top. A sufficient quantity of fibrous, moderately sandy peat, is next selected and placed on the top of the drainage, being first broken into various forms and sizes, but none of them less than a walnut; in placing these, care is taken to dispose of each, so as to leave a passage for the escape of water; this is more effectually secured by putting in, as the process of potting goes on, a few pieces of broken pots, say, between every layer, more or less, according to the size of the plant; indeed, I find it an excellent plan to continue a connection of broken pots all the way up the centre, to the bottom of the pseudo-bulbs. After the peat becomes level with the pot, the successive external layers are made fast by means of small pegs, varying from 4 to 6 inches long, these pegs run through the layers of peat, and thus secure the whole firmly together. At 8 inches above the line the plant is placed on the top; the roots are carefully laid out and covered up to the base of the bulbs very carefully with smaller pieces of peat and potsherds, continuing to fasten the peat as before described, until the whole is finished, when it will be a foot or 15 inches from the top of the pot; small plants are not potted so high. At each shifting the plant is raised a little higher. When I commence potting a small plant it is not raised more than 3 or 4 inches at first, but as it grows larger it is progressively raised in building up as here described with peat; it does not terminate in the shape of a cone, but is carried up nearly square, being merely rounded a little at the top. Unless the plants are very healthy, but very little water is given at the roots, and in winter very little or none, the great desideratum in the cultivation of orchidaceae being *to preserve the roots* which, by overwatering, especially in winter, are almost sure to be destroyed.

'I cannot conclude this statement better than by recommending those who wish to grow terrestrial orchidaceae well, to attend to the following brief rules, in applying the four great elements of vegetable life, viz., air, light, heat and water.

'Air. — Terrestrial orchidaceae should never have a great volume of external air admitted at once, however fine the weather may be; to prevent the house becoming too hot, a thick canvas shading should be covered over it during sunshine.

'Light. — The best aspect for an orchidaceous-house is due south, and the house should be made to admit as much light as possible. In summer a thick canvas is always put on the house to prevent the bright sun damaging the plants. In winter every ray of light is advantageous to the plants.

'Heat. — During the growing season orchidaceae require a moderately moist heat, varying from 65 to 85 degrees; in the dormant season from 60 to 75 is quite sufficient; in the season of rest the house should be kept dry.

'Water. — With this element more damage is done than by all the others put together. Orchidacea in pots should be sparingly watered in the growing season; in the dormant state little or no water should be given. The secret of growing these plants is to take care *never* to kill the old roots; when too much water is given while the plants are not in a growing state, almost all the old roots invariably perish.

'N.B.: The brief account here given refers entirely to plants potted in peat soil; those grown in moss and on bits of wood require quite a different treatment.'

A few points in the above are worth noting. The orientation of the house toward the south would be reversed to face north in the southern hemisphere. So far as air is concerned, the trend in the later years of the twentieth century is to reverse Paxton's recommendations, if anything, and to admit plenty of air in the Australian or other sub-tropical and temperate climates. Naturally, in cooler climates his restrictions would still be applicable, but we have the advantage of electricity and modern air-circulating equipment that Paxton probably would have been excited about. There is no reason why a stanhopea or similar plant would not grow exactly as he recommends, trouble and all as it may be to arrange.

Modern cultivation of stanhopeas, coryanthes and gongoras and other similar orchids must follow at least most of Paxton's recommendations. They are best grown in slat baskets with a fairly wide and free bottom space for the flower spikes to pass through. The bottom layer of the container may be of sphagnum moss thinly laid, most fibrous materials including coconut fibre in a similar thin layer or the outer husk of stag or elk horn ferns. This layer is simply to hold the potting mix, which may be anything from cymbidium mix coarsened up a little to specially prepared formulations to hold and feed the plant. There must be some form of decay material included so that the natural habit of the plant establishing in rotting forest detritus may be encouraged.

When growing, the plants should be freely watered and then allowed to almost dry out before the next application. In general, all Paxton's recommendations may be followed and in this regard it is obvious that over more than 130 years of cultivation we have learned little that he did not already know. There is also a modification in his recommendations for shading, for although the leaves will burn easily if allowed exposure to Australia's summer sun, we would hardly be likely to use a screen of anything near the thickness of canvas. A ratio of at least 50 to 70 per cent should be used, depending on the type of climate in which stanhopeas are grown. While the species *Stanhopea tigrina* is frequently recommended as a cold-growing subject and indeed has been grown and flowered that way, it will be found that it does better in a glass enclosure or plastic-roofed bush-house. None, if tried really cold, with temperatures sliding below the 10 degrees Celsius mark (about 50 degrees Fahrenheit), will grow well or flower. They are sub-tropical to tropical plants.

Fertilisers may be organic or inorganic type but any carry-over into the dormant season of the plant should be avoided. In this regard such things as old hard lumps of animal or fowl manure are far better than nutrient solutions. If placed on top of the growing medium and the water applied through them the plant gets full benefit of a natural fertiliser and any residue may be removed at the end of the growing season or left on the surface and its function taken up again when the plants are again freely watered.

Coryanthes

It is impossible to write about unusual orchids and their unique life styles without introducing coryanthes. They are seldom seen in cultivation, a fact noticeable ever since they were found in the Central and South American jungles. The word jungle probably originated in India and is indicative of impassable masses of vegetation of all kinds, from creepers and ground cover to trees. It is best to go back to some original notes from people who knew the coryanthes and their particular habitats in the American jungles.

F. C. Lehmann, who is mentioned in regard to masdevallias and other genera, was impressed by the extraordinary features of different orchids and none intrigued him more than coryanthes. He stated:

'*Coryanthes wolfii* was named by me in honor of Professor Dr Wolf, formerly of Guayaquil (Ecuador), now of Dresden. In his house I had the pleasure of seeing, examining and sketching the first flowers of this marvellous plant, although it was known to me many years previously as an Ecuadorean species. It grows very sparingly, mostly on cacao trees, all over the littoral districts of the Guayas, where it flowers in February and March, when these level lands are mostly inundated. During this season it is beyond the power of man to penetrate the woods there — a circumstance that accounts for the plant not having been seen before. It produces thick, upright flower spikes 40 to 50 centimetres high with three to six large, wonderfully constructed flowers which are yellow, mottled and stained with brownish red.

'There are but few plants in the entire vegetable kingdom which are more interesting and which afford such a varied amount of material for the student of vegetable physiology. Everything relating to coryanthes is curious and arrests the attention of the observer, even its spontaneous mode of growth. Whenever a large mass is found in the tropical forests of South America numerous ants surround its root masses. This ant is a small species of myrmica possessed of a strong, aromatic smell and which bites very severely, so that it requires some courage to meddle with the plant. These ants seem to be indispensable to the well-being of the plant, for if these animals do not collect around the roots it appears not to do well. Even in a cultivated state, as well as in the house of my friend Dr Wolf at Guayaquil, as in my own country residence, I have observed the same facts. But nothing surpasses the flowers.

The very peculiar organisation of the whole flower, the position each organ assumes in relation to another, the secretion of the sweetish fluid always retained in great quantity in the bucket, all is highly interesting and invites both to study and investigation.'

Lehmann was responsible for the transport of coryanthes plants to England, particularly to the Liverpool Horticultural Company. Some of these grew and flowered and later passed into oblivion because of incorrect culture and not, as generally supposed at the time, because of lack of ant power.

Even more unique than the association with ants is the pollinating system. Perhaps it is best to go back again to another observer, J. Rodway, also previously mentioned in this book, for his account of the function of bees in carrying out their perhaps involuntary role of pollinators:

'Hanging from a creeper or branch,' he remarks, 'may be seen here and there an oval, bag-like mass of aerial roots, something like one of the nests of the troupials so common in the silk-cotton tree, above which are the pseudo-bulbs and leaves of that wonderful orchid the coryanthes. After throwing out two or three roots to attach itself to its support, it develops an interlacing network all round in a way almost peculiar to the genus. At first sight it would be hard to say what purpose could be served by such a contrivance; but shake or strike the plant and it will be seen that it is nothing less than a veritable ants' nest. The orchid is, like other plants, subject to the attacks of many foes, such as cockroaches and larvae, which are particularly fond of the aerial roots. To protect itself against these, the coryanthes has chosen to provide a comfortable nest, wherein a garrison of carnivorous ants find shelter; they, in return for the accommodation, being ready to come out and fight at the first alarm of an enemy...

'Having provided a guard against crawling vermin, the coryanthes proceeds to develop a wonderful flower, in which every part is obviously formed to attract a particular insect... It has laid itself out to catch, without hurting it, a beautiful metallic-green bee (Euglossa aurata). From the base of one of its pseudo-bulbs a long flower stem is produced, which pushes itself straight downward. Upon this hangs a number of beautiful cups, into each of which a liquid drips from two horn-like processes in the upper part of the flower. Take a china teacup with a spreading mouth, hang some little flags over the handle and stick a model of the figurehead of a polynesian canoe opposite and you have something like one of them as it opens itself in the morning from a bud resembling the swathing of a Chinese lady's foot. The species vary in color and markings, being generally whitish or yellow, blotched and spotted with crimson. Their odor, as judged by our standards, is not pleasant, but nevertheless it is very attractive to the bees, which immediately swarm round in great numbers. Flying towards the flower as a moth to a candle, the bee falls into the liquid which covers the bottom and, wetting its wings, is unable to use them. Look into the cup and you will see a dozen bees swimming round and round or vainly trying to climb the slippery sides and, if it be the second day after opening, one or two may be seen drowned. It was never the intention of the flower, however, that their lives should be sacrificed; but, on contrary, that they should escape and in doing so perform the office for which the whole contrivance has been arranged. Under the flags, where the column comes near but does not actually touch the cup, is a narrow opening through which the bee can push its way out. In doing this it has to use sufficient force to widen the gap (which opens out like a spring door), when it comes in contact with the pollen-case, ruptures it and carries off the male organ on its back. Not being able to fly, there is nothing to be done but to crawl over the flower spike, where, heedless of its former trouble, it soon finds itself inside another flower.

In making its way out the pollen masses are rubbed on the stigma and the ovary fertilised, after which it may carry out the pollen masses of this flower in turn to fertilise another.'

Dr Crueger, director of the Botanic Gardens in Trinidad about 1900, spent long hours watching the antics of bees buzzing around coryanthes flowers and swimming in the nectar pool. He watched them gnaw at the edible material of stanhopea flowers and other plants. He remarked:

'... some cellular tissue which these humble-bees gnaw off exists also in the hypochil of the lip of *Coryanthes macrantha*. They are seen in great numbers disputing with each other for a place on the edge of the hypochil. Partly by this contest, partly perhaps intoxicated by the matter they are indulging in, they tumble down into the "bucket" half-full of a fluid secreted by organs situated at the base of the column. They then crawl along in the water towards the anterior side of the bucket where there is a passage for them between the opening of this and the column. If one is early on the lookout, as these hymenoptera are early risers, one can see in every flower how fecundation is performed. The humble-bee, in forcing its way out of its involuntary bath, has to exert itself considerably, as the mouth of the epichil and the face of the column fit together exactly, and are very stiff and elastic. The first bee, then, which is immersed will have the gland of the pollen mass glued to its back. The insect then generally gets through the passage and comes out with this peculiar appendage, to return nearly immediately to its feast, when it is precipitated a second time into the bucket, passing out through the same opening and so inserting the pollen masses into the stigma while it forces its way out and thereby impregnating the same or some other flower. I have often seen this and sometimes there are so many of these humble-bees assembled that there is a continual procession of them through the passage specified.'

Dr Crueger was also the victim of careless spelling, his name variously appearing as Cruger, Crueger, Kreuger and Kruger in the mass of research material leafed through and studied in regard to coryanthes.

Owing to the enormous colonies of ants which infested the root ball of coryanthes they were never popular with collectors and it is easy to understand perhaps their horror when their employers, knowing nothing of the involvement, ordered perhaps 200 or so coryanthes and stanhopeas. The collector Roezl was well acquainted with the hazard and described the mode of operation. It must have taken a considerable bribe to get the natives to hack the plants down from the vines to which they sometimes clung. They had to be cut down and at the slightest vibration or disturbance the ants swarmed out to the attack. With the plants at ground level the usual practice seemed to be immersion in the river until the last of the ants had been evicted and the plants then recovered and dried out for transport. It seemed to early cultivators that the plants needed the ants to grow; that there was some relationship between the two. The truth, of course, was that the early imported plants were divested of most of the great root ball and they died before they could reconstitute this in the type of environment to which they were consigned by growers.

Gongoras

These orchids, like their two companions are fairly numerous in the Central and South American region, but generally they will withstand much brighter light than the stanhopeas and coryanthes. They also have in common the habit of completely reflexing the beautiful sepals and petals, so that it is only in the unfolding of the flowers of stanhopeas, coryanthes and gongoras that their true beauty is apparent.

The naming of the genus presents utter confusion, with even modern taxonomists in disagreement on identification. There is no certainty that the labels on plants are correct or merely synonyms and at times it is certain that they are sold without identification at all. As an instance of this confusion, *Gongora quinquenervis,* which was discovered by Ruiz and Pavon in 1798 and named by them, was also named by Lindley in 1833. He called it *Gongora maculata* and this orchid, according to Dunsterville and Garay in their book *Venezuelan Orchids,* has at least twenty synonyms, including many which are recognised as true specifics by other taxonomists. Pabst and Dungs in *Orchidaceae Brasilienses* note that it has fifteen synonyms. All that, of course, has little to do with the appreciation of these curious orchids in the eyes of growers.

Gongora atropurpurea, which is also native to Brazil, was one of the first to be sent to England, possibly with many other genera, from Trinidad in 1825. It was flowered at the Liverpool Botanic Gardens. Some years later Warscewicz, collecting in Peru for his European contractors, sent *Gongora scaphephorus* in a mixed consignment and it came into the hands of G. W. Schiller in Hamburg, frequently referred to as Consul Schiller but with no enlightenment on that title. Schiller had an extraordinary collection of glass-houses and they are illustrated in a woodcut in *The Orchid Review* of 1925. In all he had a collection of 156 genera and this comprised no fewer than 1268 species. No doubt he had more than one plant of each of these species, as was common in that period. His glass-houses were all heated, and with coal at about £1 to 30 shillings a ton who cared? He noted in his book, which would now be a museum piece, that his friend Reichenbach determined the names of his orchids for him. It will be noted in passing that several orchids were named in his honor, such as *Lycaste schillerana* and the phalaenopsis already mentioned. Like most of the gongoras, *Gongora scaphephorus* is scented. On his death, Schiller's collection passed to the Hamburg Botanic Gardens, where it was totally destroyed in the Second World War.

Gongora maculata, synonymous with *Gongora quinquenervis,* was introduced to England by the Harrisons, notable in the 1830-40 period as entrepreneurs and innovators in the realm of orchids, although it was originally introduced by another grower from Colombia in 1832. In the Harrisons' hands it produced spikes of flowers which hung down some 'two and a half feet long'. Lindley said of it: 'Many a strange figure has been met with among orchidaceous plants and numerous are the animal forms which botanists have fancied they could recognise among their singular flowers. Some are said to bear little men and women swinging below their canopy of petals; others have appeared to carry the likeness of lizards, frogs and other reptiles crouching among their leaves; while some have been compared to Oberons and Titanias hanging by their tiny arms from the bells where they have concealed themselves. To what the flowers of the plant now figured can be likened we profess not to know, unless to some of the fantastic animals of heraldry; a griffin segreant, as they term it, would do as well as any other for a comparison.'

Well, fanciful and all as it may appear to see things in flowers, Lindley was at least right about the gongoras, despite the ridicule which some taxonomists and authorities on orchids pour on the suggestions that their flowers have resemblance to animate objects which at times even flirt with them.

Gongoras have in common with some other orchids, such as *Dendrobium speciosum,* for instance, and catasetums, the habit of producing masses of vertical roots which may reach as high as 10 to 15 centimetres above the crown of the plant (about 4 to 6 inches). An example is illustrated in the color section on a dormant catasetum plant. In the growing season these roots are tipped with a green point which, however, does not lengthen. As some observers have remarked, at times these tips glisten with drops of condensation or dew. When these plants approach dormancy the tips seal off and turn white, a sure indicator that the plant requires less moisture until they again become green in the growing season. It is a pale green, not a dark color. So far as *Dendrobium speciosum* is concerned at least, it is quite obvious if the plants are grown epiphytically that they develop this system and it becomes a food trap, with the tips always just clear of the detritus which such a root pattern collects. In the dormant season they also turn white and seem inactive, returning to a green tip again in the growing period. Plants growing lithophytically or grown as rockery plants do not develop this system.

Gongoras should be grown in the same way and in similar temperatures as stanhopeas and coryanthes, with no latitude below about 15 degrees Celsius (about 60 degrees Fahrenheit) in the cooler period of the year, despite the fact that the plants may be dormant. Gongoras, however, may be pot grown, as their spikes, even though pendulous, do not force their way downward into the potting material. They travel horizontally until they reach the edge of the pot or container and then hang.

All of these orchids are greedy feeders and in the make-up period, which may be short in the later part of summer, should be fed with nutrient liquids in weak form in addition to top-dressings of animal manure or blood and bone. Such top-dressings should be capable of removal once the plant is fully developed. Mostly the flowers appear on new growth and it is unlikely that they will come from the older parts of the plant.

The usual pests which infest glass-houses, such as scale, aphids and red spider, will attack the young growths of these orchids and they should be kept out or controlled with any of the usual methods. Good eyesight is a necessity and from time to time the leaves should be turned over and examined underneath to see that the pests do not get a foothold.

Watering can scarcely be overdone when the plants are growing, but once they mature more care will be needed. A good soaking about once every two weeks should be sufficient to keep the plants in a stable condition until new growths start. But it is only when new roots are showing that more water should be given. In repotting it is fairly certain that a large amount of root on the older parts will be lost and this stage in their cycle should be attempted only when the plants are growing strongly in the summer, even if it means sacrificing the flowers for a season. Most of the old roots should be taken away when repotting, leaving just enough to hold the plants firm. If inclined to be unstable a stake should be used to tie the remaining leaves firm so that new root tips are not damaged.

Stanhopeas and coryanthes will burn in less than 60 to 70 per cent shade, but gongoras are much more hardy and when I grew the plant illustrated it hung well up toward the roof, which was whitewashed and had no additional shade-cloth in summer.

Coelogynes

This genus was named by Lindley in 1822, based on the species cristata. The derivation of the generic name is from two Greek words, *koilos* (hollow) and *gyne* (pistil or woman), referring to the deep receptive cavity for implanting of the pollen.

A large number of orchid growers will admit that among their frustrating experiences has been cultivating *Coelogyne cristata* and of looking at well-grown plants and wondering where they have been wrong as the flowers so consistently failed to appear. At least that was my experience.

One of the most appealing things about writing a book on orchids and their culture is the lapse of memory suffered about failures and the ease with which cultural directions can be put on paper.

The genus as a whole is fairly widespread throughout Indo-Asia, possibly extending as far south as the islands off the Niugini mainland. Although they have never been generally popular in cultivation they have much to recommend them. So far as hybridising is concerned, little work has been done on the genus and what cross-pollinations took place occurred in the period between 1900 and 1923. In *The Orchid Review* of October 1901, the editor noted a small batch of seedlings at Charlesworths from coelogynes *speciosa* and *cristata,* but apparently they were not named until about 1907, when the cross-pollination was registered as *Coelogyne* Colmanii.

While some of the coelogynes have erect racemes of flower, others are completely pendulous, some are scented and some are not, some flower from the apex of the pseudo-bulbs, others from the base of the new growths. Buds of those which flower from the apex of the bulbs usually appear in the immature growths. This means, of course, that there are several separate cultural requirements and it is impossible to grow them all in the same conditions.

A number of the species occur at high elevations of from 2000 to 3000 metres (7000 to 10 000 feet) but even these can seldom be cultivated in cold conditions of, say, 10 to 12 degrees. William Hooker, botanist and one time director of Kew Gardens, England, or his son Joseph who also occupied the same position, described the incidence of both coelogynes and pleiones in the Himalayan foothills and anyone reading their descriptions could not fail to be impressed with the wealth and beauty of these orchids in the habitat.

As most coelogyne flowers are white or pale colors and bloom in a dryer period of the year, in cultivation they must be given slightly arid conditions and care in watering or the flowers spot quickly. Most of the genus are more suited to temperate climates and are not recommended for tropical or even semi-tropical culture. As with many genera the country of origin is not really a guide, as elevation could be just as important.

Equally important is non-disturbance once a plant is acclimatised. While some coelogynes like the species *cristata* will pile pseudo-bulbs on top of each other in containers, it is only on plants like this that shows of flower such as illustrated are gained. The root systems, too, seem sparse on many species and poor understanding of their annual cycle results in loss of most of them.

Coelogyne fimbriata (Lindley) was the first of the genus to withstand trans-shipping from its habitat in southern China to England, sent by J. D. Parks to the Horticultural Society of London, in whose garden it flowered in 1824.

Some magnificent specimen plants of various species have been grown in the past, one of them a plant of *Coelogyne dayana* which in 1893 had twenty-four spikes of flower with over 800 individual flowers, a photograph of which appeared in *The Orchid Review* in October 1929. It was included with other magnificent orchids, some of them specimen plants, in the exhibit of Baron Schroder whose orchid grower, a man named Ballantine, was an obvious master, in the Temple Show of that year. The Temple Show was not confined solely to orchids, but included magnificent examples of horticultural craft from all sections.

The cultivation of specimen plants is possibly the ultimate accomplishment in orchid growing and takes time, patience and good equipment. It is not easy to attain in either small collections or small glass-houses.

Coelogyne cristata, from northern India and Burma, is probably the most widely cultivated species. There are two varieties more commonly noted in orchid collections, one with rounded small pseudo-bulbs growing on a rather short rhizome which crowds the plant as a mass of occasionally large dimensions; the other variety has taller slightly tapered pseudo-bulbs and a longer gap in the rhizome between each bulb. While environment where the plants are grown must rank as the strongest influence on their flowering, it is often thought that the last mentioned type is more easily flowered than the small rounded bulb type. It was named by Lindley.

The flowers on all the varieties are similar, pure white with either an orange or yellow splash on the centre of the labellum and with a pure white variety also known. The type flower is that with the orange labellum, the lemon-yellow labellum type known as *Coelogyne cristata* var. *lemoniana*, not from the color but from Sir Charles Lemon, who originally flowered the variety about 1880. The pure white form, naturally, is an albino, common in many orchid genera.

Coelogyne cristata was discovered by the collector Wallich in 1824 in the Himalayan foothills, where it grows as a lithophyte and epiphyte at about 1200 to 2000 metres (4000 to 6500 feet). It also occurs in several areas of Nepal and other Indian states. The collector Gibson sent or took plants to England about 1837 and it first flowered in a collection near Birmingham about 1841.

Sometimes, rather than concoct a set of conditions for an orchid, it is possible to quote past authorities who in a brief sentence can say all there is to be said. From *Sanders' Orchid Guide* comes something applicable to *Coelogyne cristata:* 'To obtain the best results a slightly higher temperature than that accorded odontoglossums should be given, water should be withheld for a short period when the pseudo-bulbs mature, usually about March or April — a slight shrivelling will do them no harm — and infrequently and carefully given till after the flowering period.'

More must be added to that, however, as the months are related to the state of the plants and could vary from country to country and even state to state. The type of potting is also important. As the root system is inclined to be short in cultivation, deep pots should be avoided and the plants grown in shallow dishes or pans, either clay or plastic, with a good drainage base. The roots grow from the rhizome and not from the base of the pseudo-bulbs. They are inclined to be tough but brittle and after growing they simply act as feeders without as much additional budding or extension as the roots of other orchids.

Position in a glass-house is critical and a certain amount of plant movement may be necessary from year to year to find out a little about light and air movement. In summer *Coelogyne cristata* should be grown in fairly bright light with good air movement about the plants. The humidity should not be too high or the leaves may develop spots indicating condensation burn. The foliage also marks badly in winter if allowed to remain wet in a temperature drop such as may occur at night. This rarely applies to plants grown outdoors, which develop a foliage hardness not possible in glass-house culture. It is impossible to recommend a position for *Coelogyne cristata* plants in general, as glass-houses vary so much in their position and light availability. A spot must be found to suit each circumstance.

At one time, and possibly still in some minds, *Coelogyne cristata* was considered an ideal beginners' orchid. Nothing could be further from the truth, as it is a challenge which has defeated most experienced growers. None of the morphological variants is easier than another, nor do the plants from any specific area of Asia or India offer easy approaches to flowering. The spikes show almost as soon as the pseudo-bulbs mature, pale straw-colored tips emerging from the sides at rhizome level in much the fashion of new growths, which are darker. As the spikes grow and the buds show, the straw-colored sheaths wither and almost disappear on the stems. The buds and opened flowers should be kept dry and the humidity low or they may spot badly.

Provided the root system is functioning well, liquid fertilisers applied sparingly during bud progress to opening seems to suit this orchid. In growth and before flowering hard old chunks of cow or sheep manure placed on the surface of the potting material cannot do anything but good, but the liquid fertilisers should be cut down to compensate. Over-stimulation or over-watering should be avoided or the root system may be lost. Little attention should be paid to shrivelling of the pseudo-bulbs if the leaves look healthy. They should be a glossy mid-green and remain so until the plant enters dormancy, by which time they may have dulled a little and perhaps gone darker.

Potting material should be related to culture and not to the habits of the grower. A starting point for combinations may be tried of one part of coarse bark with a little finer residue mixed in, a little coarse charcoal with a similar fine part and a fairly generous amount of dry leaf such as oak leaf rubbed into shreds. The mix should finish in an open condition which would retain a little moisture but no free water. Hard-grown plants sometimes outstrip softer counterparts at flowering, but as a method of culture it is not recommended. It always gives the impression of an 'Are you going to flower or die?' ultimatum. An ego-building process if successful, but most destructive at other times.

Potting materials should not end up as a challenge to these orchids because they exist naturally in their habitats on decaying vegetation and the nutriment existing in the bark of trees. Various changes should be thought up to suit individual environments and with coelogynes there must be a slight reservoir capacity for water incorporated into the potting mixes. This can be fulfilled by decaying leaf content as well as by such sterile things as peat-moss or even sphagnum moss. The dry or dormant period in the cycle of most coelogynes is a testing period for potting materials and reabsorption capability should be thought about. Some bark mixes are very hard to reconstitute and perhaps a little added peat-moss may help this. Preservation of a vital root system through this period is necessary and it is here that the test of growers crystallises.

Some coelogynes have completely pendant flower spikes. They hang anything up to 40 to 50 centimetres below the rim of the pot (15 to 20 inches) and can cause accommodation problems. While the plants may be benched until the spikes start to lengthen, eventually somewhere must be provided for them to hang and develop. They are delightful additions to orchid collections, although a little difficult to manage when taken to exhibitions or society meetings.

Two of these coelogynes in particular are worth a mention. *Coelogyne dayana* (Reichenbach f.), a native of North Borneo, naturally needs a little better than cultivation in a cool glass-house and does not mix well with the coelogynes from cool climates. *Coelogyne massangeana,* originating in Assam, northern India, also needs the same consideration to get the best from it, although it will give a little less in results in a moderately warm glass-house. It was also named by Reichenbach.

Coelogyne dayana was imported or brought into England by Charles Curtis and named after the artist-grower John Day, some of whose illustrations and scrapbook pages have been reproduced in *The Orchid Review* from time to time. It was found in the tropical lowlands and in cultivation proved to be a little variable in flowering, principally depending on the environment in which it was grown, producing its flowers anywhere from late winter to late spring. It is faintly perfumed.

Coelogyne massangeana remained practically unknown in England for many years after it was first cultivated in the glass-houses of Europe. It was thought to have originated in Malaya, according to Veitch, but Sanders gave its origin as Siam. We now know, of course, that it grows in Java, Borneo and other Indo-Asian islands as well as the first two regions.

Both these coelogynes are best grown in wire fern baskets lined with the tough outer husks of stag or elk ferns or similar materials. As the leaves are stout and long, something after the fashion of aspidistra leaves, they should not be suspended too close to the glass-house roof when young and developing, as there would be a strong possibility that they would burn. Like most of the coelogynes, the leaves are fairly permanent, lasting for upward of three years. The plants go through much the same type of dormancy as the general run of coelogynes, but it is not as marked in the tropical species as in the group from cooler regions.

Coelogyne pandurata (Lindley) is among the larger plants of the genus, with pseudo-bulbs up to 15 centimetres high (6 inches) and complementary large leaves. The flower spikes are usually semi-erect and the plants better accommodated on large flat rafts. As the rhizome extends by as much as 10 or 12 centimetres (4 to 5 inches) for each new pseudo-bulb a plant of *Coelogyne pandurata* is most unsuitable for a small glass-house. Found in Sarawak by Sir Hugh Low about 1850 and flowered by Loddiges in 1853, it grew in the hot and humid areas of the Borneo swamps and lowlands and needs warm culture.

The potting material would be similar to that for most of the genus, coarsened up a little for the large slat containers most suited for such a large plant. Like many tropical orchids there is very little dormant period in natural habitats, but in artificial culture it would probably drop into this pattern following flowering. The root system is most vigorous and not all will enter potting material, following the habit of most epiphytes and clinging to the exposed surfaces of its container. *Coelogyne pandurata* flowers are not long lasting, but the unusual color combination of green and black is most attractive and unusual. Despite this, intending growers should think twice before buying it, as such large plants have a peculiar habit of outgrowing their surroundings and becoming tiring after once flowering.

Coelogyne speciosa (Lindley) originated first in the Dutch East Indies, ound by Blume at about 1500 metres (5000 feet). A cool-growing orchid, it was later collected by Lobb and sent to Veitch in England about 1846. Unlike *Coelogyne pandurata*, it is a neat small-growing orchid, very easy to cultivate in a moderate glass-house and with attractive flowers borne mostly singly in the spring to early summer, the color varying from pinkish-brown to deeper ones. The labellum is the part which is most conspicuous, as the illustrated flower indicates. Most epiphytic potting mixes would suit this orchid, plant dormancy the only stage to be watched.

For those who know the genus, *Coelogyne mooreana* (Sander) probably fills the place of best and brightest. Its pure white flowers with the orange stain on the labellum is typical for the genus generally, but the flower is about laelia size and long lasting. It was a rather late discovery in 1905 in Siam (now Thailand) and is referred to in *Growing Orchids — Book One* in the cymbidium section in a quote from a letter from the collector Micholitz, whose name is commemorated in a coelogyne hybrid. *Coelogyne mooreana* is one of the more difficult of the genus to cultivate, needing moderate cattleya conditions for growing. Where most of the genus are rather easy to stage through dormancy, this one appears to be more troublesome and not all growers will be able to cultivate it well.

Naturally, Micholitz sent his plants of *Coelogyne mooreana* to Sanders, where some flowered in 1906 and gained a First Class Certificate for that establishment. It was named after F. W. Moore, of the botanic gardens in Dublin. He was known world-wide as Moore of Glasnevin and knighted for his services to horticulture. Micholitz found *Coelogyne mooreana* growing at about 1200 metres (4000 feet) on the Lang Bien range in Thailand.

Some of the coelogynes produce their flower spikes from the centre of the new growths when they are about 8 centimetres or a little higher (3 inches). In artificial conditions water should be kept from the centres of these leaf whorls or the spike and possibly the new growths will be lost. It may be a useful habit with these and other coelogynes to use a spray such as Capthion on the new growths as soon as the leaf shoots open up. It prevents decay from fungus infection and kills off moth or other larvae which may hatch and attack the soft, tender leaves. Capthion is a three-way spray — it is said to be capable of leaf penetration to give control over sap-sucking pests, it is a surface protector and also a guard against fungus infection from spores which may germinate and grow in moisture remaining in the leaves after watering. However, do not fill the cavity with spray, simply mist it.

There are several other worthwhile coelogynes, all needing varying degrees of warmth to grow and flower well. Minimum temperatures of above 12 degrees Celsius (54 degrees Fahrenheit) should be aimed at, although in some favored instances they will tolerate lower temperatures in the dormant period. Adequate shade in summer is a necessity, which in average climatic conditions would be somewhere from 60 to 80 per cent in the brightest of conditions.

Watering is the most critical feature to be watched, particularly in relation to its pH or acid level. Few glass-house plants will tolerate alkaline water and in centres where this is reticulated, rain-water storage is the only possible solution. The ordinary supply should be used for damping down, but rain-water should be used for both misting and watering.

All coelogynes are epiphytic and this should be the guiding factor in fabricating potting materials. While many growers prefer to rely on inorganic fertilisers for their growing systems, perhaps for their easy preparation and handling, there is little doubt that epiphytic orchids of all types thrive far better and produce more consistent results from organic decay materials. Naturally, these must be backed up by similar non-decay materials such as the plants are accustomed to and have been so accustomed through the millions of years of their evolution. These organic materials in nature are simply the recycled decay products that have been going around and around in the system for the same period of time. They have lost nothing in the process and one could quote perhaps the primary formula that nothing is ever lost ever in nature.

The attempt at modifying glass-house techniques to fall into line with this natural law may perhaps take a little more time in a busy world and the temptation is always there to look at what inorganic fertilisers do for the flowers. But scratching a little deeper usually finds the effects of such programs on the plants and this may be more fully appreciated when such a plant is bought and taken into a different world... sometimes an unhappy experience for both plant and buyer.

Bifrenaria

The genus named by Lindley in 1833, the name referring to the two tiny attachments of the pollinia to the glands on the column of the flower, which is one of the minor distinctions between the bifrenarias and the maxillarias and other members of the total family.

The variation in the colors and shapes of bifrenaria flowers is not usually appreciated by orchid growers, their conception being based solely on *Bifrenaria harrisoniae*, with which this cultural résumé is mainly concerned. Two other similarly shaped species are *Bifrenaria atropurpurea* (Lindley) and *Bifrenaria inodora* (Lindley). Like *Bifrenaria harrisoniae* they bear one or two flowers to a stem, seldom more. But several other bifrenarias have a raceme and the flowers are much smaller, some with the synonym stenocoryne.

There are some twenty-five species in Brazil, five in Venezuela, two in Peru and several in other South American countries. Bifrenarias are related to lycastes and other members of the sub-tribe maxillarieae.

The genus is little known in cultivation except for *Bifrenaria harrisoniae*, which grows in the provinces of Minas Geraes, Espirito Santo, Rio de Janeiro, Guanabara, Sao Paulo, Parana, Santa Catharina and Rio Grande in Brazil, which indicates a very wide-ranging habitat. The type mostly noted in cultivation is probably that originally collected and illustrated in the color section, but there are several varieties, including one with pink-tipped petals and sepals and a red-barred labellum or a purple labellum covered with lamellae.

Like so many of the Brazilian species, it was collected in enormous quantities, with little known of its original discovery and cultivation. It also suffered the eclipse common to so many species and one writer about 1914 said of it that 'few growers now cultivate it'. There was a double reason for this, however, as beyond the difficulty of getting it to flower the products of hybridising took all or most of the time of collectors and cultivators.

Bifrenaria harrisoniae was named by Sir Joseph Hooker, who, like most of the botanists of the time, was entranced with each new species brought into flower in England in the collections of the wealthy fanciers. It was sent to England from Rio de Janeiro by William Harrison, a merchant. The source of the plants or the habitat was not described and the whole story has two or three versions, with Mrs Harrison, the grower who first flowered it, having a confused part in it all. Although nominated as the sister of the merchant, it would appear with a little thought that she may have been married to his brother. Mrs Harrison's collection near Liverpool was extensive and she was also the recipient of plants of *Cattleya harrisoniae* as mentioned in *Growing Orchids — Book Two.* No doubt she had a competent and interested gardener.

Hooker's Exotic Flora of 1825 featured a drawing by Mrs Arnold Harrison of the plant and flower, at that time known as *Dendrobium harrisoniae*. It was described as follows: 'Mrs Harrison received it two years ago from her brother at Rio de Janeiro; and the species appearing entirely new to me, I cannot do better than honor it with the name of the individual who has not only introduced this but many other new and rare plants to our gardens and who cultivates them with great success.'

Bifrenaria harrisoniae was collected in quantity by George Gardner some time after the original plants were sent to England and he described its habitat as 'some 2500 to 3000 feet, growing on moist, shady rocks'. Most growers of later years in the nineteenth century realised that they could never flower it in those conditions and Gardner's description could perhaps be equated with experience of his discovery and detailing of the habitat of *Cattleya labiata* in *Growing Orchids — Book Two*. It was again collected later by another trader and he described its habitat as a north-facing almost sheer rocky cliff, the plants growing in full sunlight for much of the day, the foliage yellow-green and hard-looking. He noted that the plants flowered freely and one of the anachronisms of orchid growing is that it could be for two reasons that they did so — it was a survival bid in harsh conditions or that it really suited the particular variety which he gathered. His lucid climatic description of the habitat also reveals sufficient for the basis of modern cultivation. He noted that for some six months the climate was dry and cool, during which the plants were dormant. At the onset of the rainy season the weather was warm and the plants made fast growth, maturing and flowering at the end of this period.

Experience in cultivation may indicate a totally different sequence, however, and a lot of individual treatment seems necessary from grower to grower, with many failing to get the results aimed at — the flowers. Whatever its history, *Bifrenaria harrisoniae* has frustrated many orchid growers in its cultivated history. The root system is almost as coarse as that of cymbidiums but not as extensive. Some attempt should be made to work on the plants to induce flowering. The most probable time for this will be in the late Australian spring to early autumn, with a quick season of growth and then a dormancy, which is nothing like the type of program noted by the gatherer of the hard-looking plants. During the growth stage the plants should be kept wet and supplied with fertilisers and it may be a good idea, if such equipment is available, to set an automatic heat cut-in for the odd chance that temperatures may fall below about 15 degrees Celsius (77 degrees Fahrenheit).

Bifrenarias should be grown in common cymbidium mixes to which a little more than usual leaf content has been added. Some growers use dried eucalypt leaves, as they are very hard and durable and do not decay to a sodden mess as quickly as some softer foliage like oak leaf.

Plastic or clay pots may be used, but considering the root system and the extended period of dormancy clay pots have a lot to recommend them, as they may be stood during this dormancy on closed bench systems with moist to wet gravel under the pot. During the whole of the dormant spell the plants need never be watered and the pots will take up moisture by capillary action and prevent much of the shrivelling common from dehydration or root loss in plastic pots.

While these orchids are naturally epiphytes or lithophytes they do not thrive very well mounted on cork or wooden slabs. There is little reason to take much notice of Gardner's brief summary of their habitat, either, as if this is correct it is totally unsuitable for glass-house culture.

Most of the flowering plants exhibited at society meetings or shows look extremely poor, with sunburnt and badly marked foliage, but it would appear that this is the only condition in which the plants may be forced to flower. They do not look very attractive, but usually the heavily textured flowers are fresh and beautiful. It is common for growers to apologise for the condition of their plants, but they are no doubt very pleased to have flowered them at all.

The right place for all confessions is at the end of something. For me the confession is that although I have flowered both *Bifrenaria harrisoniae* and *Coelogyne cristata*, it was done in conditions directly opposite to what I have advised. *Coelogyne cristata* was hung well up toward the roof of a very bright glass-house to promote flowering as the pseudo-bulbs swelled to maturity and it flowered on almost every new pseudo-bulb. *Bifrenaria harrisoniae* was grown in a half fruit case made of soft pine wood some 45 centimetres long (18 inches), 25 centimetres wide (10 inches) and 20 centimetres deep (8 inches). It was grown well down in the glass-house on a low bench with plants hanging overhead, never dry right through the year. Although it never flowered until the box was full, the show of flowers was magnificent, with the box practically rotted away and pseudo-bulbs and their roots holding the remnants together. Satisfied, I never grew it so again and sold all the plants resulting from the break-up to other people to try their luck.

The obvious lesson offered by that last paragraph, of course, is that no one really is able to put a program on paper for the cultivation of any orchid. The ultimate success or failure of any grower is largely dictated by willingness to experiment and improvise, always, of course, obeying the ground rules for building a collection suited to the climate from which they come and the climate in which they are expected to continue growing, regardless of their species or hybrid status.

Ada

The name is of Greek origin, derived from a Carian woman. An epiphyte, it was named by Lindley in 1853, and is not recommended for semi-tropical or tropical climates.

Ada aurantiaca belongs to a small family of only two members. It was discovered on the eastern sector of the Cordilleras in Colombia about 1851 by the Belgian collector Schlim, growing at about 2500 metres elevation (about 8000 feet). At this altitude the average daytime temperature is about 14 degrees Celsius (55 degrees Fahrenheit). At night this would drop to almost freezing at times, but the plants will not stand this type of treatment in cultivation, preferring something about the 14 degrees Celsius mark.

James Bateman was probably the first grower to flower it in England and he remarked that it seemed to be flowering out of season for him. This may have been the result of flowering a plant not acclimatised or fully developed into a northern hemisphere seasonal routine. In the southern hemisphere it flowers from about the end of July to late September, quickly disappearing at the first sign of summer and commencing its new growth. Schlim sent the first plants to Linden, the Belgian nurseryman, who placed it with the brassias. Lindley, however, relegated it to separate status with the name ada, and morphologically it is related to the odontoglossums and oncidiums among other genera.

Ada lehmannii, the other member of the duo, is infrequently noted in collections. It first appeared in England about 1888, when a plant was forwarded to Kew Gardens by an English grower named O'Brien. His plants came from Europe after being sent there by F. C. Lehmann, the German consul in Colombia. Although similarly colored, *Ada lehmannii* flowers later in the year and is considered a summer orchid in cooler areas of the northern hemisphere. There are also morphological differences between the two species. *Ada aurantiaca* is illustrated in *Growing Orchids — Book Two*.

Both species were used in hybridising. In the period 1880 to 1900 anything in the way of orchids brought into Britain and Europe were immediately on flowering subjected to the most extraordinary cross-pollinations that could be imagined. However, the adas combined with both odontoglossums and cochlioda, to produce such hybrids as *Adaglossum* Juno (*A. aurantiaca* x *Odonto. Edwardii*), which probably has long since disappeared from cultivation. It was a dull crimson spotted with dark purple and with a reddish-brown labellum. The cochlioda association occurred in the cross-pollination of *Ada aurantiaca* with *Cochlioda noezliana* producing *Adioda* St Fuscian, which had red-scarlet flowers about four centimetres (1½ inches) in diameter. *Ada aurantiaca* was also cross-pollinated with *Odonto. nobile* (syn. *pescatorei*). More recently it has been crossed with *Brassia verrucosa* to produce some very attractive hybrids, though with few flowers on the raceme, also illustrated in *Growing Orchids — Book Two*.

The flower spikes appear in the immature growths of *Ada aurantiaca* in late autumn and winter at times and at this stage are succulent and tender and hould be protected from pests such as slugs and snails. These spikes develop slowly until they flower in August to September, with the opened flowers always appearing half-dead because they do not fully open out like other orchid flowers. The spikes are arching and at times may be semi-pendant. They are durable and may last for some weeks in suitable conditions. The pale green leaves develop to their full length over the flowering period, by the end of which the pseudo-bulbs should be fully matured and be recommencing growth.

Coolness and moisture during the warmer periods of the year are essential and neither of the species will grow in warm climates. While the plants should never be allowed to dry out at any stage of their annual cycle, overwetness or cold allied with high humidity soon causes the leaves to mark badly, much after the manner of masdevallias. Leaf-tip burn or browning is more frequently the result of stress and dryness in warm conditions. The root system is more like that of masdevallias than of other genera and is markedly durable in suitable conditions, lasting for four years and more.

A good potting mix should be made up of constituents similar to those used for masdevallias and should include some leaf decay material such as dry oak leaves which have not commenced to decay. All sorts of variants may be fabricated, but they should have in common the ability to retain moisture for long periods and in the growing season the mix should be topped with a thin layer of growing sphagnum moss to use as a 'tell-tale' for the moisture content.

Pot size is not critical, but overpotting should be avoided. The type of pot used is not important, but for growing on a closed bench clay pots may be best, as there would be no necessity to water the plant at all in winter so long as the bench material was kept constantly wet to damp.

Either of the adas would be suitable companions for odontoglossum collections or any other orchids which do not need a hot, sometimes dry temperature, such as oncidiums or cymbidiums.

Chysis

The generic name alludes to the self-fertilising ability of the flowers. An epiphyte, it was named by Lindley in 1837.

Chysis bractescens, commonest of the cultivated species, was introduced to Britain from Mexico and flowered in the collection of a Birmingham grower named George Barker about 1840. The species *Chysis aurea* pre-dated that flowering, however, on plants which bloomed for James Bateman about 1836, collected in Venezuela by Henchmann and consigned to Messrs Low & Co. Both these original species, however, are considered as one and are known as *Chysis aurea*. Although they were the first of this numerically small genus to reach Britain and Europe, Bateman did not use either when he published his book on the orchidaceae of Mexico and Guatemala. He used *Chysis laevis,* which was also named by Lindley.

Chysis aurea var. *bractescens* came from the coastal forests of Mexico, while *Chysis aurea* originated in forest areas at elevations of 500 to 1000 metres (1600 to 3500 feet). Some confusion still occurs in identification, but most of the plants labelled *Chysis bractescens* appear to be creamy white to pale pink-tinted flowers and the descriptions of the Mexican and Venezuelan species vary from book to book. The two photographs in the color illustrations give some idea of the possible variations. They are very beautiful orchids which, despite their rather solid appearance, do not last long in flower.

Apparently some species last longer than others, as the Horticultural Society's Journal of 1849 states: 'its flowers remain long in perfection and have a slight odor. Of all the plants this is the best for decorating ladies' hair. Its flowers may be used once, twice, thrice and even four times if skill be applied to their preservation and yet are fresh and sweet'.

In common with most genera imported into Britain, chysis were cross-pollinated and produced three hybrids as early as the turn of the century. But according to *Sander's List of Orchid Hybrids* in 1945 only two were valid, *Chysis* Chelsoni and *Chysis* Sedenii. Others were simply cross-pollinations of different varieties of the same species and were rejected.

One of the most curious mistakes in illustrating the species occurred with *Chysis bractescens* and *Galeandra baueri* in James Bateman's book. Miss Drake, one of the outstanding artists in depicting orchid flowers and plants in the early years of the nineteenth century, perpetrated the error quite unknowingly. She depicted the flowers of *Galeandra baueri* most beautifully as usual but attached the inflorescence to the plant of *Chysis bractescens*. Lindley, the ever perceptive and intuitive botanist, wrote on the relevant page of his copy of James Bateman's *Orchidaceae of Mexico and Guatemala*: 'This is made up of two very different plants.'

Reichenbach expressed his opinion in Latin, understandable even to anyone with no knowledge of the language: 'Icon. Phantastica horribilis florulenta foliis cauleque minus correctis.' However, the mistake was understandable for one knowing very little about the plants but a great deal about their delineation in color.

A note from the orchid enthusiast Hermessen in 1907 has relativity to conditions prevailing in Australia when this book was in production. It concerned the destruction of the coastal area in which he was living at the time of 'development' of South and Central America: 'Eight hundred acres of virgin forest were felled in February and March for rubber planting. This ground was burnt over in May and planted in June (with rubber). During the past ten days it has been my duty to supervise the clearing of the young rubber ... and it has almost broken my heart to see the numerous charred remains of orchids, no doubt many of them very rare, on the burnt tree trunks scattered over the ground... The establishment of sanctuaries for the preservation of the wild orchid flora in certain districts may some day be necessary.' Substitute wood-chipping for rubber planting and the corollary is perfect.

J. C. Harvey's orchid grower

On a slightly happier note, James Clay Harvey, whose name is to be noted in other parts of these books, writes of a collecting trip to southern Mexico at altitudes of about 1500 to 1800 metres (5000 to 6000 feet):

'One of the guides who knew I was coming had sent an Indian out to collect plants of *Chysis bractescens*. He had gathered almost 600 of the plants and had nailed them all on a long plastered old wall. They were all in fine condition.'

They had been there for some weeks when Harvey arrived and were all in full flower on their new growths. He remarked: 'Never had I seen such a display before, the lovely white waxy blooms in superb condition and in such numbers, exhaling a pronounced delicate odor reminding me, as I fancied, of gardenias but less heavy. Some of these plants had monster pseudo-bulbs and carried thirteen flowers to the single shoot flower stem. I have never seen more than five or six in cultivation.'

Harvey also stated that it grew best in high forks and on high branches of trees at about 800 to 1000 metres (2600 to 3200 feet) in temperatures of 24 to 35 degrees Celsius (75 to 95 degrees Fahrenheit) in daytime and 21 to 26 degrees (70 to 80 degrees Fahrenheit) at night in the dormant season, with little if any rain but good night-time humidity.

In cultivation *Chysis bractescens* should be grown in cattleya conditions. It flowers from the enclosing leaves of the new growths, appearing when these are quite short. The spike develops quickly and the flowers open in late spring, usually only two or three unless the plants are exceptionally well grown and mature. Even with this number it is a beautiful orchid. As the flowers fade and die off the pseudo-bulbs continue to grow, much faster in the warm summer days than if prevailing weather is dull and cloudy. The plants should be hung where they will be regularly watered, but not allowing water to lodge in the centre of the leaf whorl when they are in the preliminary growth stage after flowering, as this may rot out the new shoot. The root system is tough and suede leather-like on the outside, about the same diameter as that of dendrobiums.

The growth is similar to the catasetums in appearance, but leaves are regularly carried the full length of the growths, occasionally cast as the growths elongate, the lower leaves soon showing effects of lack of water. Weak fertilisers may be used in the growing season, but care should be taken to see that the potting mix is not overloaded. It is surprising how stout the pseudo-bulbs will become on very little and should grow to about 30 centimetres or more (12 inches plus) in good cultivation.

As the leaves are cast at the end of the growing season the plants should be suspended where they may slowly dry off into maturity, a stage they go through entirely leafless. A certain amount of shrivelling may occur and this should be offset by standing the plant over a dish or saucer of water but not wetting the compost. The evaporation of the water will create enough humidity to keep the plant virile.

The plants will grow better if they are suspended so that the pseudo-bulbs may become pendulous or semi-pendulous. The best container in which to do this is a wooden slat basket, topping the potting material with a few strands of sphagnum moss to hold the surface. Potting material should be rather coarse, with fibrous material like chunks of tree-fern, coarse bark and dry leaf such as oak leaves. The root system may attach to the wooden slat container as well as to the lumps of potting mix and one of the real measures of success is to maintain a virile root system through the dormant period to start the plants off again in spring. Wintering over should preferably be in temperatures about the 15 degree Celsius mark (55 to 60 degrees Fahrenheit) and while an occasional lapse may be harmless, prolonged low temperature in the colder months will certainly set *Chysis bractescens* and its relatives back to a degree which may take a lot of careful growing to overcome. In summer there is no reasonable limit for the plants and the leaves will withstand bright light.

Endnote

In the three books *Growing Orchids* most of the mainstream of cultivated orchids are considered. In addition to these genera many thousands of species are grown by orchidophiles all over the world, some simply because they are names, others for their beauty, miniaturism, exclusiveness and any number of incentives which may enter the sphere of human behavior. In all there is some appeal to two things, the money which may be made from the plants without having the least liking or consideration for them on any other grounds or the second stage in which orchid plants and flowers are grown for their singular appeal and the time and money outlaid on them has no limit. The latter group of people are the most fortunate because their orchid-growing life is filled with beauty.

The history of orchid cultivation began in peculiar fashion following the movement over the sea of merchandise and people. Until the beginning of the nineteenth century the cultivation of plants was confined mostly to gardens, with concentration on those which would withstand the climates in which the cultivators lived. Then came the stage where protection of glass roofs allowed more delicate subjects to be grown, sometimes fruit as well as flowers. Naturally, this was beyond the reach of the majority of the population. It was the pastime of the wealthy and they spent great sums of money in filling the glass-roofed structures with exotic plants, of which orchids were at first an insignificant proportion and later assumed the greater role. As people and merchandise moved more freely and in greater quantity more and more orchids became known and were collected and despatched to distributors, as outlined here.

In the late years of the twentieth century, 200 years later, the craft of orchid growing has spread and become available to almost the total population of the more 'westernised' and developed countries if they so desire. In some ways it has become commercialised and cheapened in the worst sense of the words, but the significant drive is still in the minds of most growers — the appreciation of beauty, the sense of achievement in cultivating plants which are challenging and the strangest sensation of all — however old one becomes, it is always possible to look at an unflowering plant and say, *'There is always next year to look forward to'*.

Bibliography

A Guide to Australian Native Orchids, R. Bedford, 1969

A Manual of Orchidaceous Plants, James Veitch, original editions, Vols. 1 and 2, 1887

An Introduction to the South African Orchids, E. Schelpe, 1966

Australian Indigenous Orchids, A. Dockrill, 1969

Australian Orchids, FitzGerald, Vols, 1 and 2, 1977 reprint, Lansdowne

Beautiful Thai Orchid Species, Rapee Sagarik, 1975

Encyclopaedia of Cultivated Orchids, Alex Hawkes, 1965

Epiphytic Orchids of Malawi, Brian Morris, 1970

Formosan Orchids, Chow Cheng, Taiwan

Generic Names of Orchids, Schultes and Pease, 1963

Growing Orchids—Books One and Two, J. N. Rentoul, 1980-82

Histoire Particulaire des Plantes Orchidees, Du Petit-Thouars, 1822

Humming Birds and Orchids of Mexico, author unknown, English version edited by N. P. Wright, 1963. Original author supposed to have been Rafael Montes de Oca, circa 1870, who painted the illustrations

Illustrated Treasury of Orchids, Frank, J. Anderson. (Reproductions of old lithographs. Text in conflict with other versions in parts.) 1979

Indian Orchids, Guides 1 and 2, Udai C. Pradhan, 1976-1978

Johnson's Botanical Dictionary, 1917 edition

Orchidaceae Brasilienses, Pabst and Dungs, Vols. 1 and 2, 1975-77

Orchids, Lewis Castle, 1887

Orchids of Australia, Nicholls, 1969

Paxton's Botanical Dictionary, 1868

Pears Shilling Cyclopaedia, 1900 edition

Peruvian Orchids, Vols. 1-4 and Supplement, Charles Schweinfurth, 1958-1970

Refugium Botanicum edited by W. Wilson Saunders, 1869-1882

Sander's List of Orchid Hybrids, Sanders (St Albans) Ltd and the Royal Horticultural Society

Sanders' Orchid Guide, 1927 edition, Sanders (St Albans) Ltd

Sertum Orchidaceum, John Lindley, 1838 (Johnson reprint)

Southern African Epiphytic Orchids, John S. Ball, 1978

T Orchids catalogue, Bangkok (vandas), 1978

The Australian Orchid Review, 1936-81

The Genus Lycaste, J. A. Fowlie, 1970

The Orchid Review, 1893-1981

The Orchid Stud Book, Rolfe and Hurst, 1909

The Orchid World, Vols. 1-6, 1910-16

The Orchidaceae of Mexico and Guatemala, James Bateman, 1837. (Johnson reprint)

The Orchids of Burma, Bartle Grant, 1895.

Venezuelan Orchids, Dunsterville and Garay, Vols, 1-6, 1959-1976.

Reference maps: South America, Kummerly and Frey; Indonesia, Malaysia, Vietnam, by Robinson; Pakistan, Bangladesh and Sri Lanka, including Burma, by Bartholomew

Index

239